Sexual Assault of Children and Adolescents

Ann Wolbert Burgess
A. Nicholas Groth
Lynda Lytle Holmstrom
Suzanne M. Sgroi

Lexington Books
D.C. Heath and Company
Lexington, Massachusetts
Toronto

Library of Congress Cataloging in Publication Data

Main entry under title:

Sexual assault of children and adolescents.

Includes index.
1. Child Molesting—Addresses, essays, lectures. 2. Incest—Addresses, essays, lectures. 3. Sex crimes—Addresses, essays, lectures. I. Burgess, Ann Wolbert.

HQ71.S397   364.1'53   77-10217
ISBN 0-669-01890-2—Casebound
ISBN 0-669-01892-9—Paperback

Ninth printing, August 1982

Published simultaneously in Canada

Printed in the United States of America

Paperbound International Standard Book Number: 0-669-01892-9

Casebound International Standard Book Number: 0-669-01890-2

Library of Congress Catalog Card Number: 77-10217

Dedication

To Allen G. Burgess, who has maintained my airspeed for this project.

A.W.B.

To my mother, Sophie M. Groth, and my aunt, Helen M. Konicki, with love and devotion.

A.N.G.

To Olivia Cabannẽ Lytle, who provided a model.

L.L.H.

To Charles W. Parton, M.D., who has set an outstanding example for hospital-community involvement and permitted me the freedom to follow it.

S.M.S.

Contents

Foreword

Concern for the victims of sexual assault has become a national priority only during the past five years. In that time, both public awareness of and knowledge about sexual assault and its victims have grown immeasurably. Despite this awareness and community involvement, however, work in the field has been limited primarily to adult victims. The problems of child and adolescent victims have been largely unaddressed. In fact, the extent of sexual abuse of these victims has remained unknown.

In 1973 the Children's Division of the American Humane Association testified before a Senate Committee estimating that 100,000 children are sexually abused each year. Many estimates go higher, but they are just that—estimates. No national statistics on child sexual assault exist. And statistics that do exist, of course, reflect only reported crimes. Likewise, major studies in the field of child sexual assault are few, and those which do exist usually focus on the offender more than on the victim.

Few studies concern the special problems of the juvenile victim in relation to the official world. Few representatives of the judicial process are expert at the techniques needed to interview children, and defense attorneys often use the same tactics on juveniles as they use on adult victims.

The controversy surrounding attempts to initiate rape prevention programs at both the elementary and secondary school levels has virtually killed such efforts in many communities throughout the nation. Where programs have been initiated, they are generally geared toward female students only, resulting in a failure to reach many potential offenders. In light of the high number of youths arrested for rape, this may be a serious omission indeed.

Recently, convicted child-rape-murderer Arthur Goode was quoted as saying that he tested his victims for their politeness and helpfulness. The prevention dilemma this poses for parents is enormous. How, in fact, do we teach our children to protect themselves without giving up all the social values we may wish to instill in them?

Today, there is an increasing interest in the treatment and prevention of sexual assault of children and adolescents. Yet, many gaps exist in the approach to providing these services. Theories abound, but hard data are difficult to find. Clinician and agency staff are faced with the crucial need for treating both young victims and their families in a preventative way when little is known about appropriate treatment or the long-range effects of what they seek to prevent. *Sexual Assault of Children and Adolescents* attempts to provide some of those treatment answers in a manner which is easily understandable and adaptable to both professional and lay counselors and their individual programs. By providing specific "how to's" for treatment personnel, this book should have an impact on both the improvement of victim services and the amelioration of the traumatic aftereffects of sexual assault on its youthful victims.

Ann Wolbert Burgess and Lynda Lytle Holmstrom were among the first to systematically identify the needs of adult victims of sexual assault and were pioneers in the field of developing treatment strategies for meeting those needs. Now they have expanded their work to include the very special needs of children and adolescent victims. As both a victim advocate and a mother, I am grateful for the continuing dedication of these two women and their coauthors, A. Nicholas Groth and Suzanne M. Sgroi.

Mary Ann Largen
Former Coordinator, National Rape Task Force,
National Organization for Women and
Member, National Rape Prevention and Control Advisory Committee (HEW)

Preface

The sexual assault of children and adolescents is an increasingly visible social problem that is beginning to impact on many disciplines. This book is designed as a handbook to guide those people whose work brings them into contact with either the victim or offender. The major themes of this book are as follows:

1. *The human dimension.* Individuals who are involved in a sexual assault need to be viewed as people under stress; that is, they matter as people. The task of the intervenor is to attempt to understand the situation and to apply techniques and skills in such a way as not to add to any existing trauma.

2. *Community program planning.* Communities, as they complete a needs assessment, can begin to plan for education on prevention and treatment of sexual assault, the implementation of programs to assist the people involved, and the evaluation of outcomes.

3. *Interagency cooperation.* The success of a community project depends on its ability to form and maintain working relationships among community agencies.

One major difficulty in writing a book on this subject is coping with the terminology in the field. Professionals use the terms *sexual abuse, sexual assault, sexual misuse,* and *sexual molestation* interchangeably. For the purpose of this book, we have chosen the term *sexual assault* to refer to the forced, pressured, or stressful sexual behavior committed on a person under the age of 17. This act by a victimizer may lead to physical and/or psychological aftereffects. We use this term more broadly than is found in the legal statutes of many states.

This book has been written in response to the many requests received from people in the field. It seemed most useful to combine our work and present an interdisciplinary approach to the subject in the hope of encouraging multi-agency collaboration in working with child and adolescent victims.

We have written this book from our own work with victims, their families, and offenders. The specific experiences of the authors are as follows:

A. Nicholas Groth, Ph.D.: Offender data are derived from three different groups:

1. *Offenders who were convicted of sexual offenses against children.* Information about these individuals was derived from clinical work and research (1966–1976) at the Center for the Diagnosis and Treatment of Sexually Dangerous Persons in Bridgewater, Massachusetts. Convicted child offenders who were ajudicated as "dangerous" (that is, likely to repeat their offenses and, in doing so, inflict harm on their victims), and who were civilly committed for an indeterminate period—from one day to life—in lieu of, or in addition to, a prison sentence constituted this population sample.

2. *Offenders who were apprehended but either ajudicated incompetent to stand trial or not guilty by reason of insanity.* Information regarding these

individuals was acquired through research at the Whiting Forensic Institute in Middletown, Connecticut, a security treatment center whose patient population included such subjects.

3. *Offenders who were identified or detected but who were either not prosecuted or convicted for a variety of reasons.* Information about these individuals was obtained through private referrals and through requests to the Forensic Mental Health Department of Harrington Memorial Hospital in Southbridge, Massachusetts, for court diversion evaluation.

Ann Wolbert Burgess, D.N.Sc., and Lynda Lytle Holmstrom, Ph.D.: The child and adolescent victims of sexual assault presented in this book are derived from three different target groups:

1. *Subsample from Boston City Hospital.* During a one-year period (1972–1973), the authors were on 24-hour call to the Emergency Department of Boston City Hospital to see anyone who came to the hospital with the complaint of sexual assault. A total of 37 child and adolescent victims under the age of 17 comprise this subsample (34 females and 3 males).

2. *Supervision and consultation cases.* Supervision and consultation have been provided by the authors to the Boston City Hospital Victim Counseling Service since 1973 and to the Norfolk County Rape Unit, Massachusetts.

3. *Referral cases.* Referral cases for crisis counseling and victim therapy have come from the mental health community.

Suzanne M. Sgroi, M.D.: Clinical material relating to medical evaluation and child protection is drawn from four different populations.

1. Cases seen in the Emergency Room and Outpatient Clinics, Mount Sinai Hospital, Hartford, Connecticut.

2. Cases seen in the Hartford Health Department Communicable Disease Clinic.

3. Cases seen in consultation with child protective services staff from the Connecticut State Department of Children and Youth Services.

4. Cases referred by municipal and state police.

Also, valuable contributors to specific issues in child sexual assault were made by Anna Giaretto (M.A.), Henry Giarretto (M.A.), Mary L. Keefe (M.C.J.), and Maureen P. McCausland (R.N., M.S.).

Acknowledgments

We wish to acknowledge the many people and agencies who have helped us with this project. We wish to acknowledge the Boston City Hospital Nursing Department for their cooperation in allowing us to base the victim counseling and research project in the Emergency Department. In particular, we wish to thank Anne G. Hargreaves, Executive Director of Nursing Services and Nursing Education, Department of Health and Hospitals, City of Boston, and Pamela MacLean Johansen, Assistant Director of Nursing, Emergency Services, Boston City Hospital.

We wish to express our thanks to the following people who have contributed to our work at various times and in various ways: H. Jean Birnbaum, Frank Bridges, Murray L. Cohen, and Richard A. Siegel.

We are appreciative of the following student research assistants from Boston College who helped with the library and court work: Marie Beatini, Deborah Blum, Mary Terrio Burroughs, Linda Evans, Thomas S. Gary, Dianne Kenty, and Anna T. Laszlo.

We very much appreciate the assistance in typing and manuscript preparation provided by Deborah Blum, Anne Hathaway, Irma Henk, Cynthia Hill, and Dianne Simonelli. And we wish to thank John N. Wolbert for the final proofreading of the pages. We appreciate the fine assistance provided by Darina Williams of Lexington Books who directed the editorial production of our book.

All case examples in the text represent actual clinical situations. The material is accurate, but names and identifying data have been changed to protect the client and clinician identities. We are especially grateful to these clients for contributing to our knowledge and understanding of this subject.

Introduction: A National Needs Assessment for Protecting Child Victims of Sexual Assault
Suzanne M. Sgroi

Sexual abuse of children is a crime that our society abhors in the abstract, but tolerates in reality. This is a strong and intentionally provocative statement about a topic that is still taboo in many circles. However, an examination of the ways in which child protection issues in child sexual assault are commonly addressed in every state both illustrates and supports this sorry assessment.

We tolerate sexual abuse of children because it is the last remaining component of the maltreatment syndrome in children that has yet to be faced head-on. Even now, protecting children from sexual assault receives far less community sanction than prevention of, and protection from, physical abuse or neglect. It seems to be "too dirty," "too Freudian," or perhaps "too close to home." Those who try to assist sexually abused children must be prepared to battle against incredulity, hostility, innuendo, and outright harassment. Worst of all, the advocate for the sexually abused child runs the risk of being smothered by indifference and a conspiracy of silence. The pressure from one's peer group, as well as the community, to ignore, minimize, or cover up the situation may be extreme.

Approach

Stereotypes and misinformation about sexual abuse of children abound in the United States and significantly hamper our overall approach. For example, we continue to approach the problem as if it always involves a violent, forcible attack on the child victim. This view prevails despite a large body of evidence showing that child sexual abuse often involves nonviolent, nonforcible contact between the victim and the perpetrator. So we expect child victims to "act traumatized" and discount the possibility of sexual assault if they do not. Needless to say, many cases are missed for this reason.

In addition, we continue to behave as if most cases involve perpetrators who are strangers to the child and who fit the mythical "dirty old man in the alley" stereotype that seems to be indigenous to our culture. Yet we *know* that many child sexual abuse cases are perpetrated by individuals who are known to the

---

This introduction contains excerpts from S. M. Sgroi, M.D., "Sexual Molestation of Children: The Last Frontier in Child Abuse," *Children Today* 4, no. 3 (1975). Reprinted with permission.

child. Indeed, most child sexual abuse involves intrafamily perpetrators—fathers, stepfathers, uncles, mothers' boy friends, etc.—people who have ready access to the child in his or her home. Many offenders are individuals whose primary sexual orientation is not toward children. However, because we expect perpetrators of child sexual assault to look the stereotyped part, we often miss or discount many cases.

It follows, then, that we approach most cases of child sexual abuse as if they were capricious and catastrophic one-time-only events—yet many of these cases actually reflect a continuum of sexual contact between children and adults over time. We tend to act always as if the incident we encounter is the first such incident that has occurred and frequently overlook indicators that it is not. Meanwhile, the child victims pay the penalty for our society's collective ignorance.

Reporting

It is impossible to assist a sexually abused child unless we identify his or her plight and report it properly. We tolerate sexual abuse of children in our society because we permit gross underreporting of this phenomenon. Sexual assault of a minor is a reportable crime in every state in the United States. If the perpetrator is a family member or caretaker of the child, or if a family member or person responsible for the child's care permitted the perpetrator to have access to the victim, then the situation must also be reported to the statutory child protective services agency within that state. Most states' child abuse reporting legislation requires such reports. In many localities there are penalties for failure to report child sexual abuse to police and protective services. By failure to report, we deny effective intervention to the victim. Nevertheless, society looks the other way as reports are suppressed and withheld.

Recognition

We tolerate sexual abuse of children in our society because a low priority is placed on acquiring the diagnostic skills necessary to recognize the phenomenon. *Recognition of sexual molestation in a child is entirely dependent on the individual's inherent willingness to entertain the possibility that the condition may exist.* Physical examination of the child to obtain medical corroboration of sexual abuse is extremely important. Lack of corroborating medical evidence frequently hamstrings positive intervention efforts on behalf of young children. However, the medical profession is frequently not prepared to obtain this information because of the long-term perpetuation of two myths related to sexual abuse.

Medical Myth Number 1 is that a genital examination of a child is intrinsically traumatic, and that special medical expertise is required to perform an adequate examination to identify the physical indicators of sexual assault. This is a "cop-out"—rooted in the basic hangups about human sexuality that physicians, alas, share with the rest of society. Genital examiantions of children are *not* intrinsically traumatic; any practicing physician should be qualified to perform them competently. Medical examination is *essential* for every child in whom sexual assault is suspected.

Medical Myth Number 2 involves "kids with clap," children who acquire gonorrhea after the neonatal period. Children, of course, acquire gonorrhea just as adults do, by person-to-person sexual contact with someone else who has an infection. Yet doctors have clung to an erroneous double standard for years by postulating a nonvenereal mode of transmission of gonorrhea for children only! Children do *not* acquire gonorrhea from doorknobs, toilet seats, bathwater, or bedsheets. Any physician who cites a nonvenereal mode of transmission for genital, urethral, or pharyngeal gonococcal infections is doing so because he or she cannot cope with the reality of adult-child sexual contact. Gonorrhea in childhood should always be regarded as an indicator of sexual assault. The toilet seat–bathwater–bedsheet myth should be annihilated because it is hurting children badly. So long as it is perpetuated, we will miss cases of sexual abuse of children.

Interviewing Children

We tolerate sexual abuse of children in our society because, thus far, we have largely ignored the teachable and transmittable body of existing knowledge about investigative and therapeutic interviewing techniques. Every community needs to have a few individuals who are skilled in these techniques available to do investigative interviewing of children when sexual assault is suspected. These individuals should be professionally competent, and they need to be able to serve as credible witnesses in court, if necessary. Yet, to date, most communities do not possess these skilled individuals, since developing interviewing techniques in child sexual assault has not been a high priority either.

Investigation

Our society tolerates sexual abuse of children because we have not yet accepted the premise that special training and skills are absolutely essential for police and child protective services workers who investigate cases. In most law enforcement agencies, cases are investigated by individuals in the detective or juvenile division who have no special training in child sexual assault. This is, unfortunately, equally true of child protective services agencies—the workers who investigate sexual abuse cases usually lack the specialized skills, experience, and supervision required to deal with the most delicate, volatile, and highly demanding child protection problem yet to be identified. Small wonder that many other professionals cringe at the idea of turning sexual abuse cases over to law enforcement and child protection agencies whose employees lack the necessary expertise. Yet it is a mistake for the private sector to attempt to bypass the existing statutory agencies in handling child sexual abuse cases.

Professional Cooperation

Time and again, the police, child protective services, medical professionals, therapists, and counselors attempt to investigate cases unilaterally—without input from the other disciplines. It is *impossible* for a doctor alone, a police officer alone, a social worker alone, a counselor alone, or therapist working alone to determine if sexual abuse of a child has actually occurred and—the all-important *and*—if the child and other children similarly situated are at further risk. We must work in concert. And yet for a number of ancient and dishonorable reasons (including mutual distrust, ignorance, and "defending of turf"), we professionals fail to work together. To the extent that we refuse to utilize each others' skills and expertise on behalf of the children who present to us, we tacitly tolerate further sexual abuse.

Access to the Child

In most states it is often extremely difficult to gain access to a minor in order to interview, examine, and treat him or her for child sexual assault without prior parental consent. However, in the majority of cases, parents are involved by either commission or omission in the sexual abuse and can hardly be expected to give consent willingly for any process that would tend to incriminate *them.* Accordingly, obtaining access to the child to collect evidence in an incest case usually requires a judicial custody order that is not likely to be issued unless or until compelling evidence is presented to the court that corroborates sexual abuse. We tolerate sexual abuse of children in our society to the extent that we permit such "catch-22" situations to exist. For the most part, society's failure to enable access to the sexually abused child is rooted in archaic laws and customs that subordinate the best interests of children to property rights of adults. *One exception:* Nearly every state in the United States permits minors to obtain diagnosis and treatment for venereal disease without parental consent. Few child advocates utilize these statutes to expedite examination of minors for sexual assault. To date, a statutorily permitted physical examination of the child to identify sexual assault *and* venereal disease without prior parental consent, combined with assistance from sympathetic school officials, day care center personnel, and, occasionally, clergy, are the only methods by which access to the child for investigative purposes can be obtained prior to introducing corroborative evidence to the court. Until we achieve better access to children who are suspected to be victims of sexual abuse, we will be unable to intervene effectively in a great many cases.

The Criminal Justice System

We tolerate sexual abuse of children in our society because we continue to process cases through an adversary system of criminal justice that is overwhelmingly weighted against the child victim at virtually every level. Consider how our criminal justice system operates against children who are sexually abused.

1. Few cases are pursued on the strength of the evidence alone unless an adult family member, usually the mother, is willing to press charges on behalf of the child. Yet the usual scenario in father-daughter incest cases is that the mother will ally herself with the father and refuse to act as an advocate for the child in court by serving as complainant against her husband.

2. When charges are filed, accused perpetrators are often released immediately on low bond pending trial with no enforceable injunction to stay away from the family. Yet, again, the scenario in most cases features the father or a father figure as perpetrator. The likelihood that he will harass and pressure the family to drop the charges and recant their allegations is very great. If, indeed, the defendent does stay away from the family, he may also cease to support his wife and children, in some cases, even locking *them* out of the home. Law enforcement and social agencies have little protection or concrete assistance to offer these beleaguered people over time.

3. Cases that do go to court may take an unconscionable amount of time to be processed and heard. Frequent appearances in court and continuances may prolong the intrafamily crisis to unbearable lengths for many families. Again, the frequent result in many incest cases is withdrawal of allegations and dropping of charges.

4. The evidence collection and adversary court process may require the child victim to repeat his or her testimony frequently before and during the trial and to undergo cross-examination by a defense attorney whose sole interest is to discredit damaging evidence against his or her client—the suspected perpetrator. This process may well be more traumatic to the child victim than the sexual abuse itself, yet we frequently fail to exercise available options to minimize this trauma. More important, we do not make changes in our criminal justice system to ensure more sensitive and appropriate handling of intrafamily

sexual abuse cases. Instead we behave as if all these unfortunate procedures and their consequences are truly inevitable and immutable. We will all tolerate sexual abuse of children so long as we continue to act as if those aspects of our criminal justice system that victimize children are inalterably engraved in stone instead of subject to change by a free society.

Penalties

When convictions against perpetrators of child sexual abuse are obtained, the penalty prescribed by law may vary widely from state to state. This is especially true for incest, the penalty for which may vary from 1 to 50 years imprisonment, depending on the jurisdiction. There are even two states whose penal code invokes the death penalty for child rape (this may well be unconstitutional). The extreme variability of penalties for convicted child sexual offenders further complicates intervention on behalf of the child or children involved. In most incest cases, the more severe the penalty, the less cooperation can be expected from other family members.

Treatment

Perhaps the greatest lapse of societal concern for sexually abused children lies in the failure to link punishment of the convicted offender to treatment. For too long we have accepted only one "therapeutic" option in parent-child incest cases—family breakup and separation. This is most often accomplished by removing the target child from the family, or, if a conviction is obtained, sending the perpetrator to jail. Understandably, members of the helping professions are reluctant to participate in such a destructive option. On the other hand, the track record in persuading perpetrators and families to undergo voluntary therapy for incest is abysmal. Although referrals to a psychiatric or counseling agency may be eagerly accepted at the outset, perpetrators of incest rarely remain in an effective treatment program when the pressure to participate slackens.

Why do we ignore compelling evidence that an authoritative incentive to change his or her behavior is absolutely essential for the adult perpetrator of child sexual abuse? Why are we so slow to establish a network of family sexual abuse treatment programs patterned after the highly successful Child Sexual Abuse Treatment Program in San Jose, California? It has been demonstrated that there *is* a humane alternative to separation, family breakup, and incarceration for incest. It requires concern, caring, skill, and an authoritative "or else" to ensure family participation. Ideally, there should be direct referral into a family treatment program from a criminal justice system that acknowledges that punishment consisting of incarceration of the perpetrator may well penalize

the victim further by causing irretrievable family breakup. Although a successful
family treatment program may, in time, attract voluntary or even self-referred
clients, it will be necessary to *build in* an authoritative incentive to participate
in order to begin treatment programs in most communities. Direct referral of
clients from the police or the courts to a nonpunitive treatment program is not
likely to begin spontaneously. Professionals who seek to establish effective
sexual abuse treatment programs will have to work cooperatively and persuasive-
ly with those in the criminal justice system. A hearts-and-flowers approach is
likely to receive short shrift. Initially, it may well be necessary to persuade
judges to permit participation in a treatment program aimed at reuniting the
family in conjunction with (rather than in lieu of) punishment. The treatment
program will almost certainly have to establish a successful track record before
most judges will be willing to shorten criminal sentences or accept participation
in the program as a condition of the perpetrator's probation rather than being
sent to jail. This will require enormous effort. Leadership will have to come from
the very therapeutic community that has worked so poorly with the criminal
justice system in the past and tends to be so uncomfortable with authoritative
incentives for treatment. However, we will tolerate sexual abuse of children as
long as most of us live in states and communities where no family treatment
programs for sexual abuse exist.

Recommendations

How can we become a society that constructively opposes sexual abuse of
children by our behavior as well as by abstract principles?

National Leadership

We need to be on national record against sexual abuse of children, as well as
against child abuse and neglect. The National Center for Child Abuse and Neglect
(or any other statutorily defined national child maltreatment center) needs to
have a specific mandate empowering it to take a leadership role in public education, research, demonstration, and funding of programs to deal with child sexual
abuse. In addition, there needs to be a national movement to standardize penalties for sexual assault of children.

State and Community Action

It is on the state and community level that effective action can and must take
place. All components of the intervention system must eventually become

involved. Police, child protective services personnel, prosecutors, and judges must become better informed about sexual abuse of children. Every community needs a small group of well-trained and highly skilled individuals who are experienced in the investigative and interviewing techniques required to work with families. Legislation must be introduced on the state level to permit sufficient access to child victims to determine what level of intervention is required. The criminal justice system must be reformed on the state and local levels to ensure speedier, more knowledgeable, and more humane processing of cases. Last, but not least, offender treatment and family treatment must be linked to punishment. A humane alternative to separation and family breakup in incest cases is feasible only at the community level. Its establishment will depend on a hitherto unheard of level of cooperation between the public and private sector, with a blending of voluntary and mandated roles and expertise. The time is ripe to gather known skills and information from a variety of disciplines and bring them together for a concerted and constructive approach to this universal and tragic problem.

The following chapters describe known clinical data on sexual abuse of children from the disciplines of psychology, nursing, sociology, and medicine. The authors sincerely hope that the readers will be able to apply some or all of the information presented to child sexual abuse situations in their own professional practices and communities.

Part I Offenders

The purpose of this first part is to focus on experiences, observations, and ideas derived from working with child offenders, as a client group, for more than a dozen years. This part does not present a formal study of the child offender, nor will it offer a definitive solution to this form of sexual psychopathy. Instead, the material offers an approach to structuring clinical work with such a client population.

1

Patterns of Sexual Assault against Children and Adolescents
A. Nicholas Groth

A sexual offender against young people (commonly referred to as a *child molester*) is a significantly older individual whose conscious sexual desires and responses are directed, either partially or exclusively, toward prepubertal children (pedophilia) and/or pubescent children (hebephilia) to whom he or she may be directly related (incest) or not. It is a widely held assumption that such contacts constitute a risk to the sexually immature child, whether that risk be ethical (the misrepresentation of the moral standards of the community), psychological (the development of emotional disturbance and distorted ideas and attitudes toward human sexuality), and/or physical (the jeopardizing of the child's safety). The exposure and introduction of a child to adult sexuality is regarded in the American culture as especially serious and something from which children should be safeguarded. Unlike other aspects of adult-child interactions, it is regarded as inappropriate and potentially traumatic for an adult to instruct a child in human sexuality experientially. There is the legitimate assumption that the adult's motive is self-serving in such situations rather than an expression of a genuine investment in the child's needs and welfare. Given such strong social and legal sanctions against such behavior, why would any adult turn to a child in search of sexual gratification rather than other, more acceptable outlets? Such behavior seems unreasonable.

Myths and Realities

In order to answer such a puzzling question and to explain such behavior, a number of myths and misconceptions have developed about the child offender both on the part of the general public and by professionals as well. The layperson imagines the child offender to be a stranger, an old man, insane or retarded, alcohol or drug addicted, sexually frustrated and impotent or sexually jaded, and looking for new "kicks." He is "gay" and recruiting little boys into homosexuality or he is "straight" and responding to the advances of a sexually provocative little girl. Perhaps the most insidious myth is that the offender himself is the victim of a provocative and seductive child, for here the victim is blamed for being victimized, and the actual offender is not held fully responsible for his behavior. He is sometimes regarded as a brutal sex fiend or as a shy, passive, sexually inexperienced person. He is oversexed or he is undersexed; and so on. These are popular notions, appealing in their simplicity—even if they

3

are self-contradicting—and they offer the advantage of making the child offender as different and unlike the ordinary person—ourselves, our parents, our children, our relatives, friends, and teachers—as possible. These same basic views are offered by many professionals—psychiatrists, psychologists, nurses, physicians, social workers, sociologists, police, lawyers, and judges—who may view the child offender in terms of a sexually prohibitive, repressive, and ignorant society that mistakenly labels him as deviant—the social attitudes toward his behavior rather than the behavior itself being inappropriate. Or the child offender may be seen as the product of a sexually permissive and immoral society with lax attitudes and laws regarding sexuality that stimulate and encourage him through the availability of pornography, prostitution, drugs, alcohol, and sex outside of marriage. Some see such behavior as reflective of lower-class mentality and morality, poverty, and the lack of education. Others attribute it to a criminal personality. And still others, when the offender is an adolescent, take the position that this behavior is typical for a sexually maturing male—nothing more than experimentation.

No doubt we could find case examples that would tend to support each of the above notions, yet it becomes quickly apparent when working with child offenders and their victims that these examples prove to be the exception rather than the rule. The appeal of these views is that they reduce a very complex, multidetermined behavior to a very simple, single cause. It is difficult and frustrating to conceptualize the many complex, interrelated factors underlying sexual involvement between adults and children and then to find a clear, practical, and effective solution to this problem. The myths, the stereotypes, the generalizations are easier to understand and accept, and, therefore, more satisfying than the reality.

In contrast to the notion that the child molester is an old man, we found all our clients had committed their first known offense before the age of 40; over 80 percent were first offenders by the age of 30 and almost 5 percent had committed their first sexual assault before they reached adolescence. Rather than being a stranger, the majority of offenders knew their victims at least casually. Likewise the role of alcohol in the commission of the offense appears to be overemphasized. Less than one-third of our clients could be described as alcohol or drug dependent. The majority did not abuse alcohol or drugs and were not intoxicated at the time of their offenses.

The stereotype of the pedophile as a retardate is unsupported by our data, which reveal no significant difference in intelligence between child offenders and the general population. The idea that the pedophile is psychotic or insane is likewise incorrect. Less than 5 percent showed clinical evidence of some psychotic process operating at the time of the offense. Finally the belief that homosexuals are particularly attracted to children is completely unsupported by our data.[1] The child offenders who engaged in adult sexual relationships as well were heterosexual. Those offenders who selected underage male victims either have always done so *exclusively* or have regressed from adult *heterosexual* relationships. There were no homosexual, adult-oriented, offenders in our sample who turned to children.

Incidence of Sexual Abuse

No clear idea of the extent or the dimensions of this serious social problem yet exists. Its incidence is difficult to estimate since much of this abuse may go undetected or unreported for a variety of reasons and the detected and apprehended suspect is not always convicted. Furthermore, known instances of sexual assault against children may be prosecuted under a number of different statutes, some of which would also apply to offenses against adult victims: indecent exposure, indecent assault and battery, open and gross lewdness, contributing to the delinquency of a minor, unnatural acts, carnal abuse, sodomy, rape, incest, and so on. Therefore, the available crime rate statistics for this offense may be highly unreliable. However, it is our impression, as people working in the field, that we are dealing with a problem of considerable magnitude.

The theoretical contributions on pedophilia have related the etiology of the sexual desire for underage persons either to psychological concepts of arrested psychosexual development;[2] intellectual deficiency;[3] or mental illness (psychosis);[4] or to physiological conditions of functional disturbance, such as impotency;[5] degenerative diseases, such as alcoholism[6] and senility;[7] or organic insult, such as cerebral trauma.[8] However, for the most part, writers have tended to regard this condition as a single clinical entity. Even more significant, none of these theoretical conceptualizations has given rise to any systematic body of research.

Instead, most of what we know about the child offender has resulted from empirical data derived principally from analyses of prison populations of convicted child molesters.[3,9] However, these studies, for the most part, have been limited to a presentation of a number of accumulated behavioral observations without any subsequent attempt to verify the resulting classification schemes experimentally.

Classifications have been proposed based on a wide variety of criteria: some focus on the characteristics of the offender himself, such as age; others focus on the characteristics of the victim, such as age or sex; some emphasize the type of sexual act; others, the aim or intention of the impulse; still others consider the offender's level of sociosexual adjustment and situational factors. In addition to using these criteria as a primary basis for differentiating among pedophilic sex offenders, the reported research has typically presented data regarding such variables as the nature of the overt sexual activity, the conscious sexual attitudes and responses of the offender, the relationship between offenders and the victims, the places of offense, the degree of participation on the part of victims, and a number of personal and social characteristics of the offender, such as family background, medical history, intelligence, education, occupation, marital status, religious affiliation, and so on. However, the state of knowledge regarding this form of sexual deviancy has not progressed beyond clinical and statistical observation. To date, the bulk of the literature on pedophilia consists of case reporting, in which it is difficult to differentiate relevant material from irrelevant, or large-scale statistical research, in which individual differences are regarded as error. There is very little research available that relates the statistical findings to the theoretical data. As a result, the psychology of pedophilia remains pretty much an enigma.

Even though definitive research in regard to this area of human sexuality is lacking, there is, nevertheless, a demand placed on clinicians to bring to bear their knowledge and experience to deal with those offenders who directly or indirectly come to the attention of law enforcement, mental health, social service, and other community agencies.

Patterns of Pedophilic Behavior

Adults who become sexually involved with children or adolescents can be classified into two groups on the basis of whether this involvement constitutes a persistent pattern (a fixation) or a new activity or change (a regression) in their sexual orientations or lifestyles.

The Fixated Pedophile

Fixation is defined as a temporary or permanent arrestment of psychosocial maturation resulting from unresolved formative issues that persist and underlie the organization of subsequent phases of development. A *fixated child offender* is a person who has, from adolescence, been sexually attracted primarily or exclusively to significantly younger people, and this attraction has persisted throughout his life, regardless of what other sexual experiences he has had. As a teenager the offender tends to avoid the usual pattern of socialization with age-mates typical of adolescence, such as dating and competitive sports, and as an adult he generally does not initiate or actively pursue mature sexual relationships. If sexual involvement with another adult in fact does occur, it most frequently originates from the efforts of the partner. The fixated pedophile may respond to sexual invitations or demands from age-mates but generally does not initiate or actively pursue them. When they do occur, they are clearly a departure from his usual pattern of sexual encounters and are precipitated by external events or circumstances. For example, a young man, age 20, who was accused of an indecent assault on an 11-year-old boy had earned a living as a male prostitute and had modeled for pornographic films. In this capacity he had sexual relations with adults, both men and women, but his own sexual preferences were for preadolescent boys. Such involvements are situational in nature and never replace the primary sexual attraction to and preference for underage persons. For the most part, these pedophilic desires are not disturbing to the fixated offender; that is, he is comfortable and satisfied with such activity and experiences no intense feelings of guilt, shame, or remorse in this regard. Even when the fixated offender is distressed by such desires, he experiences the attraction as a compulsion, something that cannot be resisted or avoided. He or she feels controlled by a need for sexual contact with a child and not in command of such wishes. Sexual thoughts and fantasies about children or young adolescents preoccupy the offender, and interest in them often reaches the level of an obsession. The offender appears sexually "addicted" to children. Conversely, sexual relationships with adults tend to be avoided out of fear of rejection and/or punishment; feelings of inadequacy or inferiority; experiences of shyness, guilt, anxiety or embarrassment; or simply because he does not find adults to be sexually desirable—they just do not "turn him on." Sexual activity with adults is not as emotionally gratifying as sexual activity with underage people, and this immature orientation does not appear confined to his sexual life. It frequently reflects a psychosocial adjustment that characterizes the fixated offenders' whole style of life. He appears to be a marginal or inadequate individual who is somewhat overwhelmed by the ordinary demands of life. He feels compelled to interact sexually with children, and he finds or creates opportunities to be in their company. Rather than a reaction to an acute crisis situation in his life, this offender's pattern of repeated sexual contacts with children or adolescents seems to constitute for him an attempted resolution—albeit a maladaptive one—to specific life issues or conflicts encountered in his psychosocial development. Pedophilic interests have become part of his nature. Jeff is such a person.

Clinical Case 1

Jeff is a 20-year-old, single, white male convicted of indecent assault and battery on a child under 14. He is the second oldest of four children and the only boy. His father worked as manager of a warehouse and provided well for his family. His mother worked part-time as a secretary until Jeff was 10 years old and then went to work full time, entrusting the care of the children to their maternal grandmother. Jeff's parents describe their marriage as compatible and harmonious. His father does not drink and tends to leave many of the family tasks up to the discretion of his wife.

Jeff's birth was full term and normal, but he developed asthma during infancy and suffered from this until age 7. He was a sensitive, affectionate, and obedient child who developed a strong attraction to his older sister. For the most part he preferred to play by himself and rarely showed any desire for play activities with other children. His mother tended to "baby and cater to" Jeff, but his father showed a greater fondness for his three daughters and was rather strict and somewhat rejecting toward his son. Jeff was enuretic and incontinent up to the third grade. During his early years of school he chewed crayons and complained of headaches. He was of average intelligence and ultimately graduated from a trade school where he studied printing.

As a preadolescent, about the age of 10, Jeff experienced his first sexual activity. Two 16-year-old boys forced him to perform fellatio on them. He was scared by this experience and told no one about it, but feels that it was the impact of this event that ultimately led him into his later legal predicaments. He explained that these older boys clearly enjoyed the act and that he wanted to experience the same feelings they had. Jeff reports that at age 14 his father discovered him involved in sexual play with his 6-year-old nephew and that, on the pretext of providing sexual instruction, took Jeff to bed and engaged in sexual relations with him. (At this time Jeff's mother was in the hospital giving birth to her youngest child.) Jeff relates feeling troubled by this event, which occurred twice on subsequent nights. "I was frightened. I thought my dad was a fag."

Jeff did some casual dating during his later teen years but remained emotionally isolated from age-mates; and although an opportunity for sexual relations occasionally presented itself, he would find some excuse to avoid them. Jeff realized he was sexually interested in young boys and began clipping pictures of them out of magazines and newspapers and drawing genitals on them. At age 20 he approached a 13-year-old boy at a local swimming hole, engaged him in conversation and walked into the woods with him. He then grabbed the boy, put his hand over the boy's mouth to stop him from yelling, and pulled off the boy's swim trunks. He made some threatening remarks to the boy, then got undressed, and forced the boy to perform oral sex on him. Jeff simultaneously performed fellatio on his victim, after which he let the boy go, warning him not to tell anyone. Jeff was arrested, and while out on bail awaiting trial committed a similar offense on a 12-year-old boy. Jeff masturbates to fantasies of young boys whom he finds physically attractive because "their bodies are soft and smooth and they are sexually innocent." He fantasizes that they will enjoy the sexual encounter and seek further contact. He is repelled by the thought of adult men and women as sexual partners and finds adult homosexuality particularly offensive.

The Regressed Pedophile

Regression is defined as a temporary or permanent appearance of primitive behavior after more mature forms of expression have been attained, regardless of whether or not the immature behavior was actually manifested earlier in the individual's sexual development. A *regressed child offender* is a person who originally preferred peers or adult partners for sexual gratification. However, when these adult relationships became conflictual in some important respect, the adult became replaced by the child as the focus of this person's sexual interests and desires. Throughout his sociosexual development the regressed offender exhibits an appropriate interest in age-mates. Yet his development appears to be undermined by a sense of inadequacy that increases as he approaches the responsibilities of adulthood. His self-image and sense of identity is then further impaired by some challenge to his sexual adequcy or threat to his sense of competency as a man. The situational crisis may be physical, social, sexual, marital, financial, vocational, etc.—or a combination of such factors—but it precipitates the sexual involvement with a child. His offense is an impulsive and desperate act that is symptomatic of a failure to cope adaptively with specific life stresses. The regressed offender has not exhibited any predominant sexual attraction to significantly younger people during his sexual development. If any such involvement did occur during adolescence, it was situational or experimental in nature. Instead, this individual's sociosexual interests have focused on peer-age or older people either primarily or exclusively. Typically this offender is married and a situation develops that threatens this relationship. Feeling overwhelmed by the resulting stresses, this man becomes involved sexually with a child. Quite often he is distressed by this behavior, that is, he may experience feelings of guilt, shame, disgust, embarrassment, remorse, or dissatisfaction about what he has done, but these feelings occur after the fact. At the time of the sexual activity, this offender is usually in a state of depression, in which he doesn't care, and/or a state of partial dissociation, in which he doesn't think about what he is doing—he suspends his usual values, his controls are weak, and he behaves in a way that is, in some respects, counter to his usual standards and conduct. During this period of regressive sexual behavior, this offender's sexual encounters with adults usually continue to coexist with his sexual encounters with youngsters. His pedophilic behavior appears to be an effort to cope with specific life issues. Gary is such a person.

Clinical Case 2

Gary is a 20-year old, single, white male convicted of unnatural acts on a child under the age of 14. He is the second oldest of eight children and has six brothers and one sister. His father operated a small-appliance repair business and his mother worked occasionally as a cleaning woman in a nursing home. The family had a low-income standard of living, and Gary's mother suffered a series of "mental breakdowns" requiring repeated hospitalization during his development. Gary never felt close to any member of his family, and parental relationships were marked by considerable friction and antagonism.

Gary's medical history is unremarkable and, apart from some truancy, he presented no serious behavioral problems in school. He appeared to be of average intelligence. At age 15 he was picked up by the police for being a runaway and for stealing and was committed to a youth detention center for one year. At this facility he was forcibly sodomized by an older boy. He returned to school after his release but then dropped out to join the service. He served in the Army for four years, during which he was stationed in Korea where he became actively involved with both prostitutes and native women. He received an honorable discharge and worked at a series of unskilled jobs.

At this time, he left home because of difficulties with his parents and began living with a cousin as man and wife. She was divorced and had a 6-year-old daughter. This relationship quickly proved to place more demands on Gary than he was prepared to handle. However, any attempts he made to end it were successfully discouraged by his cousin's threat of suicide should he leave her. They had been having sexual relations regularly, and his cousin became pregnant. Mounting financial problems, increasing stresses with his parents, and continuing pressures with his cousin led to some heavy drinking. Then one day the little girl brought some of her young friends into the apartment while Gary was taking a shower. He felt a sudden sexual urge to expose himself to the three girls, ages 7, 6, and 5. He undressed them, put them on the bed, and fondled them. He had them play with his penis and perform oral sex until he ejaculated. Prior to the incident Gary had had a couple of drinks but stated that he wasn't drunk. He was depressed and discouraged and felt trapped and desperate. He was lonely and saw the girls as undemanding and loving. Gary had no previous history of any sexual involvements with underage people or any unconventional sexual experiences. His interests focused on adult women. He pleaded guilty and was given a sentence of one year to the House of Correction and two years probation on and after.

Summary

In summary, sexual offenders against underage people can be differentiated on the basis of whether their pedophilic behavior is a chronic condition (a fixation) or an acute situation (a regression) in their sexual lifestyle. The fixated offender, in contrast to the regressed offender, has had little or no meaningful involvement in peer-age or adult sexual relationships, nor does he experience any strong desire for such. Instead, he consistently selects an underage person as his primary and preferred source of sexual activity. His is a chronic and persistent sexual compulsion. In differentiating the regressed sexual offender from the fixated sexual offender, you find a primary sexual orientation toward people of equivalent (adult) age, a precipitating stress, and a consequent displacement of sexual impulses onto children. The regressed offender has had positive adult sexual relationships and has made active efforts to establish these relationships. He turns to children only when these adult relationships have become conflictual. His is an acute and reactive sexual involvement, often more impulsive than premeditated. For both types of offender, the sexual involvement with a child is symptomatic of an internal, psychosocial crisis. For the fixated pedophile, this peaks at adolescence and results in the formation of a sexual orientation in which a child becomes the preferred sexual choice. For the regressed offender, the onset of the crisis is the impact of adult responsibilities and life demands that he experiences as overwhelming and from which he retreats to the psychological safety of a sexual involvement with a child. Obviously the regressed offender, who has had comfortable and satisfying peer age sexual relationships at some point in his life, has a better prognosis for rehabilitation than the fixated offender, who never has had this experience.

Motivational Intent[a]

In addition to categorizing offenders in terms of whether their sexual involvement with children is preferred or only resorted to under stress, we can also categorize offenders in regard to the psychological aims underlying their behavior. Child sexual assault is equivalent to a symptom, and like the dynamics of any symptom, it serves to gratify a wish, to defend against anxiety, and to express an unresolved conflict. The nature of the interaction between the offender and his victim reveals his motivational intent and the determinants prompting his selection of a child for sexual contact. Such offenses can be classified into two basic categories: pressured sex contacts and forced sex contacts.

Sex-Pressure Offenses

This offense is characterized by a relative lack of physical force in the commission of the offense; in fact, the offender generally behaves in counteraggressive ways. His typical modus operandi is either *enticement,* in which he attempts to indoctrinate the child into sexuality through persuasion or cajolement, or *entrapment,* in which he takes advantage of having put the child in a situation in which he or she feels indebted or obligated. This offender makes efforts to persuade his victim to cooperate and to acquiesce or consent to the sexual relationship, oftentimes by bribing or rewarding the child with attention, affection, approval, money, gifts, treats, and good times. But he may be dissuaded if the child

---

[a]Parts of this section are excerpted from "Motivational Intent in the Sexual Assault of Children," A. Nicholas Groth and Ann W. Burgess, *Criminal Justice and Behavior* 4, no. 3 (September 1977):253–264. Used by permission of the publisher, Sage Publications, Inc.

actively refuses or resists because he does not resort to physical force. His aim is to gain sexual control of the child by developing a willing or consenting sexual relationship. At some level, he cares for the child and is emotionally involved with him or her. The pedophilic interest can be understood as the result of a projective identification on the part of the offender with the child in which dependency and affiliation constitute major components of the motivational aim. In sex-pressure situations, sexuality appears to be in service of needs for physical contact and affection. Such offenders appear to desire the child as a love object and typically describe the victim as innocent, loving, open, affectionate, clean, attractive, and undemanding. They feel safer and more comfortable with children. Very often victim and offender know each other prior to their sexual involvement, and sometimes they are related. This involvement can be continuing and fairly consistent over time. The following cases illustrate sex-pressure by enticement.

Clinical Case 3

Henry is a 60-year-old, single, white man who was observed sexually fondling a nine-year-old boy in a movie theatre. He had a prior record of 10 convictions for similar offenses with young girls and boys, and to date has spent over 25 years in prison for his pedophilic activities. At age 15 he was initiated into sexuality by a 27-year-old woman; however, he found his interests focused on children between the ages of 9 and 13. He would approach them and offer them money, sometimes exposing himself. "Most relationships were hit-or-miss at first. I wasn't comfortable with adults and I'd turn to kids for love and affection. I wanted a steady relationship with a kid. I'd take them horseback riding, boating, fishing, to carnivals and zoos—things like that. I'd ask them to have sex and would touch them, but if they refused, I wouldn't go any further. It wasn't so much the sex. What I wanted most was hugging and kissing—this gave me more satisfaction than 'coming off.' They were getting to like me and that satisfied me. I cared about them and was concerned that they got something out of it. Usually I'd masturbate the boys and fondle the girls. I didn't care to have them masturbate me. Once in a while, when the kid wanted it, I would 'blow' them, and sometimes I would rub my penis against them or between their legs, but I used to prolong the sex, the kissing and hugging and fondling—I wasn't interested in climaxing. At first I was interested in boys and girls, but little girls talk a lot and little boys don't, and I became happier with boys; the girls were more demanding. What especially attracted me were boys that looked like girls. Sometimes the kids got involved with me for the money—newspaper boys were good prospects—but I always tried to turn it into a friendship, and they would introduce me to other kids who would engage in sexual activities with me."

Where there is an ongoing involvement, this can usually be understood as the result of a mutually advantageous arrangement; and "giving" on the part of the offender is more bartering than real sharing. The following cases illustrate sex-pressure by entrapment.

Clinical Case 4

Jack is a 49-year-old married, white male who was referred for evaluation in regard to his sexual involvement with a 14-year-old neighbor girl. He was convicted of statutory rape but denies the charge, admitting only to having taken "snapshots" of the girl undressed. His victim, Debbie, was neglected by her family and "she would come over to our house and have meals with us or would drop in to watch television or just spend time with us. Debbie was always dressed in rags and my wife would sew her clothes or I would buy her new ones. When she needed eyeglasses, I got them for her and I would take her and her friends on picnics and to the movies. Her parents were alcoholic, and she started to get mixed up with drugs. I got a new camera and asked her to pose for some pictures, and she agreed, but that's all that happened." Debbie, however, stated that during the picture taking session Jack fondled and caressed her and this progressed to intercourse. She said she didn't know how to handle the situation, and although she didn't want to get Jack arrested, she didn't want the sexual activity to continue; so when he again made advances toward her, she threatened to report him. The incident, however, was uncovered when Jack's wife accidentally discovered the photographs of Debbie hidden in her husband's workshop. Under questioning Debbie acknowledged the sexual involvement.

Sex-Force Offenses

The sex-force offenses are characterized by the threat of harm and/or the use of physical force in the commission of the offense. The offender's method of operation is either *intimidation,* in which he exploits the child's relative helplessness, naivete, and awe of adults, or *physical aggression,* in which he attacks and physically overpowers his victim. This category of assaults may be subdivided into two groups: (1) the *exploitative* assault, in which threat or force is used to overcome the victim's resistance, and (2) the *sadistic* assault, in which force becomes eroticized.

The exploitative offender essentially forces himself upon the victim. He typically employs verbal threat, restraint, manipulation, intimidation, and physical strength to overcome any resistance on the part of the victim. He may strike the child, but whatever aggression exists is always directed toward accomplishing the sexual act. It is not the intent of the offender to hurt the victim, and he will usually use only whatever force is necessary to overpower the child. The physical risk to the victim is inadvertent rather than deliberate injury. This offender uses the child as an object for sexual relief. He makes no attempt to engage the child in any emotional way. Instead he sees the child as an outlet solely for self-gratification. The child is regarded as a disposable object, one to be used and then discarded. The sex act constitutes the extent and duration of the relationship, and thus, usually, it is a temporary and unstable involvement.

This offender relates to his victim in an opportunistic, exploitative, and manipulative way. Self-entitlement characterizes his orientation toward the child, and sexuality appears to be in the service of a need for power. Such offenders describe their victims as weak, defenseless, helpless, unable to resist, easily controlled and manipulated. They feel stronger and more in charge with children.

The majority of exploitive child offenders intend no actual injury to their victims, submission being their objective, but at the same time there are also no strong defenses against hurting the child, if necessary. This type of offender exhibits a lack of concern for the consequences or cost to others of his sexual activity; he experiences his motivation to be strong sexual needs that he is incapable of delaying or redirecting. Children are objects of prey; they are stalked and hunted; and any resistance on their part can quickly release anger and hostility in this offender. He will usually not take "no" for an answer and will enforce his sexual demands through coercion, often employing physical force, the use of a weapon, or intimating that the victim will be harmed if he or she does not cooperate. The following cases illustrate the exploitative type of sexual assaults:

Clinical Case 5

Ron is a 27-year-old white male, legally separated from his wife after five years of marriage. He was convicted of the rape of two boys, aged 10 and 12. "It started out with just looking at a young boy's nude body, then with playing with his privates. About the age of 20 I started asking kids to perform oral sex on me. This didn't happen too much until I got my driver's license so I could get away from home. I found out an an early age that you get caught too easily if you go too near home. After my marriage I started performing oral and anal sex on boys. This has happened many, many times. I haven't always been caught. I don't know if the kids sometimes don't tell anyone, but even if they do report it, it's too late to catch me and probably their parents say, 'We don't want to make a big deal out of this because it's going to affect Junior.' And if they do call the police, how will the police know where I came from. The kids don't see me drive off. I'm careful about this. It's just a one-shot deal. I never see the *same kid again. Occasionally I would take pictures of the boys in the nude with a Polaroid camera. I would make them have sex together and take their pictures. What happened in this case is that I spotted two boys walking across a field, so I parked my car and went up to them and told them that my kids had lost their pet dog and I was offering a $10 reward to anyone who would help me find it. We walked into the woods and I reached over and grabbed the older boy by his arm and slid my hand into his pants. I told them I wouldn't hurt them and then I undressed them and myself. They were kind of edgy, but since I was an adult they cooperated. I performed oral sex on them both and then told the blond boy to lie on his stomach and I sodomized him. Then I ordered the dark-haired boy to also sodomize the blond boy. At first they objected, but they said 'Will you let us go if we do this?' and I said 'Sure, once you do it.' So they did, and I took their picture and I asked them if they enjoyed it. Then I got dressed and left. I've been attracted to kids since I was 7 years old. At that age I was sexually involved with a 2-year-old boy, and all of my victims have been no older than 12. I'm attracted to their young, youthful appearance, smooth bodies, no hair— things like that. I've also had sex with women, but guys turn me off—it's not natural."*

There is a small group of sex-assault offenders who derive pleasure in actually hurting the child. Sexuality and aggression become components of a single psychological experience: sadism. The sadistic child offender inflicts sexual abuse on the victim, who becomes a target for rage and cruelty. Physical aggression is eroticized. Consequently the physical and psychological abuse and/or degradation of the child is necessary for the experience of sexual excitement and gratification in the offender. The youngster is attacked or assaulted. He or she is generally beaten, choked, tortured, and sexually abused. It is the intention of the offender to hurt or punish the child in some way. More force is used in the assault than would be necessary simply to overpower the victim. The sadistic offender finds pleasure in hurting the child, and typically the assault has been planned out, thought about, and fantasized for some time prior to its actual commission. It is not an impulsive act; it is premeditated. Sexuality becomes an expression of domination and anger. In some way the child symbolizes everything the offender hates about himself, and thereby becomes an object of punishment. The victim's fear, torment, distress, and suffering are important and exciting to the sadistic pedophile, since only in this context is sexual gratification experienced. The complete domination, subjugation, and humiliation of the victim is desired, and typically, a weapon, such as a gun, knife, rope, chain, pipe, or belt, is used for this purpose in the commission of the offense. The offender relates to the victim in a brutal, violent, and sadistic fashion. His intention is to hurt, degrade, defile, or destroy the child. Sexuality and power are in the service of anger. The extreme of this condition results in the "lust murder" of the victim. The following case is an example of a sex-force, sadistic-type assault.

Clinical Case 6

Paul is a 19-year-old, single, white male who was convicted of four rape charges, but he reports that in fact he had attempted or committed over 20 such assaults within a three-year period. Paul would seek a girl victim around the age of 12 who was "innocent looking" and force her into the woods at knifepoint. "Then I'd give her a choice: I would rape her or cut off her hair. I'd tie her hands behind her back with my belt, put the point of my knife between her eyes, and threaten to kill her. Then I'd get undressed and make her lick my body and blow me because I knew she wouldn't want to do it. I'd get all shaky and excited. I would keep her scared and frightened—her fear and suffering gave me pleasure. Sometimes while the girl was blowing me I'd burn her with a cigarette on her shoulder and ass and "come off" in her mouth, sometimes I would punch her and stomp on her hand with my workboots."

Paul states that when he was 8 years old, he was molested by two female cousins who would babysit for him, and that around the same age "two girl, strangers in their twenties grabbed me and tried to carry me to a car, but I got away." His parents describe him as becoming a difficult, stubborn, and rebellious youngster around age 9, and his fifth grade teachers noted that he needed help because of his hostility. Paul began masturbating at age 10 to fantasies of beating and raping females. He also began peeping in windows and making obscene telephone calls. He noticed an increase in aggression over time. "I could have killed. I would masturbate while peeping, and I felt like walking right through the window and attacking and killing the girl. When I was 13 I tied up my younger sister (age 10) in the basement and touched her and felt like hurting her. When I began dating, around age 16, I'd mess up somehow. I was afraid, shy, withdrawn, sexually frustrated. I wanted to get back at women, and that's when the assaults began. Even now, when I think about a girl getting beat up, or see it on television, I get a 'hard-on'."

What is evident in the sexual assault of children is that sexuality is never the offender's only motivating force, nor does it appear to be the primary issue. The dynamics of aggression appear to be more germane. The sex-pressure type of offender tends to exhibit a general inhibition and suppression of aggression. The sex-assault exploitive-type pedophile channels aggression into issues of power and control. For the sex-assault sadistic-type pedophile, aggression in the form of anger and power becomes eroticized.

Sexual involvement with a child on the part of an adult is a complex and multidetermined act. It may constitute an effort to compensate for feelings of inadequacy and to retreat from conflictual or intimidating relationships with adults to safer, less-threatening nonadults. It may serve to assert power and strength, to express anger and retaliation, to achieve mastery and control, and to gratify needs for affection and sexuality. It becomes a way to avoid competition, to retain status and identification, to enhance a sense of worth, to discharge tensions and frustration, and to achieve attention and recognition. In short, the pedophile expresses multiple psychological needs by acting them out sexually.

Incest

Incest, in its broadest definition, refers to sexual relationships between people in a kinship pattern that prohibits marriage by law. Usually it refers to sexual relations between members of the immediate (nuclear) family, that is, sexual activity between a parent and child or sexual intercourse between sexually mature siblings. Incest is difficult to operationally define. Noncoital sexual involvement among prepubertal or adolescent siblings—for example, sexual play between a preadolescent brother and sister or two 16-year-old brothers who occasionally engage in mutual masturbation—is not generally regarded as incest, nor is sexual activity between a foster parent and child. On the other hand, sexual relations between a stepfather and his child are commonly thought of as incest.

Most of the referral cases in this regard appear to be sexual offenses committed by a father against his children. Mother-child incest seems to be rarely reported, perhaps in part because there are strong stigmas and taboos attached to males who have intercourse with their mothers, and brother-sister sexual relationships appear to be more likely reported when the brother is significantly older than his sister. Incestuous relationships may also involve grandparents, uncles, cousins, and so on, and are more likely to be viewed in this fashion if there are ongoing, repeated sexual contacts over a period of time.

In this section, the focus of attention will be on the parent-child incestuous relationship, specifically the father-child involvement. Such involvements can be dichotomized into *actual parent incest,* where the child is the biological offspring of the parent, and *functional parent incest,* where the offender is the stepfather of the child or a boyfriend or common-law husband of the child's mother and primary male authority figure to the child. Incest and pedophilia are not synonymous, since incest refers to sexual involvement with a relative, and pedophilia refers to sexual attraction to children. There is overlap and similarity, however, when the child becomes the sexual victim of his or her parent. Again there is a wide variety of incestuous behavior. In some cases the incestuous behavior appears to be exclusive.

Clinical Case 7

Charles, age 39, had married a woman whom he described as a "periodic nymphomaniac." After 17 years of marriage and six children, she abandoned the family. Charles had lived with his mother until he married, and she now moved in to care for the children after his wife's desertion. He began having sexual relations with his oldest daughter, age 14, whom he described as the initiator of the relationship, offering herself to him in place of her mother. The relationship lasted two years, progressing from the daughter masturbating her father, to performing oral sex, to submitting to intercourse. It ended when the daughter's boyfriend accidentally discovered her and her father engaged in the act of intercourse. Charles confined his sexual activity to his oldest daughter. He did not become involved with the other children or, in fact, with anyone else, adult or child, during this two-year period.

In other cases, the incestuous behavior appears to be associated with other pedophilic activities.

Clinical Case 8

James, age 52, and his wife were married about 15 years when she first noticed his "perverted sexual desires." He would beat her on the buttocks with a strap until he would reach an orgasm. At one point, his wife noticed one of their daughters fondling her husband's penis through his trousers and asking, "Daddy, is this what you want me to do?" On another occasion, another daughter reported that she awoke to find her father naked in bed and kneeling over her, and that he forced her to suck his penis. On still other occasions, James forced all three of his daughters to perform oral sex on him. His wife separated from her husband, and six months later James was accused of sexually approaching two little girls, aged 7 and 9, in the basement of a school, exposing himself, and saying "suck it." James admitted to these and other offenses involving his own daughters, neighborhood children, and other children who were strangers, explaining that his wife had refused him sex for the past six years following the death of their son at age 3 from polio.

In a few situations the incestuous behavior appears to be only one aspect of an indiscriminate or pansexual orientation.

Clinical Case 9

Brian is a 28-year-old, divorced father of two who was arrested for raping his 15-year-old brother. When he was 13, Brian became sexually active with male peers and also engaged frequently in sexual relations with animals. At age 17 he became sexually involved with an older woman and then with another girl his own age, whom he impregnated and married. After two years of marriage,

Brian began forcing his 12-year-old sister to have intercourse with him in the presence of his wife, following which he would then have intercourse with his wife. Later he began forcing his wife to submit to intercourse with his brother, who was 14 at the time, and Brian would watch them and masturbate himself. After his wife left him, Brian turned his sexual attentions to his brother, now 15 years old, and would perform oral and anal intercourse on him. In addition to these relationships, Brian also engaged in extramarital homosexual and heterosexual affairs.

Although the dynamics of parent-child incest and pedophilia are similar, there are some differentiating factors. A major issue is that in pedophilia we are primarily dealing with the dynamics of an individual, whereas in every case of parental incest, there is some form of family dysfunction. The interrelationships among all members of the nuclear family must be examined, the structure of the family network as well as the dynamics of the participants.

In assessing those family interrelationships in which father-child incest developed, we found the marital relationship between husband and wife to be characterized by dependent attachments on the part of one or both parents. The marriage was not characterized by mutuality, reciprocity, attentiveness, understanding, and empathy. Instead, unspoken expectations met with frustration, and immature needs sabotaged the marital relationship.

In some family constellations, the husband appears to be looking more for a mother than a wife in his marriage. Although he may provide financial support for his family, he does not provide emotional support for his wife. Instead, he relates to her more as a dependent child than as a partner, and the wife feels emotionally deserted and burdened. She has not found the capable, competent companion that she needs and wants, and eventually she turns elsewhere for male companionship. She becomes self-sufficient and independent and may feel some contempt and resentment for, or indifference toward, her husband. The wife is no longer attentive to him, but looks to her own interests. He then turns to his daughter as a surrogate wife-mother. The daughter may have the responsibility of preparing his meals, doing his laundry, and spending leisure time with him; eventually a sexual relationship evolves. Just as he was dependent on his wife, in time he becomes dependent on his daughter and fears her abandoning him for another male when she reaches adolescence and starts dating. Discovery of the incestuous relationship provides the wife with an opportunity to terminate the unsatisfying marriage.

Clinical Case 10

Tom is a 40-year-old man whose difficulties involve his interpersonal relationships. In other areas, such as schooling and work, his performance, while not outstanding, has been adequate. It is in the area of his human relationships that he is unsuccessful. Tom's first marriage ended in divorce, the result of his in-laws moving in with him and disrupting his life. He felt his wife chose her family over him, and he divorced her on the grounds of mental cruelty. His second marriage has lasted for about 15 years. Prior to this marriage, his wife had a 3-month-old illegitimate daughter by another man. Tom married her after going with her for six weeks. They appear to have married out of mutual loneliness. Tom's mother has never accepted his wife because of her illegitimate child, and Tom feels estranged from his family.

Although his marriage was reasonably happy at first, the birth of a son after 5 years of marriage marked the beginning of its deterioration. As Tom describes it, his son replaced him. His wife has slept with their son for the past 10 years, and he was forced to sleep in an upstairs bedroom alone. Their sexual contacts were reduced to once or twice a year. About four years ago, Tom discovered his wife and her boss "making out" on the living room couch at about two o'clock in the morning. She admitted they were having an affair, and on a couple of subsequent occasions she remained out all night. She talked about taking the children and leaving, and Tom said he felt "crushed." It was at this point that he began having sexual relations with his adopted daughter, Betty. He describes her as a provocative and promiscuous girl who had been getting into sexual difficulties since puberty: sex-play with boys her own age, exposing her breasts, etc. She also got involved in shoplifting, and Tom states that he informed her that he would "ground" her. She then promised him anything if he would only allow her to go out. He reports that she played up to him, grabbed him between the legs when they went swimming, and played one parent against the other. Tom said he had become increasingly lonely and depressed and turned more and more to his daughter for affection. At the same time, he felt she was getting more and more control over him, and states that when he objected to her going steady with an older boy, she informed her mother about the sexual relations with her father.

Betty's version: *"I am 15 years old. Since I was about 11 my father has bothered me in sexual ways. By that I mean he would touch my breasts and my private. He would always make me give him a hand-job. When I was about 14, my father began to have sexual intercourse with me about once every two weeks. He would also make me suck his private, and he would put his tongue in my private. When I would refuse, he would tell me I couldn't go out or he would send me to do some extra work. The past two summers I had to wake him up for work in the morning, and when I went into the bedroom to get him up, I would sometimes have to submit to him. For the last year, my father has had intercourse with me every Wednesday night when my mother went bowling and my younger brother was asleep in bed. On Saturdays he would have sex with me when my mother was out shopping and my brother was out of the house. I finally told my mother what my father had been doing to me because I was sick of what he was doing and saying about me. I felt he was wrong. I was also afraid of my father, and when he first started doing these things to me, I told him I was going to tell and he said I better not because my mother would divorce him right away and that was something that frightened me. I was also frightened that he might hurt me if I told on him. At one time, my period was late and my father said that if I was pregnant I should say that he had let me out of the house and that I met this guy and had intercourse with him."*

In a separate interview, Tom's wife and stepdaughter both denied there was any force or threats used by Tom. His wife expressed guilt over "cheating" on him, and both wife and daughter were quite concerned over his incarceration.

In other situations, the wife appears to be very dependent on her husband emotionally (and sometimes financially as well). She is an insecure woman who is unable to face the prospect of taking care of herself and her children alone. She may have had a previous marriage end in divorce or abandonment and feels this reflects on her adequacy or worth as a wife. The husband feels overwhelmed by the emotional demands he feels from his wife and turns to his daughter for attentiveness to his needs. Even when the wife discovers his incestuous behavior, she may be reluctant to take any decisive action and risk losing her husband.

Incest may in some situations constitute one aspect of a pattern of child abuse.

Clinical Case 11

Larry is a 20-year old, single, white male who was arrested for sodomizing a 6-year-old boy for whom he was babysitting. He also confessed to having intercourse with a 10-year-old girl and to performing fellatio on an 8-year-old boy, as well as having two other children (ages 6 and 7) masturbate him, all within the space of a week.

Larry is the oldest of three children and the only boy. He described his family life as "weird." Beginning when he was about 8 years old, his parents became involved in the manufacture and marketing of pornographic photographs and films in which Larry and his sisters were used as models. This went on for about seven years and involved having Larry perform sexual acts with his sisters and other children. Photographs were also taken of Larry and his sisters having sexual encounters with their father. When Larry reached adolescence, his father began prostituting him. He would bring home older men with whom Larry would be forced to perform oral sex and submit to anal intercourse while being photographed and filmed by his father. If Larry objected or resisted, he would be beaten. His uncle noticed the bruises one day, and Larry confessed what had been going on. Shortly thereafter the police raided the house, and his father was arrested and convicted on pornography charges. It was learned that in addition to the sexual exploitation, the parents had often physically abused and neglected their children. His mother would give Larry and his sisters mustard sandwiches for their school lunch, and as Larry described it, "I had no clothes, no money. I wore my father's old work clothes to school. I had sneakers with holes in them and had to wear a summer jacket in the winter. Some days I'd go to school with no socks on. I've kinda had a rough life." His parents would go away for a weekend and lock their children out of the house. The State took custody of the children and placed them in foster homes.

Larry, by this point in his teens, did poorly in school. Rumor had gotten around about his past. Girls would not socialize with him, and a group of older boys would force him to perform oral sex on them. Eventually Larry dropped out of school to join the Army. While in the service, he accepted some sexual propositions in exchange for money but established no genuine relationships with men or women. After his discharge he worked at some low-level jobs and supplemented his income by babysitting.

In regard to the instant offense, he reports he had been "thinking back to when my father brought that first guy back to the house and was taking pictures, then the little boy came into the room. . . ." While being held in jail awaiting trial, Larry performed oral sex on a group of 10 fellow inmates in succession. In court he asked for commitment to a treatment center, realizing he "wants to 'go down' on every guy or kid I see."

Incest, like pedophilia, is multicausal. With regard to the motivational intent underlying such behavior, one common theme appears to be retaliation on the part of husband against wife for her actual or imagined unfaithfulness. Another is the sense of entitlement in regard to one's own children—that they are one's (sexual) property. Loneliness and the need for intimacy and affiliation with another appears to underlie some incest behavior. Themes of isolation and depression are also frequent. The attraction to the child in incest appears dynamically to be the same as the determinants underlying pedophilia, with the additional factor that the child is also the means through which the husband reacts to his wife's behavior.

General Observations

Some general observations can be made about the incidents of sexual assault by an adult against a child that have come to our attention.

Characteristics of Pedophilic Behavior

There appears to be an approximately even distribution of fixated and regressed offenders. Female children are victims almost twice as often as male children, yet based on the sexual lifestyle of the offenders, males seem overrepresented as victims. Most offenders are very specific in regard to their choice of victim with respect to age, sex, and type of sexual act committed. They tend to choose either prepubertal or pubescent girls or boys with whom they focus either on the sexual areas of their victims' bodies (touching, fondling) or on their own genitals (penetration), rather than combining both. The offenders characteristically commit their offenses alone—codefendants are atypical. Recidivism is characteristic. For some offenders the offense constitutes an exception to an otherwise law-abiding and adaptive life, whereas for others it is simply one of many life-adjustment problems. Some offenders are retarded. Some are psychotic. Most are neither. If they share any common psychological traits or characteristics, these tend to be a sense of isolation or alienation from others, an ineptitude in negotiating interpersonal relationships, deep-seated feelings of inadequacy, and a tendency to experience themselves as helpless victims of an overpowering environment.

Although, clinically, child sexual assault cuts across all diagnostic categories, the majority of offenders who came to our attention would be included under a personality disorder classification. The diagnostic impression that emerges is that of a person who has achieved a tenuous adjustment to life demands, an inadequate individual whose sexual assaults serve a number of compensatory aims or purposes in his psychological life. The child offender appears handicapped by poor impulse control, especially in regard to sexuality; poor ability to tolerate frustration or to delay immediate gratification of his needs; and low self-esteem. He is relatively helpless in meeting psychosocial life-demands and appears to be concerned only with his own needs and feelings. There is a relative insensitivity or unawareness of the needs and feelings of others and little insight into or understanding of his own behavior. In essence, he is a psychological child in the physical guise of an adult.

Reaction to the Offense

One of the striking characteristics about many of these offenders is their relative lack of distress about their attraction to children. Genuine remorse or shame is uncharacteristic. More likely, they are distressed at the consequences to themselves of having been discovered. The impressions derived from listening to their versions of the offenses are that some clearly are intentionally lying, others are less consciously distorting or misperceiving the incident, and still others are aware of exactly what is going on. They employ defense mechanisms that serve to repress the anxiety or guilt resulting from their sexual desires rather than to repress the desires themselves. When confronted with their offenses child offenders employ a variety of techniques to exculpate themselves: Some may fully admit to their offense, but more characteristically they deny ("a false accusation") or minimize ("I accidentally touched her when helping her change into her pajamas.") their behavior, claim they have repressed the event and have no memory of it ("I was in a blackout"), project the responsibility onto some external factor ("I was drunk and she approached me") or rationalize the offense in some way ("She looked much older").

In summary, the sexual misuse and abuse of children constitutes pedophilia. One of the most basic observations that can be made about child offenders is that they are not all alike. They do not all do the same thing, nor do they commit similar offenses for the same reasons. Sexual encounters between adults and children may range from situations at one extreme in which there is only visual contact (as in exhibitionism, for example) to those at the other extreme which result in the intentional death of the child (as in lust murder). Our aim in this section of the book has been to identify and differentiate various aspects of pedophilic behavior. If we are to be of help to the victims, we must understand the offenders—for the etiology of a victim's trauma lies in the offender's pathology. Only by understanding the psychological makeup of the offender, the nature of his offense, his method of operation, and his motivational intent can we fully appreciate what his victim is a victim of.

References

1. A. Nicholas Groth and H. Jean Birnbaum, "Adult Sexual Orientation and the Attraction to Underage Persons," *Archives of Sexual Behavior* (forthcoming).

2. Anthony Storr, *Sexual Deviation* (Baltimore: Penguin Books, 1964).

3. Paul H. Gebhard, John H. Gagnon, Wardell B. Pomeroy, and Cornelia V. Christenson, *Sex Offenders: An Analysis of Types* (New York: Harper and Row and Paul B. Hoeber, 1965).

4. Morton L. Kurland, "Pedophilia Erotica," *Journal of Nervous and Mental Diseases* 131 (1960):394–403.

5. Alfred Kinsey, Wardell Pomeroy, and C. Martin *Sexual Behavior in the Human Male* (Philadelphia: Saunders, 1948).

6. S. W. Hartwell, *A Citizen's Handbook of Sexual Abnormalities* (State of Michigan, 1950).

7. Manfred S. Guttmacher, *Sex Offenses, the Problems, Causes, and Prevention* (New York: Norton, 1951).

8. L. C. Hirning, *The Sex Offender in Custody: Handbook of Correctional Psychology*, ed. R. M. Linder and R. V. Seliger (New York: Philosophical Library, 1947), pp. 223-256.

9. J. W. Mohr, R. E. Turner, and M. B. Jerry, *Pedophilia and Exhibitionism: A Handbook* (Toronto: Univ. of Toronto Press, 1964).

Guidelines for the Assessment and Management of the Offender

A. Nicholas Groth

When an individual has been identified as having made sexual advances toward a child, he is usually pressured to see a clinician in this regard. Or if criminal charges have been brought against him, the court frequently turns to mental health professionals for input in processing the case. The clinician may be asked to take part at various points in the criminal justice process (court diversion, pretrial, predisposition/sentencing, institutional screening, and probationary or parole release) in regard to a diagnostic assessment of the offender. Usually such referral questions address two issues: repetition and dangerousness. It is in this regard that the court turns to the clinician and asks for a predictive opinion in order to arrive at a meaningful disposition of the case before it—one that will serve both the needs of the community and the needs of the offender.

In order to deal effectively with adults or adolescents who become sexually involved with children, the primary task is to determine what risks—either physical and/or psychological—the offender constitutes to the victims. What safeguards are needed and how stringent should they be in order to deter any further recurrence of his sexual offenses? The clinician in this situation is being called upon to predict the likelihood of repetition of the individual's offense and to estimate its danger to the victim. It is a difficult task that faces the clinician, and one that carries a heavy burden of responsibility, for an error, on the one hand, could result in the needless and potentially destructive deprivation of an individual's freedom and, on the other hand, could result in further jeopardy to the community, specifically to its children.

Although no precise set of predictor variables are yet available in terms of repetition and dangerousness, and although clinicians have yet to demonstrate that predictive accuracy can be achieved in these areas, we nevertheless have no viable alternative at this time. Equally, however, it is premature to assume that such accuracy cannot be achieved.[1] This chapter offers some guidelines for making a predictive analyses of repetition and dangerousness in regard to the child offender. Such a process requires an extended period of study, making use of a number of professional personnel, and involves recourse to a variety of clinical, behavioral, and social sources of data.

The Issue of Repetition

To answer the question "How likely is this offender to repeat his offense?" the sexual contact with the child must be viewed in the context of the offender's

25

life history, his biopsychosocial development, the social and cultural environment in which he grew up, his current life situation, and the circumstances surrounding the offense. Before the prediction of repetition can be made, two sets of questions must be answered: (1) How much is the offense a result of external, situational factors, and to what extent does it derive from inner, psychological determinants? and (2) Under what environmental conditions is the sexual offense most likely to happen, and what are the chances of these conditions occurring? To answer these questions, assessments must be made of such internal psychological determinants as motivational needs, attitudes, values, and defenses and such external factors as precipitating stresses, victim availability, and release mechanisms. A number of issues need to be taken into consideration:

1. *How long has the sexual behavior with young people been going on?* The psychological maxim that the best predictor of future behavior is past behavior unless there has been some major intervention in the individual's life is especially true in regard to sexual behavior. Sexual activity, by its very nature, is rewarding. It is associated with physical and emotional pleasure. Therefore, it is self-reinforcing, and the longer the pedophilic behavior has been going on, the more ingrained a pattern of behavior it has become. Repetition increases the likelihood of repetition.

2. *Is the sexual interest in children a persistent orientation (a fixation) or a new behavior (a regression) in the offender's sexual lifestyle?* The prognosis for abandoning the pedophilic activity would appear to be better for the regressed offender, who has had gratifying sexual relations with age-mates, than for the fixated offender, for whom children have been the exclusive focus of sexual interest. The compulsive quality of the fixated offender's sexual activity with children suggests a higher probability of repetition than does the regressed offender, who selects a child victim for the first time.

3. *If the pedophilic activity constitutes a new sexual experience, that is, if this is a departure, a regression, from the offender's customary sexual interests, why has it started?* What are the precipitating stresses, and are they still in operation? All areas of the offender's current life situation must be carefully explored to uncover the sources of his emotional distress: physical, social, educational, vocational, marital, economic, and the like. If the sources of stress cannot be identified, the resulting pressures cannot be relieved. If the stresses have not been alleviated, or if the offender has not found better ways of coping with these stresses, then the symptom, the pedophilic behavior, is more likely to continue than not.

4. *What part do such factors as alcohol, drugs, codefendants, automobiles, isolation, leisure time, pornography, or other erotic materials play in the commission of the offense, and to what extent are these factors still in operation?* To what extent do they contribute to, encourage, or stimulate the pedophilic interests on the part of the offender, and how accessible are they? For example,

if an offender appears more prone to act out sexually with children when he is intoxicated, you then have to assess his dependency on alcohol and determine how easily available alcohol is to him.

5. *What access does the offender have to children?* Does he have a tendency to put himself in positions where he comes into contact with potential victims? What opportunities are there for unsupervised contact between him and a child? If, for example, an individual's pedophilic interests are incestuous, his potential victims are readily available to him at practically all times. If an individual functions as a babysitter, a scoutmaster, a camp counsellor, a teacher, or the like, this provides him with easy access to children. In evaluating his potential for recidivism it is useful to determine to what extent children come into his presence in the course of his daily life, and to what extent he must seek them out.

6. *How specific is his victim selection?* Who are particular target victims of this offender? How discriminate or indiscriminate is he in regard to victim choice? Does this individual select only boys or only girls as his victims, or both? Is he attracted only to prepubescent children or only to young adolescent children, or both? Is he attracted only to his own children or only to nonrelated children, or both. The broader the range of victims in regard to sex, age, and familiarity, the greater the opportunity for, and the likelihood of, victim contact.

7. *To what extent does the offender accept responsibility for his offense, and what degree of subjective distress does he experience in this regard?* The greater the denial or minimization of his behavior and the projection of personal responsibility elsewhere, the more he can allow himself to participate in pedophilic behavior without any psychological discomfort. In the absence of any subjective experience of guilt, remorse, or moral accountability for his sexual involvement with children, the risk of repetition increases.

8. *What impact has discovery of his sexual involvement with young people had on this individual?* What changes have occurred in his life and/or in his behavior as a result, and what direction have they taken? Is the offender relieved that his sexual activity has been discovered and he has been stopped, or has this created greater stress and anxiety for him? How much has he profited from this experience? How much has he become aware of what for him are high-risk behaviors (for example, drinking) or situations (for example, unemployment) and alerted to early warning signs of impending pedophilic activity? Or how much has discovery of this sexual interest jeopardized his marriage, his job, his reputation in the community, and the like, facing him with more problems and putting greater stress on his already tenuous controls? What viable external safeguards (supervision, treatment, hospitalization, probation, etc.) have been instituted in regard to this offender in order to reduce the risk of, or opportunity for, further sexual involvements with children?

In order to estimate the probability of repetition of the sexual offense—whether the offender is more likely to continue his sexual involvements with young people than not—the personality characteristics of the offender must also be taken into consideration. These include his needs, attitudes, and values; his perception and judgment; his contact with reality; his predominant mood states; his social skills; his ability to cope with stress and manage his life; his insight and self-esteem; his ability to communicate and establish relationships with others; his sense of humor and emotional expression; and so on. The assessment of these traits will be dealt with more fully in the next section. Even so, in the final analysis, it is the clinician who must weigh one factor against another and use his clinical experience, judgment, and acumen in arriving at a determination of whether the offender has sufficient internal and external resources to combat pedophilic tendencies. The fewer the internal resources, the greater the need for external controls.

The Issue of Dangerousness

The concern about repetition is enchanced by the potential danger the offense constitutes to the victim. Our current state of knowledge suggests that the risk of psychological and/or emotional trauma is a function of several factors:[2]

1. *The nature of the relationship between the offender and the victim.* The closer the emotional relationship, the greater the risk of some psychological after effect. From this standpoint, then, sexual relations with a parent are regarded as potentially more traumatic than sexual relations with a stranger.

2. *The duration of the sexual relationship.* An ongoing sexual relationship with a victim involving repeated contacts over a period of time is seen as potentially more traumatic than a single instance of sexual contact.

3. *The type of sexual activity occurring in the offense.* Sexual acts involving no physical contact, such as exhibitionism or voyeurism, appear less traumatic than those in which there is physical contact. In turn, physical contact that involves the sexual penetration of the child is potentially more traumatic than noncoital sexual activity.

4. *The degree of physical aggression, force, or violence directed at the child in the commission of the offense.* Those offenses which are marked by violence and abuse to the victim are more traumatic than those which involve verbal persuasion.

Therefore, in assessing the dangerousness of the offender, these factors must be taken into consideration. In addition, a number of other variables need to be considered in determining what risk of harm a particular offender poses to a child.[a] Additional information is required to know whether a past dangerous

---

[a]The subsequent text is in part adapted from an unpublished manuscript by Richard A. Siegel, Ph.D. We are grateful to Dr. Siegel for his kindness in permitting us to use his material for this section of the chapter.

sexual offense will be repeated in the future, or whether a past nondangerous sexual offense will escalate into a future dangerous assault. It is at this point that the evaluation of the individual becomes so crucial. It is also at this point that the evaluation becomes extremely complex and, therefore, very hard to describe. The goal is to achieve a sufficiently thorough understanding of an individual and his circumstances that one can predict the future course of his behavior—a feat that, in general, the behavioral sciences have rarely accomplished with any consistency. The task of predicting human behavior is enormously intricate and subject to considerable error. Debates over the best methods for making predictions have occupied the literature of the field for decades, not to mention the question of whether in fact clinicians should even be regarded as experts in the prediction of human behavior.[3]

Nevertheless, clinicians are required to make such predictions, and in accordance with the prevailing beliefs of our culture, the law grants to the profession of psychiatry and its allied disciplines considerable authority and presumed expertise.

Given the knowledge of a sexual offense against a young person, the clinician must look to the offender's psychological makeup and ask, "What do we know about this person that tells us he is a risk to the safety of children?" To answer this question, a number of personality characteristics must be assessed.

1. *Impulse control.* Based on the assumption that any person has within him the potential to commit a sexual assault, a key question arises as to the individual's ability to control his sexual and aggressive impulses. Information will be sought concerning the subject's overall sexual history, as well as his customary methods of releasing anger and aggression. Repetitive sexual assaults, frequent explosions of temper, several nonsexual assaults, and attempts to commit suicide or other violent acts all suggest a personality ill-equipped to control future dangerous impulses and, therefore, likely to repeat. Other evidence of impulsivity will also be viewed as ominous: running away; enuresis or incontinence into adolescence; dropping out of school for no apparent reason; being AWOL or having other disciplinary problems while in the service; quitting jobs on a moment's notice; having free-and-easy spending habits; being a reckless driver; having a problem with alcohol; and the like, all of which may indicate poor or inadequate self-control.

Of particular importance is the relationship between sexuality and aggression in the psychological experience of the offender. The more sexuality becomes an expression of power and anger, and the more aggression becomes eroticized, the greater the danger of injury to the victim. Especially ominous in this regard is the use of a weapon in the commission of the offense and, where there have been a series of offenses, an increase in force or aggression over time, a decrease in the ages of the victims, and a progression from relatively less serious to more serious types of acts or offenses.

2. *Tolerance for frustration.* The majority of dangerous sexual offenses appear to occur under conditions of psychological stress. A person who has

a tendency to react to pressures and frustrations through sexual assaults and who also seems to possess a limited ability to tolerate stress will be regarded as a person likely to repeat such assaults in the future. Again, the subject's case history can furnish information on this issue: his success or failure in achieving long-range goals, such as an education or a vocation; specific traumas in his life and his reactions to them, such as the death of a loved one or the breakup of a marriage; his reactions to failure or disappointments in his life.

3. *Emotional stability.* Emotional instability is reported as an important consideration in terms of offenders who repeat their sexual crimes.[4] Emotional instability and/or mental illness may be a key underlying factor in recidivism. Therefore, a careful effort should be made to determine the degree and nature of emotional disturbance in a subject. This effort is based on the assumption that the more emotionally unstable a sexual criminal is, the more likely he is to repeat his sexual offenses. Previous psychiatric history, school performance, and so forth can provide clues to the presence of emotional disturbance. Evidence of alcohol or drug addiction, learning disabilities, or habitual criminal behavior will often be seen as signs of psychological conflict. Severe depression or anxiety, sexual or aggressive obsessions, and belligerent or suspicious, distrusting attitudes may be symptomatic of emotional instability.

4. *Contact with reality.* This criterion comes closest to the conventional notion of the mentally ill or defective offender. Deficits in normal judgment and intelligence, resulting either from mental deficiency or disease, are always viewed as particularly ominous signs. If a person's criminal behavior indicates that he lacks capacity to appreciate the full nature of his actions, then he will be regarded as especially volatile and unpredictable and, therefore, a higher risk to repeat. Thus in every evaluation the questions of mental retardation and psychosis are raised. The former is answered fairly easily by a review of past school performance and current performance in interviews and psychological tests. The latter is more complex. Few sexual offenders against children are demonstrably psychotic in any obvious way; it is unusual to find signs of hallucinations, delusions, catatonic stupors or uncontrollable manic excitement, bizarre or highly infantile behavior, or any other symptoms of active, clinical psychosis. Nonetheless, many of these individuals do reveal weaknesses in reality-awareness and reality-testing that are of a near-psychotic extent. Some clues to the depth of this problem can be obtained by comparing the offender's perceptions of the offense with the victim's perception of what happened. The greater the distortions in their perceptions, or the intrusion of fantasy into their behavior, the poorer or more tenuous their grasp on reality. Borderline functioning is seen as increasing the risk of dangerousness.

5. *Interpersonal relations.* Sexual assault is interpersonal behavior, however distorted or inappropriate it may be. In such an act, an individual may give expression to certain needs or strivings within him that are in some way social or interpersonal in nature. Sexual assaults may reflect a form of vengeance,

or hatred, or fear, or desire. Such assaults may also represent the enactment of conflicts or feelings generated by some other past or present interpersonal relationship against some innocent victim. An examination of the subject's history and character can shed light on his habitual modes of relating, starting from his earliest experiences with parents and siblings to later relationships with school peers and work associates, with friends, with romantic and sexual partners, and with his own wife and children. Indications here of manipulative, narcissistic, self-serving, ineffectual, or malicious modes of relating—especially where others are regarded as objects to be used or obstacles to be overcome in the pursuit of one's own need gratification—raise concern regarding the likelihood of future sexual assault.

6. *Self-awareness and self-image.* Based on the assumption that people express in their outward behavior some of their innermost feelings about themselves, the degree and nature of a subject's self-image should be carefully explored. Particular importance is attributed to the individual's ability to make sense of his previous offenses. A willingness to acknowledge personal responsibility for past offenses, some realistic sense of guilt or other expression of concern, and a degree of insight into the reasons for such acts are all considered to lessen the likelihood of repetition. Conversely, evasion or denial of responsibility (as in claiming innocence or blaming the deed on the victim, or a co-defendant, or alcohol), absence of guilt or excessively harsh and self-punitive guilt with intense religious overtones, or the absence of insight are seen as negative indications.

Over and above the offender's view of his past offenses, there is a concern for the subject's general image of himself. Feelings of personal inadequacy, or conversely, personal omnipotence, a sense of values and life goals, and other such factors are all seen as relevant to the task of deepening an understanding of this person. How stereotyped or artificial are his role definitions of masculinity? On what activities does he depend for self-definition? In this regard, it should be noted that clinical attention is directed not only toward the subject's conscious perceptions of himself and the world around him, but also toward the less conscious elements as well, his behaviors that may signal feelings with which he is not completely in touch or does not himself understand.

7. *Adaptive strengths.* The preceding points may suggest that a clinical evaluation involves only a search for a subject's weaknesses, but this is not the case. Explicit in the sifting of the details about a person's life and personality is the sense of a balance of strengths and weaknesses. Even with the knowledge that an individual is guilty of sexual assaults in the past, the question must always deal with future behavior, with a realization that a significant number of sexual offenders do not repeat. It is reasonable to assume that many criminal acts result from a moment of weakness, a transitory state, and that the very impact of such an occurrence may mobilize an individual's resources to prevent any further recurrence.

This examination of an offender's strengths is also based on the conviction that every opportunity an individual has to obtain personal satisfaction in an acceptable and appropriate fashion lessens the risk of dangerous assaults. In other words, in almost every case of sexual assault, one can identify some form of prior frustration or deprivation. Thus, if the offender can maximize his ability to achieve satisfaction in more acceptable pursuits, he becomes a better risk.[5]

In general, the greater the impairment of an offender in regard to any of his life-management functions, the greater the risk of harm to the victim, whether it be intentional or accidental. There is no formula, however, for predicting dangerousness. Some offenders will clearly jeopardize the safety of other children. Others, just as clearly, will not. But many will fall between these two extremes, they will occupy that middle ground of "maybe" or "possibly," and it is here that the clinician must bring to bear his or her knowledge, experience, skill, and expertise in order to determine the probability of this possibility. Given the current state of the art in the social and behavioral sciences, however, the conclusion will tend to be suggestive more than definitive, approximate more than exact.

Before we leave this consideration of the danger or risk of trauma to other victims, it is important to differentiate between physical trauma and psychological trauma and between immediate and long-range aftereffects. Much of the anxiety about sexual encounters between adults and children is directed toward the psychological impact and effect this event will have on the victim. Physical trauma or injury is concrete and evident, and the process of recovery and repair is visible. Psychological or emotional trauma is not always immediately obvious, and long-range after effects are the subject of current study. It is important to realize that trauma reactions are complexly determined and multicausal. Trauma may not be inevitable to every sexual encounter between an adult and a child. Where trauma does occur, offense and offender characteristics are not the only variables that will determine the outcome of the event. The responses and reactions of parents and other social network people can serve to reduce or increase the risk of trauma to the child. Also, anyone who has contact with the child victim in relation to the sexual assault can impact on the child's reaction. It is, therefore, extremely important for all people working with child victims to be aware of their potential impact on the child.

Evaluation Procedures

It is significant that in over 12 years of work in this field, we have yet to encounter a single case of self-referral on the part of a child molester. Usually he is pressured into a consultation by his family, his lawyer, the police, the department of probation, or some other social agency; or his evaluation is mandated by the court in the course of the criminal justice proceedings against him. The questions typically asked of the clinician are, "Why did he do it? How dangerous is he? What should be done with him? What can be done for him?" There is a realization that not all offenders need to be institutionalized, and even for those who do need to be institutionalized, being kept in custodial care is at best a temporary stopgap unless effective rehabilitation services and treatment programs are available. Before one can treat a person, one must diagnose the condition and identify the problems.

Types of Data to be Collected

In dealing with sexual offenders against children, the evaluation procedure must extend beyond a routine psychiatric assessment. As full and complete a psychological investigation as is realistically possible must be undertaken. There are three principal types of data used in conducting such an investigation.[6]

Historical Data. Historical data include family, social, criminal, correctional, psychiatric, medical, educational, military, and occupational histories. The collection of such data is fairly rigorous. Although there is some reliance on a subject's history, as collected by others prior to his observation, much of the data is collected first hand by contacting schools, employers, friends and relatives, and others who can supply pertinent information.

Data Concerning Sexual and Assaultive Offenses. In many cases, data on sexual and assaultive offenses are felt to be the most compelling. Therefore, considerable time is spent obtaining the necessary information from police and hospital records, court transcripts, and the patient himself. In many cases, the data are obtained from the victims or witnesses of the assaults.

Psychological Data. It is not sufficient merely to know what has happened in the patient's past. A man may commit a seriously dangerous sexual crime, or even several more, and yet never again repeat such an act. A man may commit a series of minor, "public-nuisance-type" crimes and yet be capable, under the right conditions, of a dangerous sexual crime. Therefore, through clinical interviews and psychological tests, an attempt is made to understand the psychological makeup of the patient: his state of mind at the time of the offense, his major areas of conflict and anxiety, the strength of sexual and aggressive impulses, his capacity for judgment and self-control, and any other significant physical, emotional, or intellectual factors. Moreover, since in some cases a period of many months or even years may have elapsed since a previous sexual offense, attention must be given to possible psychological changes that have occurred over time that could lessen or increase the likelihood of dangerousness.

Steps in Conducting an Evaluation

The following procedures are those adopted by the Forensic Mental Health Department of Harrington Memorial Hospital in Southbridge, Massachusetts.

Following a referral request and prior to seeing the subject (although frequently this is not feasible), we attempt to obtain a dependable and detailed description of the offense: police reports, victim's version of the offense, the statements of witnesses, and the like. We then interview the subject, having advised him of the reason for the interview, and having explained what will be done with the content of the interview material. Generally the subject is asked for his version of the offense and carefully interrogated in regard to his account. This is followed by a more structured exploration of the subject's life experiences, assessing areas of difficulty or trauma in detail to evaluate possible consequences or aftereffects. The following schema outlines major areas of inquiry.

1. *Family background:* Information is sought about the subject's family history, his parents, the number of siblings, and the birth order; the character of the intrafamily relationships; his religious upbringing; and the psychological and economic stability of his family home. *Target areas:* violence within the family (wife-beating, child abuse); social or psychological disturbances (alcoholism, mental illness, criminal acts), unconventional or inappropriate sexual behavior (promiscuity, incest); disruption in family unity (death, divorce, abandonment); financial hardship (welfare assistance, unemployment); placement of subject outside the home (foster care, orphanage, residential institution); behavioral problems (runaway, intense sibling rivalry, chronic rebelliousness).

2. *Medical history:* Data are sought that pertain to the subject's quality of physical and mental health. *Target areas:* evidence of physical traumas, serious illness, injury, disability, impairment, handicap, or afflictions such as seizures, addiction, blackouts, enuresis, psychosomatic complaints, venereal disease, mental illness, suicide attempts, phobias, chronic nightmares, insomnia, accident proneness.

3. *Educational history:* Subject's academic progress and accomplishments are examined: the number of grades completed and the quality of performance; the relationship with teachers and age-mates; IQ measurement. *Target areas:* evidence of learning problems or disability (special classes, repeated grades, illiteracy), evidence of behavior problems, (repetitive truancy, suspensions, drop-out expulsion, school phobia).

4. *Military history:* Information is sought about the subject's quality of military adjustment and performance, the branch of the armed services chosen, the military aspirations and achievements, and the type of discharge. *Target areas:* rejection by the service; inability to adjust to military service; medical, general, or dishonorable discharge; disciplinary actions; court martials; or traumas sustained during service (combat, injury, death of comrades).

5. *Vocational history:* Information is sought about subject's occupational history, quality of performance, ability to support self and family, job satisfaction or frustration, aspirations, and relationships with coworkers and supervisors. *Target areas:* work related injuries, dismissal or suspensions, welfare assistance, or unemployment compensation.

6. *Sexual development:* Data are gathered pertaining to the subject's sexual development, education, experiences, orientation, attitudes, fantasies, and comfort. *Target areas:* evidence of sexual trauma (victim of sexual assault and/or incest); sexual dysfunction; use of force or intimidation to gain sexual access to other people; unconventional sexual interests, experiences, or attitudes; and sexual fears.

7. *Marital history:* Information is sought concerning the reason for and quality of the subject's marriage(s); the number of offspring and the subject's relationship with wife and children; and the sexual compatibility and fidelity of husband and wife. *Target areas:* evidence of marital discord, such as wife-beating, separation or divorce, or extramarital sexual relationships; evidence of school problems, behavior problems, mental disorders, drug or alcohol abuse, or delinquency of children.

8. *Social-recreational history:* Subject's social interests and leisure time activities, hobbies, club or other organizational membership are investigated, as well as the nature and quality of his friendships, regard for possessions, and sports activities. *Target areas:* social isolation, susceptibility to the influence of others, leisure time interests that focus on drinking or high-risk activities.

9. *Criminal history:* Information is sought about the subject's difficulty with the law, i.e., arrests, charges, dispositions, institutional history, and parole or probation history. *Target areas:* crimes of violence, recidivism, institutional adjustment problems, parole or probation violations or revocations.

In exploring each area of the subject's life, not only is the factual material important but his accompanying attitudes and feelings are equally, if not more important. In addition to the physical and behavioral characteristics of the subject, his perceptions, defenses, affective reactions, and ability to relate to the interviewer during the examination are also significant.

Inconsistencies in the material presented by the offender and that obtained from other sources must be resolved. Therefore, it is necessary to interview other significant people in the subject's life to validate, contest, or expand the information given. A parent, wife, or relative can offer another perspective or supply additional information about the subject's behavior. School, medical, psychiatric, military, and work records are obtained from their respective sources. Law-enforcement officers involved in the investigation of the offense are especially good providers of observations and information; and the material the victim(s) can supply—details of the offense, results of medical examination, and the like—are indispensable. The data are then "lived with," studied, thought about, discussed, challenged, deliberated, examined, and reexamined. Further information may be sought through psychological testing, additional field investigations, consultants, physical and neurological examinations, and the like.

In conducting our psychological investigations we function in teams of two or three staff members. Not only does this expedite the procedures involved but also offers a multidisciplinary approach to the task and ensures a thoroughness in the processing of data.

We request permission to tape record our interviews. Not only does this expedite the interview itself, since the examiner is not encumbered by having to take notes, but also in this form all the data, together with the subject's affective tone, quality of verbalization, style of speech, and the like, are retrievable. Further, we are often called upon to interview two or more subjects in succession at the courthouse, and a taped interview works against blending impressions or confusing information.

Where feasible, a visit to the subject's home can provide firsthand impressions about his family, style of life, neighborhood, and climate or atmosphere of surroundings that are only vaguely approximated when he is evaluated in an office setting.

We always consult with the police and probation departments, not only for information and observations but also for their views, suggestions, and recommendations regarding the accused. They have a wealth of experience, very practical attitudes, and sound, intuitive ideas as to the situation.

Where possible, we also interview the victim of the offense and/or his or her parents, not only to obtain information about the sexual offense but also to permit the victim to express how he or she would like to see the situation handled, what he or she would like to have happen in regard to the offender. (This is especially crucial in cases on incest.)

Where confidentiality is not at issue, we conduct many consultations over the telephone. It would be too time consuming, inconvenient, and impractical to make field investigations in regard to every area of the subject's life, but a telephone call to a teacher, employer, clergyman, doctor, or lawyer can expedite clarification, verification, or negation of some information or produce some observations and answers to important questions.

Finally, when we complete our assessment and formulate our recommendations, we discuss the results with the parties involved—offender, victim, police, and probation—and consider their reactions. Our procedures, then, are not only multidisciplinary but interagency as well. The data are interpreted in regard to the referral questions, and the results are condensed and summarized in a report. The format for the type of report generated by our department appears in Figure 2-1.

Treatment and Management Issues

Whatever the degree of risk a child offender poses to the community, ultimately the best protection for society is some form of treatment. Different legal

HARRINGTON MEMORIAL HOSPITAL

FORENSIC MENTAL HEALTH DEPARTMENT

SUBJECT: DOCKET NUMBER (S):

ADDRESS: CHARGE (S):

BIRTHDATE: (AGE:)   COURT:

SOCIAL SECURITY #:   JUDGE:

EXAMINERS: DATE OF REPORT:

PSYCHOLOGICAL EVALUATION

REFERRAL: Date, source, and reason for the referral; purpose of the examination; referral questions; nature of the charges; subject's plea; name of court, judge, probation officer, and subject's lawyer; date of trial.

INFORMATION SOURCE: Persons consulted or interviewed, date and place or type of contact, their relation to subject; records, documents, or reports examined and their source; psychological tests administered, date and place of administration.

INSTANT OFFENSE: An account of the charges against the subject including both subject's and victim's version of the offense together with related information such as police reports, witnesses' statements, medical reports on the victim, and the like.

BACKGROUND INFORMATION: A description of the subject's behavior during his interview(s) including his appearance, physical characteristics, quality of verbalization, attitude, mood, affect, cooperation and rapport with the examiner; an account of the subject's background and life history, describing his bio-psycho-social development and noting any significant strengths or difficulties, accomplishments or traumas, in managing the various aspects of his life.

ASSESSMENT: Clinical significance and interpretation of the descriptive material reported above together with the results of the psychological tests with regard to the psychological makeup and functioning of the subject, his self-esteem, impulse control, contact with reality, quality of his major mood states, defenses, and interpersonal relationships.

VICTIM'S ATTITUDE: A description of the victim's feelings and attitudes towards the subject, what the consequences of the offense have been in regard to the victim, how she/he would like to see this matter handled.

SUBJECT'S ATTITUDE: A description of the subject's reaction to the offense, his subjective feelings regarding it (remorse, embarrassment, justification, etc.), efforts at restitution, what disposition she/he feels is appropriate or useful.

CLINICAL IMPRESSION: Diagnostic impression of subject, an analysis of the offense with regard to precipitating stresses, releasor mechanisms, and motivational intent, an estimation of the likelihood of repetition and the degree of dangerousness of such behavior, answers to the referral questions.

RECOMMENDATIONS: Suggestions for what can be done to help the subject, treatment needs, type of rehabilitation services required, placement of choice, further issues to be evaluated.

SIGNATURE
TITLE

Figure 2-1. Form of Report on Sexual Offender.

sanctions can be imposed in line with whatever jeopardy offenders present to the community. For some offenders, family pressures are sufficient to encourage them to seek treatment. Others will become involved in treatment only under the threat of charges being otherwise pressed against them. Some will accept treatment as an alternative to a trial, in which case the court can continue the case without a finding for a specified period of time, stipulating participation in a therapy program as a special condition of probation. Others will accept treatment as an alternative disposition to serving prison time, the sentence being suspended, with treatment a condition of probation. In some states offenders can be civilly committed to a security treatment center indefinitely in lieu of prison sentence, and others can receive both a specified prison sentence and an indefinite civil commitment. Whatever the mandate, it should reflect the view that the crime is also a symptom—the offense may be punished, but the condition must be treated. Sexual advances toward children, whether impulsive or intentional, are symptomatic of psychosocial dysfunction, and a fine, imprisonment, or probationary supervision alone will not in itself guarantee remission of the problems prompting such sexual behavior. In fact, in some cases, such dispositions may only serve to aggravate the situation and increase the risk the offender poses by intensifying his stress. Even if the offender is removed from the community and incarcerated—and thus out of reach of children—this is usually only a temporary solution. Most such individuals will some day be released back into the community, and since few correctional institutions have adequate mental health services or treatment programs available for their inmates, these people will come out of prison no better equipped to handle the demands, responsibilities, pressures, and frustrations of their lives than they were before.

Forensic Mental Health

Having turned to the mental health professionals for diagnostic evaluation, the courts and related agencies now look to them to provide treatment. However, forensic mental health is a relatively new frontier. Psychiatrists, psychologists, social workers, and psychiatric nurses, have not been prepared in their academic training to work with such patient populations. For the most part, sexual offenders have been dealt with through criminal justice agencies. Unlike traditional patients who are motivated by varying degrees of subjective distress and seek out help for their problems, the child offender turns to children for comfort and satisfaction of his needs, not to adult authority figures. Even those who are distressed by their desires report that they did not seek professional help out of the fear that admission of their interests would lead to incarceration in a prison or mental hospital. As a result, mental health professionals have not yet developed programs specifically tailored to the treatment needs of the various types of child offenders.

What we need are forensic institutions, places that encourage research, study, training, teaching, and direct services for both offenders and victims. The treatment services should include all modalities: chemotherapy, psychotherapy, sociotherapy, behavior modification, and related programs tailored to meet the specific needs of each patient. For some offenders there should be inpatient hospitalization under various degrees of security, partial hospitalization or day care services, halfway houses, and aftercare and outpatient programs, as well as ongoing evaluation of these programs.

There have been a number of attempts to provide specialized treatment facilities for the dangerous sexual offender—about 20 such programs are currently in operation in various states across the nation—but none of them are institutes in the true sense of the word, and only now is some information about their work beginning to emerge.[7] What we wish to address in this section of the chapter are some observations, thoughts, and ideas directed toward the therapeutic management of the child offender. These are not definitive pronouncements, they are tentative proposals for consideration.

Rehabilitation

When we address the topic of treatment, we are always asked, "Do you really think a child offender can change?" We answer: "Some, yes; others, no. It depends." Clearly, given the present state of knowledge in the behavioral sciences, there are child offenders who are untreatable. They have been too seriously damaged for too long in their lives to reasonably expect that they can be repaired or rehabilitated by available treatment modalities. For others, the prognosis is much more favorable; they would appear to be good candidates for recovery through mental health treatment intervention. Perhaps the way to address this issue, then, is to approach it as a question of prevention. Given a referral case, the question we ask, or are asked, is "What needs to be done to prevent this individual from again sexually assaulting a child"—and we add—"with as few restrictions on his life as possible?" The answer to such a question will depend on a number of considerations:

Is his behavior more psychologically or physically dangerous to the victim?

Is his behavior with children chronic and repetitive or a recent and acute condition?

Is his sexual offense an exception to an otherwise relatively conflict-free and law-abiding life, or is it just one of a series of different criminal behaviors and multiple life problems?

Apart from his pedophilic interests, is he a reasonably well-adjusted individual, or does he, in addition, suffer from a major psychiatric disorder?

The meaning of his pedophilic behavior and the constellation of related problems will generally point the way to the treatment of choice. For example, for the incestuous offender whose family wishes to remain united, family therapy would appear to be the major treatment intervention modality; for the aged, intellectually dull, fixated offender, behavior modification probably would be more appropriate; and so on.

Placement

The first decision that must be made in every case is whether the offender can safely be treated on the street or needs to be institutionalized. If he remains in the community, there is the opportunity for further sexual activity with children. How much of a risk is this to the safety of a child? Obviously if the offense has been confined to indecent exposure and the offender is not psychotic or retarded, outpatient treatment would appear to be less of a risk than if the offense involved kidnapping and sexual penetration of a victim. Therefore, a decision must be made as to the most appropriate setting in which to treat the patient: outpatient, within a residential placement, within a hospital, within a security institution. The decision concerning the extent of external structure and control is determined by the adequacy of the internal controls and inner resources of the offender in structuring and managing his life—that is, how much of a danger he poses to the safety of children. When children are not physically at risk from the offender, the tendency is to treat him in something less than a maximum security setting.

Modality

What type of treatment to provide then depends upon what type of person you are treating. Some offenders may be good candidates for psychotherapy, and others would benefit more from behavior modification programs. Some need a combination of both. More often, however, the type of treatment provided is dictated by the type of treatment available. Psychotherapy or counseling is usually the more available modality.

For those patients being treated on an outpatient basis, the following conditions need to be explored. First not only is the offender's suitability for treatment evaluated, but also his living situation must be carefully analyzed to determine which features contribute to the risk of further acting-out and how these can be changed. The offender's living arrangements, his work, his leisure-time activities, and so forth must all be carefully assessed and restructured where needed and realistically feasible. External support and control systems need to be installed. These might include such considerations as identifying someone in the subject's life—a parent, spouse, or sibling—who would be in a position to observe the offender's lifestyle and identify problematic behaviors. In this way, they may become active agents in the offender's psychotherapy program. It might be more productive for the offender to have daily meetings or brief counseling sessions (maybe 20 minutes each) with treatment staff than only once-a-week sessions for an hour. Other community agencies such as state rehabilitation commissions or programs such as Alcoholics Anonymous would be helpful, where appropriate, in structuring the offender's life and strengthening his resources. Parole supervision or the probationary threat of a prison sentence can have an impact on the offender's behavioral controls. Clear goals need to be identified for the offender in the treatment plan, and regular review of the progress toward these goals should be undertaken.

For those offenders who are in acute crisis and unable to manage daily activities on an outpatient basis, a temporary residential placement or partial hospitalization program would be recommended. But for those offenders who jeopardize the physical safety of their victims, treatment within a maximum security treatment center under an indefinite-commitment status should be considered. Hopefully the offender will then not return to the community until he is no longer dangerous. There are many objections to such civil commitments, but we have no viable alternative. In such cases, then, careful supervision and evaluation of these programs and commitments must take place, and appropriate agencies ought to be mandated to research the effectiveness of these programs and to offer various other modalities of treatment.

It has been our experience that the offenders who are committed to such facilities are those who do pose a serious risk to the community. It becomes difficult to determine when such individuals are again good candidates for return to society. Many, if not all, show significant improvement in their behavior over time; and after a few years of intensive treatment in a therapeutic community milieu, the inmate-patient may appear ready for release. The difficulty is in differentiating how much of this improvement is due to changes within the offender and how much is due to changes in his environment. In such maximum security treatment centers there is no erotic stimulation by the physical presence of children. There is no responsibility to support oneself and provide for one's family. The pressure and responsibilities of handling a marriage and bringing up children are lessened, and various services are readily provided: food, clothing, shelter, treatment, education, socialization experiences, and the like. The offender does not have to structure or organize his life. It is done for him. This environment is not stressful, and he functions more adaptively. Release from such institutionalization must therefore be gradual in order to determine whether the offender's apparent improvement is genuine or merely a function of environment.

It is a fact of life, however, that there is no place in our society for the chronic repetitive child offender who uses no physical force. If he remains in the community, he continues to sexually harass children; he gets arrested and is ultimately sent to prison. There his life is in jeopardy from other inmates who view his offense as justification for his becoming the target of their own violent behavior. He is not welcome in mental hospitals, and should he be civilly committed to a maximum security treatment center, his passive-dependent orientation leads to his quickly becoming institutionalized.

Treatment Goals

Whatever the setting, we have found that the therapeutic management of the child offender must include four issues. First, the offender needs to acknowledge that he has committed the offense without projecting responsibility or blame on some external factor, such as intoxication, victim provocation, and so on. Second, the offender must be held responsible and accountable for his actions. Some form of restitution should be made. Third, the offender needs to become sensitized to the chain or pattern of behaviors that lead to his sexual involvement with children or adolescents so that he can detect early warning signs or symptoms. And fourth, the offender should develop alternative and more appropriate modes of self-expression, need gratification, and impulse management. Unless these features characterize an offender's treatment plan in some concrete fashion, his rehabilitation cannot be considered complete.

References

1. Murray L. Cohen, A. Nicholas Groth, and Richard A. Siegel, "The Clinical Prediction Of Dangerousness," *Crime and Delinquency* (January, 1978).

2. Larry L. Constantine, "Commentary," *Behavior Today,* April 4, 1977.

3. Robert L. Sadoff, *Forensic Psychiatry: A Guide for Lawyers and Psychiatrists* (Springfield, Illinois: Charles C. Thomas, 1975).

4. Morris Ploscowe, *Sex And The Law* (New York: Ace Books, 1962).

5. Richard A. Siegel, "Coercion and Compassion: Sexual Psychopathy and The Law" (unpublished manuscript, 1974).

6. Ibid.

7. Edward M. Brecher, "Treatment Programs for Sex Offenders," National Institute of Law Enforcement and Criminal Justice, Law Enforcement Assistance Administration, U.S. Department of Justice (in preparation).

3

Crisis Issues for an Adolescent-Aged Offender and His Victim
A. Nicholas Groth,
Ann Wolbert Burgess, and
Lynda Lytle Holmstrom

The question is always raised, when describing only one side of an assault, such as that of the offender, as to what the impact was on the other person, the victim. Occasionally, we have had an opportunity to study and work with the victim as well as the offender in a case. This type of multifaceted approach has allowed for greater insights into the effect of the offense on the parties involved, including victim, offender, and their families. The following case describes a 17-year-old offender and the emotional turmoil he experienced in his life before and after the sexual assaults. The case also describes crisis counseling with one of the offender's victims, a 6-year-old boy.

The Offender

Life History Data

Robert was born in Canada. His father was a North American Indian and his mother was French-Canadian. Robert was baptized with two different sets of names, one side of his family called him Robert, the other side addressed him as Louis. Later in his life he became known by a third name, Stonie, to his friends. During the first six years of his life, Robert was repeatedly hospitalized with recurring bouts of pneumonia, asthma, and bronchitis. He was enuretic until age 9. Intense sibling rivalry developed between Robert, an older sister, and two younger brothers. While still in latency, Robert began to ring in false fire alarms and steal money from his mother (whom he later described as the person closest to him in his family). During his early years, Robert's family was constantly uprooted, relocating a number of times between Canada and the United States. His father was alcoholic and physically abusive to his wife and children. This culminated in a sexual assault by the father on his 13-year-old daughter that resulted in his going to prison and his wife divorcing him. Robert, age 9, initially remained with his mother. However, financial difficulties ultimately required his placement at age 12, in a number of foster homes together with his two brothers (ages 9 and 7). His older sister remained with the mother. Four years later, the mother remarried and the family was reunited.

Robert's memory is very vague and confused about the details of his early life, and he has no recollection of his natural father at all. Among the various places in which his family lived is an Indian reservation where Robert began

43

attending a parochial (Catholic) school. He was found to be of average intelligence and maintained a B average. By the time he reached the eighth grade he had repeated two grades; he was attending an urban school where his grades dropped to C. A pattern of repeated infractions developed—fighting with students and playing hookey for long stretches of time—which ultimately resulted in his dropping out of school at age 15. At this same age, he began to drink heavily, often to the point of intoxication, and began to become involved in delinquent-criminal activities. At 16 he was charged with two counts of rape involving a 15-year-old girl, whom he had been dating and with whom he allegedly had been having consenting sexual relations. The charges were dismissed. Four months later he was convicted of the unauthorized use of a motor vehicle for which he was probated to the state division of youth services. According to Robert, as he was walking home, he grew increasingly afraid of being assaulted by personal enemies in the neighborhood, and finding a car, he hot-wired it as a safe means of transport. In connection with this offense, he was seen by a court psychiatrist for approximately five sessions, terminating when, now 17 years old, he enlisted in the Army, after the Marine Corps—his first choice—turned down his application. Unable to tolerate menial tasks and sedentary projects, and feeling threatened and frightened a good deal of the time, Robert went AWOL, but turned himself in after two days because he ran out of money and was hungry. However, Robert constantly believed he was going to be assaulted—a fear which, in the past, led to numerous fights and difficulties and which will continue to do so in the future. Robert again went AWOL, stole a car, returned to his old neighborhood, and stayed at the home of an aunt when his parents would not accept him back. He spent a weekend babysitting for friends of his family, during which he sexually assaulted and raped their 6-year-old boy. He then returned to the Army and, five months after his enlistment, received an undesirable discharge.

Sexual Development

Robert's sexual development is blurred. Initially he claimed that his first sexual interests and thoughts occurred around the age of 10, while on the Indian reservation, when he happened upon a couple engaging in sexual intercourse. Later he denied this and reported an episode in which, while on the reservation, he was approached by a "30-year-old Indian. . . . He felt my ass up, and I hit him with a bat. . . . If he tried to do it to me now, I'd break him in half." (It is significant to note that Robert was not on the reservation at this age level.) He admits to having masturbated but has no recollection of when it began or any fantasies associated with it. Today he claims that he almost never masturbates, saying he finds that it interferes with his bodybuilding exercises. When asked if he himself had ever been the victim of a sexual assault, he replies yes, but, as it turns out, the incident consisted of an older man asking him and his teenage friends if they wanted some "head." According to Robert, when he and his friends realized this was a sexual proposition, they beat the man up. Robert claims never to have had any type of homosexual experiences (in spite of the sodomy conviction) and indeed never even to have known of such things until his incarceration (in spite of other statements to the contrary). He considers such behavior disgusting and abhorrent.

Development of an Internal Crisis

An assessment of Robert's background and early life illustrates several points. We can speculate on the impact of two sets of names, a marginal minority status in a community and a cultural shift, repeated hospitalizations, a physically and sexually abusive father, a mother who found it difficult to cope with the family, intense sibling rivalry, a nomadic family lifestyle, transient peer relationships, interrupted schooling, and the lack of any genuine accomplishments or successes in terms of vocational or military achievements to his personality development. It is interesting that nowhere along the line did any people or agencies attend to the very clear signs of difficulties with the tasks of growing up. If the absence of any meaningful male or female peer relationships, the nomadic existence, his overreaction to homosexuality, and his increasing emphasis on physical size and strength (weight lifting, wanting to be a Marine, etc.) are not clear indicators of problems early in Robert's life, then what about the clearer signs: the sibling rivalry, the stealing, and the ringing of fire alarms, which escalate during adolescence into drinking, fighting, school failure, sexual misconduct, and the difficulties with the law that become even more pronounced in military service? Unsupported and unaided, the stress events in Robert's life built steadily toward an internal psychological crisis. The conflict areas centered around issues of identification, competency, self-worth, impulse management, and interpersonal relations. As Robert chronologically aged, the demands of self-reliance and responsibility increased. Ill-prepared to cope with these demands, pressures mounted, reaching crisis proportion, and resulted in a sexual assault.

The Victim

Family Background

John, age 6, was born in the United States, the fifth child in a family of four boys and two girls. The family lived in a large Eastern city where the five oldest children all attended school. They occupy part of a two-family house.

The Assault

Apparently home from the service for the holidays, Robert, a friend of the family, had been visiting and stayed overnight. The next day John said to his mother, "Last night Stonie did bad stuff to me." The mother, paying no attention to the remark, later said, "Kids are always saying things." The next day, her husband suggested that he and his wife go out and have some fun. John asked his mother not to go, but the parents went anyway, leaving Robert to babysit. While the parents were out, Robert took John into the parents' bedroom and sodomized him again. Other children in the family witnessed the act and thereby corroborated the assault to the parents when they returned home.

John reported the details of the assault as follows, "He ripped my pants and did butterfly to me. . . . He went up and down in me. . . . It hurt bad, and I tried to holler, but he kept his hand over my mouth and held my hands behind my back. He said if I told anyone, he'd hit me with a baseball bat." After telling his parents of the second assault, John refused to stay in the house with Robert. The mother had John and the other children stay with the family living above them.

The mother's immediate response was, "I wanted to stab him, to kill him, but I talked to myself to calm down." The parents confronted Robert with the allegations, and he calmly admitted three assaults, adding that he did not mean to hurt John. The husband ordered him out of the house and threatened to kill him. The mother's perception was "Suddenly he wasn't the Robert we knew— laughing, joking, and fun to be with—but now quiet and so strange."

The mother called the police, who advised that she take her son to the hospital for an examination. Next she telephoned Robert's mother, with whom she had a long relationship. Robert's mother was upset and said, "I knew something like this would happen. . . . He was AWOL. . . . If you don't prosecute, I will."

At the hospital, the victim, John, was quiet and alert, answering questions briefly. He showed interest in the hospital equipment and was cooperative during the physical examination, which was primarily visual. His parents in contrast were crying, chain-smoking, and talking obsessively about the event and their fears of the aftereffects on their young son.

Development of an External Crisis

As with adult victims, child victims and their families show disruption in the lifestyles following sexual assault. John had little appetite and did not eat. He showed no interest in his usual activities and spent his time sitting around the house staring at the television set. He refused to play outside and would go to school only after his mother insisted and accompanied him and his brothers and sisters to the local school. He had nightmares in which he would cry and mumble in his sleep but not wake up.

His siblings also reacted to the incident, especially his oldest brother, who had corroborated the assault. After disclosure of the incident, he went directly to his room and to bed. Tension was high in the family. The children refused to sleep in their own beds and would come into their parents' room at night. Once during a storm in which the lights went out, the children were terrified, fearing Robert was coming back.

The stress of a sexual assault can reactivate previous anxieties, fears, and behaviors. In this case, the victim counselor received a telephone call in the middle of the night, three weeks after the incident, from the father stating that his wife was threatening to commit suicide. Her menstrual cycle was late; she feared that she was pregnant again even though she was on birth control pills; she felt that she had not listened to her son and thus had failed to adequately protect him; she feared that her husband would leave her.

During this early phase, the family looked to significant people for support. In this case, it was the grandmother who provided the structure. She was firm and positive in her approach and advice to the situation. She advised denial as the method to handle the situation ("Forget it—time will take care of it"). She also emphasized reality: "He could have killed those kids. . . . People do . . . to shut the kid up. You are lucky your kids are alive. You can't kill yourself. Who would take care of the kids?"

The Legal Dimension of Sexual Assault

Victim

The issue of divided loyalty is always raised when the offender is known to the victim.[1] The decision of whether or not to press charges must be made. In this case, the victim's mother telephoned the offender's mother to report the incident. The offender's mother made her decision to treat her son as an assailant and had no opposition to legal proceedings. The victim's mother made the decision saying, "We will press charges. He is a dangerous person to have out."

However, the parents were concerned about the effect of the court process on the children, especially John and his older brother, who would have to testify.

Court Appearances

When the date for the probable cause hearing arrived, everyone was at the court house except Robert. The previous night he had talked his way into an apartment and, at knife point, raped two teenage girls. He had intercourse with the first victim and ejaculated. He then had intercourse with the second victim, sodomized her, bit her breast, and forced her to perform oral sex on him. He then fled but was identified by the girls through his army jacket, which had his name stenciled on it.

This latter rape case was dealt with first in court because it was considered a more serious charge than child assault. At the trial, the detective asked if Robert could have a psychiatric examination because, "He sure needs one. He has a *previous* rape." This was the first time that Robert's initial rape charge, which had been dismissed, was made known. The district attorney recommended that Robert be sent to a mental health facility for diagnostic evaluation, and the defense lawyer supported this recommendation. The judge requested recommendations from two additional sources—the probation officer and the victim counselor—both of whom also agreed. However, their recommendations were all ignored, and Robert was sentenced to prison for a maximum of 16 years. The judge stated that if prison authorities thought a psychiatric examination would be helpful, they could arrange it.

Victim and Family Reaction to Court

The courtroom experience triggered more stress on the family and victim. At the courthouse John was unable to talk to anyone. He sat quietly by himself and actually cried if anyone looked at him. His parents were silent but visibly anxious, chain-smoking and shaking. John's older brother did all the talking for the family.

John's mother was most concerned with why Robert had not been locked up immediately. After hearing of the latter offenses, she stated, "Didn't they know he would go right back out and do it again? I don't know why they let him go." Yet clearly, her feelings were ambivalent, for she said, "The last time I saw him was in court. He shook my hand and said, 'I'm awful, awful sorry,' He had such a sad face. I think about that. I don't hold it against him as a human being. He was sick."

Offender Reaction to Prison

When first incarcerated, Robert was reported as being "very scared." He twice got into fights and was transferred to a protective custody unit because of his fear of being raped. Even within this protected facility he was very uncomfortable and frightened, and reported being constantly approached sexually. An inmate was murdered in his unit, and Robert reported feeling both fear and excitement over the event. He was given work on an outside farm detail, where he did well until notified that he was to be examined at a special facility for sexual offenders. Frightened by the examination and terrified at the prospect of being sent to a place where there were "weird sex fiends," Robert escaped from his work detail only to later turn himself in when he became cold, hungry, and tired. No longer permitted outside the walls and deeply agitated by the prospect of commitment to the sexual offender unit, Robert began to have thoughts that he was going crazy; he destroyed his cell, smashing furniture and fixtures and throwing things about. The prison authorities attempted to commit him to a state mental hospital, but the court refused. The next day Robert punched an inmate who was "bugging" him. Finally, after a sequence of somewhat abnormal behaviors, possibly suggesting hallucinations, Robert was transferred to a mental hospital and examined. The hospital recommended his commitment, but the court found Robert to be a "noncommittable person" and returned him to continue serving his sentence.

Family Reaction of Offender

It is important to note the reaction of the offender's family. An aunt of Robert's, when hearing the news, said "Oh my god, he's following in his father's foot-steps," referring to the fact that Robert's father had been apprehended and con-victed of incest with his daughter. This aunt said, "I can't stand to talk about it. It's disgusting. It is hard even being related . . . having known him as he grew up." (In fact, it was this aunt who harbored Robert after the assault and before he was found and sent back to the Army.) Robert's stepfather took a stand against him initially, saying, "He's been in so much trouble, we don't want him around anymore. . . . If he ever comes back, he wouldn't be welcome here." After Robert was incarcerated, his mother and stepfather stated that they would visit him every other week. In commenting on an interview with a prison psychiatrist, Robert's stepfather said he did not agree with the psychiatrist and felt that he was "put down" in the report. Robert's mother stated that she did not feel her son to be dangerous. After he had been in prison for about three years, his parents felt they saw an improvement in him and that he was "much better." Their main complaint was that no one told them anything about what was happening to Robert and often they went to the prison to see him only to find that he had been transferred or was not available for a visit with them.

Intervention for Victim and Offender

Victim

The passage of time acts as a buffer to the initial shock and impact of a sexual assault. The victim and his family then begin the cognitive, emotional, and behavioral work of settling their feelings and reactions. One method involves mentally reviewing the incident. Questions predominate at this point of the crisis, and answers must be worked out to some degree of satisfaction to the family: Why did it happen? What will be the long-term effects on John? Why would anyone do it to a young child, a boy? In this case, the answer that was satisfactory to John's mother was that Robert must be sick. Some friends asked the mother why she just didn't kill the offender. She took a humanistic view and said, "He is a human being; he has a right to live no matter what he has done."

Very often the presence of a crisis will bring forth other information that may have been overlooked or gone unreported in a family. That this family was able to deal with the issue and respond in a decisive way against the offender gave the children the confidence to bring up additional information. The second oldest child (age 10) told his grandmother that Robert had also been after him sexually but that he had fought him off and had been left alone. John's 9-year-old sister had slapped Robert in the face when he attempted to assault her, and John reported that Robert had tried to do the same thing to the one-year-old baby sister, but that she had screamed so loud that Robert stopped. He also reported that Robert had attempted sodomy on a male cousin but was interrupted by a sister who came into the room. The victim's grandmother, who became an important person throughout the crisis, fitted many of the pieces of a prior puzzling situation together. She said,

"You know, I think this happened to [Sam] first. The [parents] took him to the doctor about a year ago. He wasn't feeling well and he was drawn and looked funny, and they had him in the hospital and everything. But the kid never told. . . . He was too scared. The children didn't dare to tell because the guy said he would kill them. But now we know what was going on and why the poor boy was so sick."

A main task in dealing with the emotional component is to sort out the feelings that various family members have. One of the hardest for the victim's mother was dealing with her initial reaction of disbelief of what John had reported to her. In referring to her denial of John's request to remain home, she said, "I paid for my fun." Her hardest task was apologizing to John for not believing him.

Betrayal becomes an issue when the offender is either a family member or, as in this case, very well known to the family and assuming the role of babysitter. The family had to come to grips with the question, "How could he do such a thing when we trusted him and had taken him in." The mother initially remarked, as one often hears from rape victims, "I won't trust a man again."

Many families deal with the issue of child sexual assault by denial; that is, it happens to others and can never happen to our family. Such was the case here. The father emphasized,

"You read about such things happening but you never think it could possibly be your own family. . . . But it has happened. What will it be like for him? Will he ever get over it?"

Admitting that it has happened is one of the positive responses one looks for in a family. As this mother said, "You read about it in the paper, but that's different. Now you know how it really feels to those people."

People start remembering and identifying with other people who have been victims of crime. In this case, the grandmother said, "I was reading in the paper where a father was prosecuting someone that hurt his daughter, and the judge put the guy on bail, and the guy came out and killed the girl. This bail thing is no good. The guy needs help. I agree to that, and I hope he gets help, but I don't want to see him out on bail." Fear of further trauma is common in victims and their families, and this is often an area for which they seek advice and support from health professionals and police. This victim's family had great difficulty in dealing with the fact that Robert was out on bail.

Adult rape victims often become more cautious and reclusive in response to a rape attack. With child victims of sexual assault, one often sees parents tightening security and becoming more protective. John's mother walked all her children to school and did not let them play outside alone. The parents refused to go out socially and would not leave the children in the care of a babysitter. The grandmother intervened in this behavior by offering to babysit for the children. She also suggested that they move out of their neighborhood to be closer to her so that she could better supervise the children.

John observed his parents installing new locks in an increased effort to make their home secure and said, "My mother kicked him out. I know how to lock the door so he won't do it again."

To assess the degree to which the family was able to return to a routine lifestyle, we note that a normal routine was resumed after the final court appearance, in which Robert pleaded guilty to the child assault. However, additional crises have developed within the family over the five-year followup. The family home was burned, and there was a move to a new neighborhood (where Robert's family also lives). The mother reports that John is "fine and doing well in school. . . . Everyone is fine except Sam." Sam, the second oldest son, at age 12, became aggressive and disruptive at school, and his mother became alarmed by his sexual interests and activity. She was most upset when she found him masturbating with his sister's underclothing. She sought psychiatric help, stating, "I am afraid of him. . . . He needs help. . . . He could rape someone." This son was institutionalized for almost a year, after extensive diagnostic evaluation, but permitted home to visit on weekends, an arrangement that greatly reduced the tension in the family. Then the mother was diagnosed with a malignancy. She underwent major surgery and a series of hospitalizations but died, leaving the father and grandmother to care for the children.

Incarceration of the Offender

When seen for diagnostic evaluation during the course of his incarceration, Robert appeared very uncomfortable. He related in a guarded and evasive manner and clearly did not care to talk about his life experiences. The most pronounced and persistent feature of his interaction in the interview was his poor comprehension of what was being asked—not that he did not understand the questions, but that he appeared to have no idea of what was being referred to; that is, he seemed almost totally unable to retrieve and accurately evaluate the past experiences. He appeared somewhat out of touch with himself and the world around him, much as if he did not appreciate, or even realize, the complexity of life events. He admitted to the rape offense against the teenage girls but claimed he was under drugs and could not actually remember what had happened. However, he asserted "It won't happen again because I don't want to have to come back to prison." He could offer no reason for his life difficulties—"things just happened"—and he denied having any problems apart from "not listening to [his] parents." His wish was to get out of prison, return home, and "help around the house."

The Offender: Internal Crisis Issue

Robert is known to the court to have four victims: three adolescent girls and one preadolescent boy. But we know from victim counseling that Robert attempted to sexually assault 5 other children, either from his family or family acquaintances. His legally charged offenses appear to progress from a pressured, "date rape" situation with a female classmate to repetitive, exploitative sexual assaults on a prepubescent boy who was a family acquaintance, to a brutal and aggressive rape at knifepoint of two female peers who were relative strangers. What determined his victim choice? Why was sodomy-rape his symptom choice? Why did Robert resort to sexual assault to express his conflicts? What motivated this behavior, and what needs did it serve? What conflicts did it express?

Clearly his offense was the result of many causes, and a definitive answer to these questions would require much more detailed information than we have access to at this point. However, we can speculate that a number of factors may have played a part in the formation of Robert's assaultive sexual behavior. At one level, it may reflect Robert's failure to achieve any stable sense of identity through avenues other than physical aggression and sexuality. Academic, military, and vocational success are absent in his life. He was unable to persist in any long-range, goal-oriented activities or to effect any emotionally meaningful, psychologically intimate relationships with others. Consequently, he put an ever-increasing premium on physical prowess for assertion and self-esteem. A child is someone he could easily control through authority, force, and intimidation.

Robert felt stronger than John, more powerful, and in more control; and in this respect, the sexual assault may have constituted a reassuring sense of mastery. As Robert became overwhelmed by the increasing stresses of his life, he reacted with sexual aggression. What did he have in the way of masculine models in his development? His father was a physically assaultive, alcoholic man who Robert so feared that he repressed all memories of him. Although it is only conjecture at this point, there is a possibility that Robert had also been, or feared being, a sexual victim of his father. What lends some credence to this supposition is Robert's early recollection of witnessing sexual relations and being sexually approached by an adult male while on an Indian reservation. This may have actually happened as reported, but it could also be a screen memory of some sexual incidents involving his father. In questioning Robert's mother about such a possibility, she replied, "I can't say it didn't happen"—an interesting response by a woman who characteristically depends on denial in discussing emotional family matters. It also seems significant in this regard that Robert's enuresis stopped when his father left the family, and Robert's sexual acting out began when his mother remarried. If Robert was in fact sexually molested by his father, his own sexual offenses could constitute a compulsive repetition of an imprinted psychological trauma. It could also account for his persistent perception of himself as being in jeopardy of assault from others, especially males. This sense of victimization may be the result of his feeling helpless in the face of frustration, neglect, assault, and abandonment from an early age. Robert finds inactivity bothersome. He is not comfortable with himself or his surroundings, and he experiences many aspects of his life as assaults that threaten his survival. His offense may then serve as a defense against feelings of vulnerability. The assault may represent his adopting the role of his aggressor ("identification with the aggressor"). Robert protected himself from assault by being the initiator rather than the recipient—rather than being the victim, he became the offender. A sexual offense is an interpersonal act, and the choice of a male child could be understood to constitute a projective identification. The victim may represent Robert's stage of psychological development. This victim may likewise symbolically represent all those features Robert dislikes about himself—weakness, vulnerability, helplessness, immaturity—and therefore his assault may constitute a projected punishment.

Robert's sexual assault may thus be serving needs of mastery, domination, anger, retaliation, in addition to sexual gratification. The particular form of the sexual assault, anal penetration, is an adult, genital sexual act, but it is performed on a prepubertal child. This regression in regard to the age of the victim, and the distortion in regard to the type of act, raises the possibility of some latent psychotic process operating in Robert. He had so few controls over his life and experienced so much stress that his sexual offenses may have been a last defense against going insane. When in fact he could no longer act out, and when he encountered the terrifying prospect of being the victim rather than the aggressor, Robert regressed into psychotic confusion. The offenses involving female peers seem to have served similar motives—sexuality in the service of power, domination, control, anger, and retaliation—and they served the added purpose of countering the homosexual quality of his pedophilic acts and reassuring Robert of his heterosexual adequacy and masculinity. The impact of his exposure in regard to his sexual acts with John may have stressed him even further, with the result that he began drinking heavily. Under the influence of alcohol his controls were further weakened, his tenuous contact with reality was further jeopardized, and his actions became more desperate. He lacked the social skills to negotiate sociosexual relationships and was now alienated from family and friends. His use of a weapon and the sadistic quality of his sexual assaults on the two teenage victims suggest that he was especially intimidated by, and harbored particular anger toward, females. Sexual conquest and degradation served to compensate for his feelings of inadequacy and to discharge his anger.

Sexual assault became the equivalent of symptom formation in Robert. Since sexual assault did not resolve his core problems, it would be a serious mistake to believe Robert's crisis has passed. He, in fact, experiences no responsibility for his behavior and shows no social acculturation. He admits to his offenses but projects responsibility for those onto alcohol and drugs. There is no experience of remorse or guilt. The only reason he can offer for not repeating his offenses in the future is narcissistic: he wouldn't want to go back to prison. His offenses, however, have been repetitive and show an increase of force over time; he has developed no alternative ways to more adaptively meet life demands. Consequently, he remains a seriously and dangerously disturbed young man.

The Victim: External Issues

There are several points to be made from the study of the victim's side of this case. These points may contradict popular stereotypes of sexual assaults of children.

Territorial Safety. Many people tell their children to beware of strangers. However, they fail to discuss the fact that their home may be unsafe as a result of the presence of people who may do them harm. Children may experience a lack of territorial safety when people renege on their responsibilities to protect them. In this case, Robert was entrusted with the safety of five children while he was babysitting.

Access of Offender to Victim. People who wish to assault children may try to gain access to children through employment or other activities. In the case of child sexual assault, frequently either family members or friends of the family use their access to assault the children. The presence of such people is not questioned by the family, and thus the children become a target for assault.

Child Reporting an Assault. Frequently, people think that they must be careful of what to believe from a child, that children make up stories or fantasize sexual attacks. In this case, the mother paid little attention to her child's report. However, when it turned out to be true, the mother had additional feelings to deal with. From a clinician's standpoint, it is important to see the manner in which a child reports an assault and the manner in which the news is received and subsequently dealt with.

Sex of the Victim. This case demonstrates that parents are concerned irrespective of the sex of the victim about whether or not the sexual assault will traumatize their child. Both male and female children experience trauma symptoms following an assault. Also parents feel upset and in need of counseling themselves, regardless of the sex of the child.

Not the Only Victim. This case points up the fact that an offender may have had previous victims who did not report their assaults for a variety of reasons: fear, guilt, intimidation.

Summary

This psychological study of Robert illustrates that forcible sexual assault can be an equivalent to symptom formation and may signal a serious psychological defect in the offender. In understanding the personality defects that ultimately result in an internal crisis in Robert, we note a paucity of psychological resourcefulness, an insecure sense of identity, deficient interpersonal relationships, inadequate impulse control, and tenuous life management skills. This appears to stem from a developmental history characterized by stress, unavailability of positive identification figures, unstable family roots, family conflicts, traumas, aggressive assaults, and few alternative means of self-expression and accomplishment. When faced with life tasks, frustrations, and disappointments, Robert experienced a sense of impending catastrophe and increasing desperation. His ego functions were overwhelmed, and he acted out in a desperate effort to free himself from distress.

This study of John illustrates how victims deal with the external crisis of a sexual assault. In comparing these cases, we see John being the recipient of a caring system in which the assault was not kept secret and the family alliance was strong and supportive; people took the incident seriously and responded to the crisis. Agency support was accepted and one can, at least, speculate that the possibility of long-term damage from the assault has been reduced. The additional tragedy of the death of the mother will undoubtedly strain the coping resources of the family and compound the problems John has to face in growing up.

Robert, the victim of a long-developing but acute internal crisis, is abandoned. Much of what was available to the victim is missing in the case of Robert: alliance, protection, intervention, support, and guidance. Perhaps even more striking is the fact that social agencies entrusted with providing safety, care, and rehabilitation of people such as Robert have chosen to repeat the same pattern of not taking seriously and attending to the signals of psychological crisis operating in him and underlying his offense. No one takes him seriously. At school he was allowed to stop in ninth grade. His parents did not actively help him establish any structure in his life. He began dating girls and started his sexually assaultive behavior. The first charges were dropped, and no one followed through. He behaved more and more in ways that called attention to himself—molesting children who knew him, often in full view of others. He was brought to court but allowed out on bail, and lacking sufficient internal (self) control to manage his life, he again raped on the evening prior to his court hearing.

However, how did the Army and the Court deal with this behavior? The Army suggested that he apply for a dishonorable discharge. They did not mention in their report any knowledge of his offense. Interestingly and significantly, it is the police who recognized Robert as a troubled young man. As one detective said, "I tried to make the Army aware of the seriousness of this. . . It looks like the Army is trying to avoid prosecution." And thus, even in a State where there is a security mental health facility designed especially to treat sexual offenders, three years go by in which Robert simply serves time in prison. The judge did *not* mandate treatment, the prison system did *not* provide treatment.

This case raises important questions. How much effort should be exerted for victims without equal input for work with offenders? How do the social institutions—school, military, court, prison—view treatment and the psychosocial components of the offense? We believe that it is important to achieve a balance in work with both victims and offenders.

Relatively little attention is being paid to the adolescent male who commits rape or child molestation. There appears to be a reluctance on the part of the courts and other agencies to view juvenile sexual offenses as significant or serious. Sometimes the concern is voiced that such a youngster will be stigmatized and that a conviction will jeopardize his plans for enlistment in the Armed Services, but more often it appears that such an offense is regarded as merely sexual experimentation, situational in nature, or as an expression of the normal aggressiveness of a sexually maturing male.

In a study of adolescent offenders, we found that in very few cases did the sexual assault appear to be the first interpersonal sexual experience in the offender's life.[2] The majority of these subjects (86 percent) had had previous sexual experiences—an observation that discredits the popular assumption that adolescent sexual offenses constitute merely sexual exploration or experimentation.

We also found that frequently there were more incidents of antisocial sexual behavior that were known to the parents, neighbors, police, or other authorities than those appearing on the offender's criminal record. Again, these incidents were typically dismissed as unimportant, especially when the victim involved was a sibling of the offender or the child of friends or neighbors.

Adolescent sexual offenses, especially those involving assault, need to be regarded as equivalent to more traditional symptoms of emotional disturbance, thus warranting careful psychological assessment by the courts and other related agencies. The all-too-frequent diagnosis of "adolescent adjustment reaction" often results in the defects and needs of the offender going unrecognized, thus allowing him to continue to jeopardize the community. There is a need for security treatment facilities for such young offenders if the courts are to make meaningful dispositions for intervention in such cases.

In conclusion, this case illustrates how a sexual assault can represent a crisis for the offender, his victim, and the families involved. In examining the crisis aspects of sexual assault, we find this offender responding to internal as well as external factors. Robert has psychological difficulty controlling his behavior and social institutions have not conveyed the message that the behavior is wrong. And we see the victim reacting to an external event and experiencing a loss of self-determination. Both are in a state of crisis and reacting to stress. The case of Robert explored the developmental crisis in an adolescent sexual offender and the reactive crisis in John, his prepubescent victim, showing the interrelationship between these crises.

Reference

1. Please see Chapter 7 for further discussion of the divided loyalty concept.
2. A. Nicholas Groth, "The Adolescent Sexual Offender and His Victim," *International Journal of Offender Therapy and Comparative Criminology* (forthcoming).

Part II Victims

In our work with child, adolescent, and adult victims of sexual assault, it became apparent that not all victims experienced the same type of attack, nor did they all react in the same way. Thus it became one of our first tasks to attempt to sort out our observations and impressions of victims in terms of the distress experienced and the problems encountered as a result of the incidents. We sought some clinical diagnoses that might be useful to health professionals working with victims. Our intent was to provide a method of logically ordering a victim's difficulties, whether physical, emotional, social, or sexual. Through this process, clinical judgment could be used to formulate treatment plans and goals.

The categories devised include: rape trauma syndrome, resulting from a forcible sexual assault; accessory-to-sex syndrome, resulting from a pressured sexual situation; and sex-stress reaction, resulting from a sexually stressful situation.

Complicating Factors in Rape: Adolescent Case Illustrations
Ann Wolbert Burgess and Lynda Lytle Holmstrom

The first type of victimization problem we observed in children, as well as in adults, we describe as *rape trauma*. In such situations, the rapist has gained access to the child or adolescent without any warning, as in a blitz attack; or the rapist has used a ploy to gain the confidence of the young person, as in a confidence attack, and then raped the child. In rape, the child is forced to have nonconsenting sexual activity under duress, threat, or intimidation. Victims experience the rape as a life-threatening situation.

The trauma syndrome that develops from this type of attack is two-phased. Immediately—in the acute phase—victims have to deal with the various disruptions in their life. In the second phase, which occurs over time, victims face the task of settling the disruptions and restoring their life to its usual state. Detailed discussions of this syndrome following rape to children and their families are included in Chapters 3 and 13.

We noted in our work, a large number of teenage rapes where there were multiple assailants involved. This chapter describes some complicating factors in rape and uses examples from adolescent victims to illustrate specific points. The complicating factors include: teenage peer rape by multiple assailants, handicapped victims, ethnic factors in rape, and family response to the adolescent victim.

Teenage Peer Rape

In studying adolescents and their offenders, it becomes clear that many teenage victims are raped by their peers. Often the adolescent offender is from the same community as the victim. Furthermore, many of these adolescent victims face multiple assailants, either a pair of adolescent males or a group of young males. Several variations of teenage peer rape may operate.

Peer Rape: Multiple Assailants and Single Victim

In this type of peer rape, several male teenagers gain access to a single victim. Usually, they all will rape the victim. In the following case, four young males from a victim's neighborhood attacked the girl as follows.

61

Clinical Case 1

A 15-year-old girl was playing with a group of five to six neighborhood friends. It was a warm sunny Valentine's day. Suddenly four youths started chasing the group, and everyone began to run. They were chased for one to two blocks, and the girl was caught. The gang of males twisted the girl's arm and forced her into an empty building. The males all raped her and threatened her if she told.

In this case, the girl told one of the friends she had been playing with when she returned home, who, in turn, told his mother, who told the victim's mother. The victim's mother reported the rape to the police and brought the girl to the hospital for an examination. The police investigated, and one of the detectives described to us how the situation was handled:

"This situation involves a triangle of about nine boys. They use this clubhouse in the area, and the boys say she has been up to it several times. The whole thing seems like [such] a complicated situation. I decided to handle it as a station matter. I went and talked with the boys in front of their parents and gave severe warnings to them that if there were any further reports of this, there would be serious trouble. We won't do anything more about this until we get another complaint. I tried to explain to the mother that it would be a difficult case in court. The boys would deny that they forced her. It would be a strain on the daughter to have to describe what happened."

Peer Rape: Multiple Assailants and Multiple Victims

In this type of peer rape, several male teenagers gain access to several teenage girls. Each male selects one victim to rape. In the following cases, there were three teenage girls and two adolescent male assailants.

Clinical Case 2

Three adolescent girls, ages 14, 15, and 15, had been shopping at a mall. They were waiting for the bus to take them home. A car pulled up to the bus stop and one youth in the car asked for directions. Then another youth stepped out of the car, held a knife to the girls, and forced them into the car. They were taken to a deserted area. The two older girls were raped. One youth raped one girl, and the second youth raped the second girl. The third girl was hysterical, and she was not raped. The assailants took all the money and jewelry of the raped girls. The three girls were then let out of the car.

The police were notified, and the girls were brought to the hospital. Eventually, one of the young men was apprehended. He defaulted at trial level.

Peer Rape: Multiple Assailants and Multiple Serial Victims

In this type of peer rape, all the assailants present will rape all the victims present. In such case, there may be a ritualistic aspect to the rape, such as who rapes first, who watches, or how many men force sexual activity on a victim at the same time. In the following case, two young women were gang raped by five youths over a six-hour period.

Clinical Case 3

Two young women were leaving a party when one of the adolescent males from the party asked for a ride home. The woman driving said OK. As they were driving, there was loud yelling, and suddenly four young men started getting into the car; three in the back seat with the second woman and one in the front seat. The driver yelled for the males to get out or she would drive to a police station. As the car turned the corner, it came to a dead end and was forced to stop. As one of the victims said: "At that moment, I knew we were in for trouble. They were like animals out of a cage." Before the women were able to turn the car around, they were dragged from the car to a wooded area.

Over the next several hours, all the youths performed various forced sexual acts, including oral, anal, and vaginal penetration. Several youths forced acts simultaneously; a beer bottle was inserted into one of the victim's vagina; insulting remarks were made about the women's bodies. The youths alternated standing around watching and laughing, making degrading remarks, and forcing sexual acts on the women.

The women were allowed to dress and then put back into the car. In the car, one of the youths threatened the women by saying, "If I see any police, I'll put money in your hand and say you're a prostitute, and I'll push you out."

The women were taken to an apartment and the rapes continued in two rooms. The telephone rang continuously, and the youths said they planned to be there all weekend and for everyone to come over and join in. The women kept screaming, which eventually brought the police to the scene.

The youths were apprehended and four of them were convicted of rape by jury trial.

Peer Rape in Tandem

There are some offenders—adolescents as well as adults—who group together specifically to rape. A number of times in our work, we observed the same pair of males systematically going through a neighborhood attacking victim after victim. Victims could be selected from within their own neighborhood or they could be brought into the neighborhood from an outside area. The assailants would rape the victim, one after the other.

Neighborhood Victims. Teenage victims within a specific neighborhood are the targets for this type of peer rape. Often the adolescent offenders have a specific location for the rapes. In the following cases, the location was an empty apartment in a housing project. It was the same pair of teenage offenders in each of the four cases presented.

Clinical Case 4

A 14-year-old girl was returning home at 10 P.M. from a party in the project where she lived. As she entered her building, two young men called out to her saying they had something to tell her. Once inside the apartment, she was slapped and then forced to submit to intercourse with one of the assailants. She screamed so loudly that she averted being raped by the second male. She was threatened with her life if she told anyone.

Clinical Case 5

On Halloween, a 13-year-old girl was returning home from school on the bus. Two young men—one of whom she had seen before—got on. The first male introduced the second, and some conversation followed, with them asking the girl to go into town with them. She refused. Later that evening, after dinner, the girl was leaving her building. As she came out of the elevator, the two young men grabbed her and, using a knife at her throat, made her leave the elevator with them. They took her to an empty apartment. In the apartment, both adolescent males raped her.

Clinical Case 6

A 13-year-old girl was walking home through the project where she lived. A youth known to her came up and said, "Would you do me a favor?" The girl said she would, and the boy gave her a note to give to another youth who lived on the fourth floor of the building. She did this, and as she gave the note to the boy, the first youth came running up the stairs and pushed her into the apartment. Both males were known to the girl. The first youth said his sister was looking for him, and they had to all hide under the bed. Once in the bedroom, the young men demanded sex. The girl was held down by one assailant as the other raped her. Then the second raped her. They threatened to kill her if she told anyone.

Case Discussion

In the case 4, the adolescent victim felt very scared about reporting the identities of the assailants. At the hospital she gave the partial names of the rapists and said she could not identify them. However, as word spread about additional rapes occurring in the project by this pair of offenders, the girl saw herself not as isolated but as one of several victims of these offenders. Four months after the rape, after learning that a friend of hers—as well as other girls—was raped by this pair, she told her father the names of the offenders. The father, in turn, notified the police again. The police did not act as fast as the father wished, and he was instrumental in locating the offenders and giving the police specific directions to where the pair was hiding.

Although two of the girls found mutual support as victims of the same offenders, the third victim did not report to the authorities nor accept counseling. She did not tell any adult for two months after the rape. By that time, she was experiencing major emotional difficulties and finally told her mother, who obtained mental health intervention.

In the court trial involving the first girl, the district attorney tried to get the third girl to testify. Her mother refused, stating that her daughter was too upset over the event. Thus the court outcomes in the three cases were: not guilty of any crime in case 4 and not guilty of rape but guilty of statutory rape (no force) in case 5. Case 6 was not reported to the police.

Not only did this pair of young offenders select victims from their own community, but they brought victims in from outside the community. In the following case, involving the same offenders, they brought an adolescent girl and a male companion into the empty apartment.

Clinical Case 7

On a hot summer evening, two young people visiting from another state, were walking around Boston. They met two young men at a park. During the course of conversation, one of the young men asked the couple what they were doing, and the male companion said they were looking for the Youth Hostel. One of the men said that they could stay at his sister's—that she had an extra room. Although the girl companion did not like the idea, the male companion said they would go with the men. All four left on a bus. It was almost midnight, and the girl could think of no alternative. As they walked into the apartment, in a poorly kept project, the door was locked behind them. Immediately the male companion was taken into a separate room, leaving the girl with one of the men, who said, "You are going to have to do me a favor. We are doing you a favor, giving you a place to stay." He took the girl to the window, and she saw at least 10 men outside who she later described as "junkies." The man said that all he would have to do was call them, and they would rob, rape, and kill her. Suddenly there was a knock on the door, and the second man said, "Hurry up, so I can come in." At that point, the man raped the girl. The second man came in and raped the girl. Then a third man entered the apartment, saying it was his turn. The male companion could be heard screaming in the other room; he was being beaten with a belt.

In this case, the girl managed to escape in the morning and obtained help by flagging down a police car. The police took her to the hospital. Her parents were notified by the hospital and police in order to obtain permission to treat her. The father, a business executive, flew to Boston to take his daughter home. The parents would not allow their daughter to testify, even though she had been able to make a positive identification of the men. The police admitted, however, that there were "problems with the case since she was a runaway at the time, she went willingly with the men, and had had some type of psychiatric help in the past." In this case, the victim never learned of what happened to the male companion who was with her that evening.

Counseling a Victim of Multiple Assailants

Counselors often do not take time to differentiate their counseling techniques when working with a victim of a single assailant versus working with a victim who has been raped or confronted with more than one assailant. This differentiation is most important to acknowledge to the victim; i.e. not only has the victim experienced one rape but has had to survive an assault by more than one assailant.

In addition to the usual counseling techniques described in Chapter 12, two factors are important to include in working with the victim of multiple assailants.

1. The victim needs to describe each rape with each assailant as a separate assault and deal with the feelings and issues involved. For example, what were the circumstances of the assault; how did the assailants gain access to her; were all assailants present to watch the rapes or did each assailant rape the victim with no one else present; was there a ritual to the rape?

2. Psychologically, each rape must be settled as a single assault, and then the multiplicity of the acts can be discussed. This process allows the counselor and victim to sort out the impact each assailant has had on the victim. Also, if symptoms develop, the link can be made, by the counselor, back to the specific details of the troublesome aspect of the rape.

A counseling analogy may be made between a victim who is forced to encounter multiple assailants and people who experience multiple losses within a family such as the deaths of several children or members of their family. The loss is overwhelming and difficult to contemplate. In such situations, the counselor must help the family member grieve each separate loss in order to facilitate the total grieving process. Similarly, a rape victim who has confronted more than one assailant needs to settle her or his feelings regarding each assailant. The victim often may have a separate set of fears and anxieties for each assailant.

Counseling Multiple Victims

There is an additional factor to consider when counseling multiple victims who have been the target in a rape; namely, it is important to talk about feelings and reactions regarding the other victim(s) present, who were either raped or who were witnesses. Each victim separately should be asked how she or he felt about the other victim(s) in terms of the rape, as well as in terms of the relationship that exists among the victims. For example, in case 2, one of the victims said, regarding one of the other victims, "We're a team." She implied that she was very friendly with one of the other two victims. One fact in this case may have influenced the two older victims' reaction to the younger victim. During the rape, the younger victim became quite hysterical and was not raped. In counseling, the two raped victims made fun of her hysteria and tended to exclude her from their supportive network. We do not know if there was a causal relationship between these two facts but most certainly the hysterical reaction and her avoidance of being raped was an issue for the two raped victims. One can speculate that the dynamics of her not being raped influenced their reaction to her.

We have noticed that victims who experience the same rape situation have varying reactions following the rape in terms of maintaining the same level of relationship they had with each other prior to the rape. For example, in case 2, the three victims became less involved with each other, especially as family pressure increased toward that end. In case 3, the two young women were casual acquaintances. Also, the victims became completely estranged when the case went to court, and one victim refused to testify.

Being co-victims can place a strain on existing relationships and should alert the clinician to be especially attentive in asking the victims to talk about this component of the rape. Then, the clinician can follow the progress or deterioration of the relationship and intervene as appropriate.

Handicapped Victims: Compounded Rape Trauma

Rape victims who suffer from a handicapped condition may be prone to experiencing additional complications from rape trauma. The issue of victim vulnerability of handicapped victims is addressed by Largen when she raises the questions: Can adequate prevention programs be developed for the handicapped? Are there special treatment needs? Can they be identified?[1]

One needs to be alert to the complicating factor of a compounded trauma reaction when a handicapped person is raped. If staff and social network are not attentive to the handicap nor supportive of the handicapped victim, the rape trauma can activate symptoms and behavior associated with the handicap (e.g. depression, acting-up behavior, or substance abuse). Handicapping situations with adolescent case examples included in this chapter are: physical, mental, or social handicaps, as well as victims who speak a different language or represent a different culture from the staff.

Physical Handicaps

Physical handicaps include limitations on a person's mobility or ability to perceive normally. Immobilizing handicaps, those including an inability to walk or coordinate body movements, generally result from neurological trauma, disease, injury, or hereditary factors. Perceptual handicaps include blindness and deafness. The following case illustrates how the offender gained access to the young victim by trading on her handicap—blindness—and then, in court, the defense lawyer traded on the same handicap as part of his defense.

Clinical Case 8

A 17-year-old young woman, blind from an injury at an early age, was learning to manage some areas of her hometown by herself. One afternoon, as she was near a park area of the town, she was pulled into a wooded area by a man and raped. There was conversation during the assault.

At the court trial, the defense lawyer inquired, both of the victim and of her father, about her blindness. He tried to use her perceptual handicap to his client's advantage, first, by challenging how blind she really was, and second, by asking how she could really be sure of the identification of the man (the victim had made the identification through voice tapes). Counseling had to focus on (1) the rape, (2) the added frustration and helplessness resulting from the handicap, and (3) the court process.

Mental Handicaps

Psychological handicaps include problems with thought and reasoning processes or problems of a psychiatric or emotional nature. Children who are mentally retarded or mentally ill fall into this category and may be especially vulnerable to sexual assault situations. They may be exploited because the offender believes they will not know what is going on and will not be able to tell in court what happened.

Family members can often provide essential information regarding the verbal and comprehension level of victims. As one father of a 12-year-old mentally retarded girl who was pressured into a sexual situation and was mute during the hospital interview said, "My daughter's problem is not so much understanding as speaking." The father made the decision to press charges for two reasons: (1) "the guy will do it again," and (2) "I wonder if he's done it to her before. I've not noticed her having her period for a while."

Supervisory staff must realize that a rape is an upsetting event to a person regardless of any handicap he or she may have. Sometimes, when staff fail to take a rape seriously, the rape complaint is frequently repeated over and over by the patient. In the following case, a hospitalized adolescent, following a rape that was not dealt with, continued to come to the hospital stating she had been raped. It was speculated that because the state hospital staff had omitted dealing with the original complaint, as well as with a diagnosed unresolved sexual trauma, the victim sought help and understanding at the place where she had been treated with respect.

Clinical Case 9

Janet, a 16-year-old patient at a state mental hospital, stated "I was raped in the basement of the Adolescent Building, and the man said he would choke me if I screamed." The assault was witnessed and staff arrived after the man left. Medical examination revealed some bruises to the neck and a negative report for motile sperm. At the hospital emergency room, Janet was very nervous, almost agitated, unable to sit still, and kept walking in and out of the interview room and up and down the hospital corridor smoking cigarettes. Janet was a tall adolescent wearing jeans that were urine soaked. She spoke in a loud voice, used graphic language, and stated, "I'm real nervous now."

Charges were pressed. At district court hearing, Janet appeared very disheveled, wearing no underwear and a badly stained dress. While testifying she became incontinent, and urine spots were visible as she left the witness chair. The defense lawyer was successful in gaining a "no probable cause" finding for his client. The 16-year-old defendant said later regarding the incident, "That big fat girl—she's not my type, and plus she's a mental woman from the mental ward. I didn't do nothing. I wouldn't mess with no girl like that. A big girl like that sitting up there in court pissing on herself."

In subsequent weeks, Janet reported being raped again and was brought to the emergency department four times. The victim counselor learned that the psychiatric staff was not taking the first rape complaint seriously and had stated, "Janet has many sexual liaisons." The counselor learned that Janet was the sole survivor of a family of six. At age 14, Janet was hospitalized for fractures, the result of child abuse, and while she was hospitalized, the father murdered the three siblings, the mother, and then killed himself. Further talks with Janet provided information that gives good reason to suspect that Janet had been the child victim of sexual assault by her father.

The reality of a mentally handicapped young person's complaint may be missed if the clinician interprets the complaint as unfounded, fantasy, or psychotic material. For example, some staff personnel have been known to dismiss a psychiatric patient's talk of rape with, "She's too crazy to have something like that happen to her" or "That isn't the real issue."

In all cases where a sexual trauma is revealed, special care should be taken to help the victim express as much of the detail and feelings regarding the experience as possible. If staff personnel are not comfortable dealing with such emotional material, the patient should be referred to clinicians who specialize in victim issues.

Social Handicap

Handicaps of a social nature include problems that bring adolescents into contact with school, police or juvenile officials. These adolescents may have histories of difficulty with their families or in foster or residential settings. Very often many agencies, as well as their parents, are involved with these children.

Defining the Handicap. There are four main ways that a social handicap may be revealed. First, the adolescent may tell you during the interview, "I have lots of problems . . . currently living in a halfway house . . . had a therapeutic abortion 10 days ago . . . am seeing a psychologist . . . as well as my parole officer."

Second, the agency may refer the adolescent to you and thus identify the problem. In one case, the director of a multiservice center called to ask a victim counselor to see one of their 15-year-old girls who had been raped.

Third, you may suspect the adolescent has had difficulties of a social nature and, during the course of the interview, ask, "Have you had any difficulties with school officials or the police or with your family? If so, have you talked with anyone about this?"

Fourth, a family member may bring this fact to your attention in talking about the current rape situation. In the following case, the father vented his problems concerning his 14-year-old daughter, whom he brought to the hospital to be examined for rape, as follows.[2]

Lying: *"My daughter lies—has lied before to get herself out of something. I wonder if the rape is a lie? If the guy did rape her, then I'd like to see him punished. But if he didn't do it, then I don't want to get him in trouble. I don't want her causing a false arrest of the guy. She has come up with a rape story before but tonight was the first time I heard her say she is pregnant."*

Foster home: *"She was in a foster home during a period when my wife and I were separated. On the prior rape story, it was supposedly the foster brother who did it."*

Syndrome of family problems: *"This daughter is my main problem. But my younger daughter is also a problem. And my son is having trouble in school."*

Police reaction: *"The police asked why I didn't put her away as a troublesome child. I told them I couldn't do that. I couldn't put her away. She is my daughter."*

After talking about his concerns, the father stated his request quite clearly: "I am trying to get help through the court—some psychiatric help—for my whole family."

Network Reaction. Family as well as other network people involved with adolescents who have a history of social difficulties often have negative reactions to the adolescent rape victim. It appears that people are able to feel that victimization is justified because the child has been "bad" before and thus deserving of rape. In this case, agency people as well as family continued to vent their feelings and reactions toward the girl as she continued through the legal process.

Mother: *"She picks the wrong friends. A psychiatrist told me when she was 6 years old that she would always be a problem. She does things to get attention. She lies about things. . . . I am angry, hurt, and resentful about her."*

Father: *"She is getting out of hot water or getting someone into it."*

Police: *"The guy is good looking—could have anyone he wanted. Wait till you see the girl—flat, skinny, and buck teeth. That guy must be an animal."*

Residential house staff: *"I don't think it will do any good to go through with this. She has been making up rape charges before."*

District attorney: *"I don't think she is mentally balanced . . . don't want to see an innocent man's reputation discredited."*

Defense: *"There have been a lot of rape charges made by this girl. . . . She has a lot of sex fantasies."*

At the time of the rape, this victim had been charged with shoplifting and had to go to court on the charge. She was declared a juvenile delinquent; she refused to return to the residential home, received three years on the shoplifting charge, and was assigned to the division of youth services. Regarding the rape charge, the defendant failed to show up at the trial. The case was eventually filed.

Intervention with Handicapped Victims

It becomes quite clear in working with victims whose handicap triggers an upsurge of symptoms that crisis counseling is not adequate. For this group, we suggest that agency people become involved—because of their familiarity with the handicap—and that both groups work together. Support for the victim in terms of the rape event can be provided by the victim counselor, and the agency staff can work with the victim on the issues relating to the handicap. For example, a counselor received a request to see a 15-year-old girl admitted to the inpatient psychiatric unit of a suburban general hospital following an overdose attempt. The psychiatrist learned that the overdose was in response to a subpoena for her appearance as a victim witness to a rape the previous month. The counselor took a victim history and, after the adolescent was discharged, continued to be in contact with the victim regarding the rape and the pending court appearance. The mental health staff continued following the girl for her emotional difficulties. The court trial process continued for 2 years. This coordination and cooperation between agency staff was successful in reducing stress for the victim.

There are several techniques that may be useful for working with handicapped victims on initial interview:

1. Identify the handicap (e.g., comprehension level, physical, speech, or hearing handicap; psychiatric or social problem).
2. Determine if the handicap will interfere with the interview and, if necessary, get help or advice from a family member or another staff person who has dealt with such clients.
3. Assess the impact of the rape on the victim's behavior (i.e., ask family members if this is a usual response to stress and/or what changes they have noted in the child's behavior).
4. Proceed with the usual protocol, adapting it to meet the stress level of the adolescent. Be prepared to take extra time with the victim and the family.
5. Be alert to avoid projecting stereotyped labels onto handicapped victims and, instead, carefully observe, assess, and talk with the victim and family

in a respectful and kind manner, fully acknowledging the impact of the victimization.

6. Record the interview in language that respects the adolescent and the family but still objectively reports your findings.
7. Be prepared to work in a collaborative way with other staff already involved with the victim. Obtain permission from the victim first to talk with the agency, and then keep the victim informed, making sure the agency knows you are reporting back to the victim and family.

It is important that counselors realize the problems that can develop when multiple agencies are involved with a client. Multiple involvement can lead to the diffusion of responsibility, which can result in nothing concrete being done for the victim. Counselors need to watch overintervention as well as under-intervention. A check on this factor can be made by talking with the victim about progress, or lack thereof, with the agency staff, as well as with her or his recovery from the rape trauma.

Language Barrier: An Ethnic Factor

The adolescent victim may represent a minority ethnic group in the community and thus speak a different language from the agency staff. A language barrier places the victim at a disadvantage in two ways: (1) the details of the rape may not be revealed because of translation problems; and (2) the cultural meaning of the rape may not be adequately understood by the counselor.

Ethnic Component of the Rape. The ethnic component of the rape includes: the meaning the ethnic group gives to the rape—it may be quite different from the meaning of rape to the majority of people in the community; the request the victim may have could be different from that of other victims in that community; and the solution the ethnic group may have to the issue may differ from that of the majority of people in the community.

1. *Meaning of the rape.* Each agency should have some understanding of the meaning the various ethnic groups represented in their catchment area have toward rape. One way that agencies have accomplished this task is to design special meetings in which staff members who represent that minority group present some information to the total staff on the issue. For example, in Spanish-speaking communities, there tends to be a high concern with a girl's virginity, and thus parents may focus their discussions of the rape on this issue. In one case conference devoted to a discussion of the meaning of rape in Catholic and Spanish-speaking communities, one staff person said:

"I was brought up Catholic. Being raped would be a sin, unless you confessed to it. To have intercourse without marriage is a sin."

2. *Request of the victim.* The ethnic factor in rape may mean that the victim has a different request for assistance than is seen in other ethnic groups. One extremely upset 14-year-old girl was brought into the hospital crying out, in Spanish, the following requests:

"I want God to take me. I want a priest. I want you to kill me. I will not be able to see my mother again."

In this situation, a Spanish-speaking counselor first worked with the girl and was able to calm her. The counselor then met the next negotiable request and called the hospital priest, who also had experience in working with young Spanish-speaking rape victims.

3. *Solution.* The solution a family makes for the situation may differ across cultures and ethnic groups. In some cases, the family talked about what to do if the daughter became pregnant. In one case, a family member said, "If my child is pregnant, I want her to have the baby." The culture placed great emphasis on the worth of a child even though it was conceived by rape.

In another case involving a 14-year-old Puerto Rican girl who was in this country with two of her sisters, the solution of how to deal with the victim was quite dramatic.

Clinical Case 10

A 14-year-old girl, Juanita, was watching her sister's two children, ages 2 months and 2 years, while her sister was in the hospital having gall bladder surgery. The father of the two children was also in the home. He raped Juanita and threatened to kill her, the two children, and the sister if she ever told. That night, unrelated to the rape, the 2-month-old baby died from sudden infant death. Juanita did not tell anyone of the rape. The sister came home, and the funeral for the baby was held.

Eventually, Juanita told another sister of the rape. This sister took her to the district court to report the rape. The detective, listening to the report, said, "Suddenly she got hysterical and started to relive the attack." She had to be physically restrained and was brought by ambulance to the City Hospital on a stretcher with arms and legs restrained, screaming loudly in Spanish.

A Spanish-speaking nurse-counselor talked with Juanita and in five minutes had her untied and sitting up quietly. She was not able to talk about the rape but kept crying and asking to see a priest. The counselor encouraged her to see a doctor, which she did, but she refused a pelvic examination. She spent most of her time talking about the dead baby, saying that she was afraid that something would happen to the other child.

This case points up several important observations. First, the flashback to the rape occurred as she was talking about the sexual details of the rape. The combined issues of the rape, the baby's death, and the offender's threat triggered an uncontrolled reaction in the victim. Second, the sister Juanita told was so upset that she was not able to talk about her sister's rape. Third, the assailant who was the boyfriend of the sister immediately disappeared. The solution the family decided upon was to send Juanita back home to Puerto Rico. Thus counseling could not be continued. Juanita was told about Rape Crisis Centers in Puerto Rico where she would be able to seek help if she wished or she could go to a mental health clinic.

Counseling with Ethnic Groups

1. *Language barrier.* If the victim does not speak English, an agency interpreter or a family member is necessary. It is less stressful for the victim to communicate in his or her own language. Be sure the translation matches the child's words and is not censored by the interpreter. It is very hard to know if you are getting a good translation but there are some clues to help alert you to the quality of translation. You should suspect you are not getting the details of the story if you hear the victim make a lengthy statement but the translator gives a short summary. You should suspect you are getting general statements rather than the child's words if the translator uses formal or sophisticated terms such as the child saying "the man penetrated me."

2. *Make ethnic factors explicit.* Find out specifically what the rape means to the child and to the family, what requests for help do they have, and what solution do they choose.

3. *Follow-up.* Try to arrange for follow-up with a counselor of the same ethnic background so that the special needs of the culture are met.

Family Response to the Adolescent Rape Victim

The news that an adolescent family member has been raped usually triggers an emotional reaction in other family members. Each parent, as well as the other children in the family—if they are told—may have a separate response. Observing the verbal as well as physical reactions of family members can provide important clues as to their thoughts and feelings on the subject. In our work with families of raped children and adolescents, we have observed three distinct behavioral responses: a consistently supportive stance, an intermittently supportive stance, and an unsupportive stance. The supportive response is essential in aiding the adolescent through the recovery phase. By observing the supportiveness of family members, the counselor can determine how much support she or he may need to be prepared to provide for the adolescent.

Supportive Stance

Support is the strength one person gives to another person in a stressful situation. Support includes trust and strength. People who are consistently supportive of young victims of rape are able to show their positive regard and concern for the adolescent, often through physical contact; they do not blame the adolescent for the rape nor the circumstances surrounding the situation; they are loyal to their child; and they are usually open to medical and counseling services for their child.

In one case involving a 13-year-old girl who had been raped at 9 P.M. in her own back yard, the support could be seen in her father's and brothers' behavior after she finished the hospital examination. She was hugged warmly by her family, and subsequently they continued the physical contact and a stylized joking family relationship. The father utilized his time with the counselor to express spontaneously his concern: (1) that his daughter might have gotten a disease from the assailant; (2) that she might become pregnant; (3) that young girls are in danger of being raped and how he could avoid being overprotective on the subject now; (4) about his daughter's present condition and how fast she should resume normal activities such as school. This family was totally concerned about their daughter. On follow-up, they talked of their daughter's progress, as well as their own reactions ("I can't stop thinking about it since it happened. I haven't slept. It's been horrible"). However, the parents were still supportive of the child's needs and requests ("She slept with us after it happened. . . . One of her brothers always walks with her now").

Parents and social network who are supportive of the child can be a tremendous help. Counselors in such situations can be available to the family and provide opportunities for the child and family to express their feelings. Parents who are consistently supportive often experience symptoms similar to the ones experienced by their child. The counselor can help the parents talk about the feelings and reassure them that the symptoms are in response to the upsetting situation their child has survived. The following examples are cited:

"I have had dreams that men are going to rape me. I wake up before it happens. This never happened before. We take precautions now . . . have the dogs; my door is locked . . . more careful of my person. Used to just be concerned of robbery."

Male members of the family may feel particularly inclined to go after the assailant. As one mother of an 11-year-old girl said:

"I have four sons. I am worried one will beat the hell out of him. That will get the family in trouble. I had the police talk with the boys."

Parents, as well as victims, need to talk about their back-to-normal reactions. One mother's statement six weeks after the assault to the question "Are things settling back to normal?" was as follows:

"I no longer think continuously about the incident, except when it is necessary to leave my daughter home alone—as in the afternoon. My pattern is to deal with one problem at a time. If I have to deal with too many at one time, I get overwhelmed. . . . Now I no longer have the court to worry about, and that is a relief."

In general, families who are able to be consistently supportive take the lead in the counseling process. They provide the direction for the recovery process for their child, and the counselor's role is one of consultation, as well as intervention and support.

Intermittent Support Stance

There are some parents and social network people who are able to be supportive to the child, but do not provide the support consistently. The support is intermittent, a constant pattern is not being maintained for whatever reason. Often these people have some ambivalent feelings that create conflict and detract from their support at key times. The parents might be ambivalent about their child in general, or they may be ambivalent over the circumstances of the rape and their child's role in it. Their ambivalence is seen in their comments and behavior, or sometimes the child reports the fact.

In one case, a 16-year-old rape victim was reluctant to see her mother following the hospital examination and interview. The police had brought her to the hospital, and the hospital notified her parents for permission to treat. The father did not come to the hospital because of a prior professional engagement, but the mother did come. When the mother and daughter met, they both hugged and kissed and cried. Later, as they were leaving the hospital, they were observed yelling at each other. The girl, swinging her long hair, could be heard saying in a loud voice that she had taken a ride because she knew the person.

It is important, from a counseling view, that parents have an opportunity to talk about their ambivalence—either what is troubling them the most about the rape or about their child. In the preceding case, the mother talked about her difficulty with the situation:

Mother: *"My concern is not with my daughter's emotional reaction but what all the legal implications are. . . . My daughter has been a problem child . . .*

difficult to manage. I know she wasn't raped. No woman can be raped. Don't you think so?"

Counselor: *"No, I don't agree. I believe people can be raped—women, men, children. Is this a problem in thinking of the legal aspect?"*

Mother: *"Yes, I don't know what to do."*

The counseling continued to focus on her ambivalence in terms of the legal issue, as well as her perception of rape.

In situations in which the parent is able to be supportive only at some times because of negative feelings, the counselor must provide the support necessary to reinforce the child. In the previous case, the father showed his ambivalence by coming to court once. At later court appearances, he excused himself because the "delays were interfering with [his] professional schedule." The mother, having access to a victim counselor, was able to be a main support for her daughter in court and was able to talk about many of her own ambivalences about her daughter's behavior.

Counselors can be most helpful in assisting parents in expressing their feelings about their child and the rape. If the parent's difficulty centers around a blurring of rape and sex, the dialogue should be guided to focus on feelings, as in the following case.

Mother: *"After all, she did go with the guy to his place and to his bedroom. How far can you go and still call it rape. I don't think he is entirely to blame."*

Counselor: *"How do you feel about the man?"* (avoiding confrontation over what is rape and focus on eliciting feelings)

Mother: *"I'd like to see him in prison. . . . He might have killed her."*

Counselor: *"It is a frightening experience to be raped . . . and you know how frightening it was for your daughter."* (acknowledge feeling of fright)

One of the issues that parents must come to terms with is their child's sexuality. With a rape, there is the reality confirmation that their child has been exposed to a sexual situation, and it becomes important how the child is treated in terms of this knowledge. For example, do the parents (1) ignore this fact and not mention the rape; (2) become extra protective of the child in normal boy-girl relationships; or (3) deny the impact of the situation? As one mother said:

"She hasn't dated since then. She is probably turned off by men. But I don't think she will have any permanent damage. After all, she was not a virgin, you know."

Parents need to talk about their feelings about their child's sexual behavior prior to the rape as well as their concerns following the rape.

Counseling is important for both victim and parents in situations where support is intermittent. The counselor can help: (1) by assisting parents in venting their feelings so that more of their energy is available for support for their child; (2) by gently pointing out how much the child needs their support; and (3) by discussing their perception of rape.

Unsupportive Stance

Some parents are unable to provide any emotional support for their child. Several things may explain this. First, this crisis may just be one more in a list of multicrises the family or child has experienced. Thus the rape crisis blurs with all the other crises facing the parents and immobilizes their ability to respond in a helpful way. Second, the parents may be overwhelmed by their own individual situations and have no energy left for providing support—a depletion of parental emotion. These parents are usually under considerable stress themselves. Third, the parents may have strong biases regarding rape and deny any significance to the event—the rape is not worthy of any attention or they may blame the victim.

In the following case of a mother who was not able to provide any support for her daughter, a police officer added his opinion of the situation, which may or may not have influenced the mother's decision in the matter.

A 16-year-old girl was brought to a hospital after flagging down a police car and stating she had been raped by a man who had offered to drive her home. The police called her mother from the hospital, told the mother what had happened, and then added, "I think your daughter is asking for it."

The daughter then talked with her mother but did not have any hopes that she would come to the hospital—it was 4 A.M.—to get her. The daughter said to the counselor after the telephone call:

"She doesn't believe me. She did the first time, but she doesn't believe this. She said she had no car and to take a taxi home. . . . I didn't think she would come down."

One of the complicating factors with this victim was that she had been raped two times previously. This fact seems to greatly influence the reaction people have to the news of a rape. People are less likely to believe a victim who has been raped before. This issue is dealt with in Chapter 11. The counselor ensured that the victim gave her home address to the taxi driver and then called the family the next day. On follow-up, the mother had an opportunity to explain her position:

"I didn't have a car and couldn't take a bus at that hour of the night. I won't go out myself at that hour. . . . It was safer to put her in a cab and send her home."

Although the mother's explicit reason was safety, the daughter interpreted another reason—that her mother did not take her seriously. The counselor was able to further assess the family in terms of support through dialogue with the mother.

Mother: *"I told my daughter she was asking for it. Walking the streets at that hour was asking for it. I'm a nurse and wouldn't go out at that hour."*

Counselor: *"How do you think your daughter is doing?"*

Mother: *"Terrible. At first she was very quiet when she came home. I was really mad at her. I told her the policeman told me you asked for it. You made me look bad. I gave you 50 cents for car fare. You were supposed to be at a coffee-house and not a club."*

Counselor: *"What did she say to you?"*

Mother: *"She went right to bed. She said, 'You don't think I enjoyed it. It was terrible.' I told her her insides would be a mess by the time she was 21. She said he threatened her with a pipe. I said why didn't you get the license plate number. Or why didn't you tell him you were being treated for syphilis."*

Counselor: *"What did she say to that?"*

Mother: *"She went to bed. She was quiet the next day. She called her therapist. She has his home phone. He calmed her down and said she was handing it well. She went to the hospital on Monday, but then today she cancelled her appointment with him."*

Counselor: *"Do you know why she did that?"*

Mother: *"She was very angry and said she was going to the beach. The psychiatrist told me he was going to discharge her on the 20th. I told him not to do that. She needs someone."*

Counselor: *"Is she under a lot of stress right now?"*

Mother: *(went into details of many issues of stress for the whole family)*

Counselor: *"How did your husband react?"*

Mother: *"He said, 'Not again.'"*

This dialogue clearly indicates that these parents are not supportive of their daughter, and thus the counselor will need to keep in close contact with the victim during the acute phase and strongly encourage her to maintain ties with her therapist.

Social network people can provide needed support for rape victims, especially in situations where the parents are unable to help. In the following case, the victim sought out her high school teachers to help her with a situation her parents failed to help her with.

Clinical Case 11

Gail, a 15-year-old U.S. exchange student living abroad, and her boyfriend were walking to the movies when suddenly two men approached them, one holding a gun, and forced them to walk to a nearby golf course. The first man asked the couple for money. Gail said, "One started getting fresh, used vulgar language, and asked if I'd like to fuck. I said 'no' and he punched me and asked me three more times, threatening to bash my teeth in if I didn't agree. The second man was holding the gun on my boyfriend and asked the first man why he didn't find some girl that wanted to. Then the man ordered me to take my pants off. I fought him and he got angry. It hurt. He raped me several times and then ejaculated. When he finished he told me to stay there and then the second man came over to where I was lying. He was not as aggressive as the first. He raped me, but finally gave up when he did not ejaculate. The first man watched the second man. Then when they were finished they said they would draw straws as to who would die first. They drew me. I turned around and was sure I was going to die. I thought of my family back home. Then they said this was a big joke and did we like it. They ran away, and we started walking home till we could get a taxi."

When they reached home, Gail told her exchange parents what had happened. The wife, a pediatrician, was concerned over a possible pregnancy, and thus the girl was given antipregnancy medication. The next day the exchange parents told Gail that they did not believe her story but rather thought that Gail had had sex with her boyfriend, was concerned about getting pregnant, and that together they had made up this story about two men and a gun.

Gail did go back to school on Monday but found that she could not concentrate and was having difficulty sleeping and eating. She called her family long distance, told them what happened, and was told to come home. Gail returned home immediately and then went back to her own high school after several weeks. She finally told a high school counselor what occurred. He, in turn, referred her to a therapist. Gail had two visits with him, but then had to terminate because the family did not believe in psychiatric therapy and refused to pay for her visits. They felt that she should be over the incident and told her to just "forget it." Gail developed disturbing dreams and nightmares, was unable to go into the city for normal activities, and was very fearful around men. The school counselor was aware of the conflict between Gail and her family in terms of treatment and was able to obtain continued victim counseling for her to relieve the symptoms and help her and her family in terms of reorganizing her life.

In terms of social network response, Gail encountered all three styles of support. First, the exchange parents, in refusing to believe her, provided no support. Next, her own parents provided intermittent support. They were initially able to respond, but they believed in superemotional strength to conquer crisis situations, and withdrew an important resource, the visits to the therapist. Gail did have access to understanding and supportive high school teachers and counselors who talked with her, supported her, and provided victim counseling. Gail's reaction to her social network was mixed. She was upset that her exchange parents did not believe her; she was ambivalent about her natural parents on the one hand welcoming her back home while on the other denying her access to some psychological help; but she was persistent and used this to advantage to gain support from school staff.

Family Response and Delayed Reactions to Rape Trauma

On occasion the adolescent will have a delayed reaction to the rape trauma. In such situations, the counselor should be monitoring the family response and may be available for intervention. Frequently the child will appear all right to the hospital staff, or to the counselor, and the family will emphasize its ability to take care of her. The family may react this way because they are so relieved that the dangerous situation is over and that the child is alive. However, they may be able to maintain these feelings of relief for only a short period of time. It is absolutely essential that parents be aware that follow-up counseling is available should they later wish either the services or telephone consultation. A delayed reaction to the rape may be triggered by a flashback. Some emotionally significant event occurs that reminds the young person of the assault. The mind then visualizes, or flashes back to, the scene, the person being emotionally flooded with the overwhelming fear and fright experienced at the time of the assault. A strong flashback has the potential to partially immobilize a person or paralyze them. Consider the following case.

Clinical Case 12

Rita, a 13-year-old student, was riding her new bicycle at 2 P.M. to a friend's house. It was vacation week, and she decided to cut through the deserted school playground. As she pedaled through a wooded area, a man who was sitting on the ground jumped up, grabbed her, and took her into the woods. He said, "Come with me. It will only take 10 minutes." The man took vaseline and rubbed it all over the girl's body, attempted to penetrate her, and was unsuccessful. The man then fled and Rita managed to get to her friend's house to tell them what had happened. She complained of her leg hurting. Her parents were notified, and they took her to the hospital and called the police.

The police emphasized the fact that Rita should receive counseling, but the family felt they could manage. The day following the assault, Rita kept fainting. Her parents took her back to the hospital where she was examined and found to be all right. Very early the next morning, Rita came into her mother's bedroom, said she felt nervous and dizzy, and complained of her leg hurting. The mother decided a cool bath would help, took all Rita's clothes off, and put her in the bathtub. At that point, Rita became hysterical and cried, "I want to go home." Rita passed out several times, saying that she could not walk and that her leg was paralyzed. The parents decided to take her to the hospital to see the victim counselor that the police had recommended.

The victim counselor met with Rita and, after some time of talking, examining the leg, and testing it, was able to help Rita express her extreme fright over the assault. The counselor discovered that Rita's leg had been curled up under her in the bathtub in the same position it had been during the rape. The flashback triggering the leg paralysis occurred when the mother took Rita's clothes off to give her the bath. Rita's mind reverted back to the rape scene, where the man had taken all her clothes off, and she reenacted her body position and verbal response. Rita finally revealed that the man threatened her by saying that if she ever told anyone, he would come back and get her. She was terrified that this would happen. Crisis counseling was continued for Rita and her mother until the symptoms subsided and they had reestablished a more regular lifestyle.

In summary, counselors can be most useful to rape victims by assessing factors influencing the *rape* (the type of rape, such as blitz or confidence; the number of assailants, such as single, pair, or gang; the age of the assailants, such as peer or adult); factors influencing the *victim* (physical, mental, or social handicaps or ethnic considerations); factors influencing *family reactions* (full, partial, or no support). The protocol should include initial crisis counseling and information for the family regarding follow-up services.

References

1. Mary Ann Largen, "Special Populations of Rape Victims" (keynote address, Special Populations Conference, sponsored by the National Center for the Prevention and Control of Rape, Arlington, Va., April 13, 1977).

2. This case is described in more detail in Ann Wolbert Burgess and Lynda Lytle Holmstrom, *Rape: Victims of Crisis* (Bowie, Md.: Robert J. Brady, 1974), pp. 63–64.

5

Accessory-to-Sex: Pressure, Sex, and Secrecy
Ann Wolbert Burgess and *Lynda Lytle Holmstrom*

Accessory-to-sex syndrome is another reaction we observed in victims, and it results from a pressured sexual situation. In this type of trauma, the victims— usually children or adolescents—are pressured into sexual activity by a person who stands in some power position over them, such as through age or a position of authority. The victims are incapable of consenting because of their level of cognitive or personality development. The emotional reactions stem from their being pushed into sexual activity and, in those cases where they are pledged to secrecy, from the added tension of keeping the secret. These victims contribute in a secondary way—as an accessory— to the offense, by agreeing to go along with it. The pressure and the victim's assistance make these cases quite different from rape, in which sex is forced upon the victim and is clearly against the victim's will.

Gaining Access

In rape, the exchange between rapist and victim consists of the offender accomplishing sexual penetration and the victim retaining her or his life. In accessory cases, the exchange is of a different nature. Bargaining for sexual contact, the offender may offer the victim several types of rewards: material goods, social activities, adult approval (through misrepresenting moral standards) and human contact.

The offender uses his position of power to help gain access to the victim. He trades on the young person's inability to make an informed decision of consent. Some young children even age six or younger may know that sexual activity between them and adults is considered wrong, but many young and even latency-age children are not yet fully aware of community norms. Many do not have a very sophisticated concept of sexuality or of the social implications of their actions. For example, in one case, a 14-year-old mentally retarded girl was on her way home from school. A 22-year-old man called out her name and took her by the hand, leading her into his building and to his apartment. He kept her

Sections of this chapter are adapted from Ann Wolbert Burgess and Lynda Lytle Holmstrom, "Sexual Trauma of Children and Adolescents: Pressure, Sex, and Secrecy," *Nursing Clinics of North America* 10, no. 3 (September 1975):551–563. Reprinted with permission of W. B. Saunders Company.

in his bedroom, locked the door, and had sexual intercourse with her twice. The next morning he tried to have intercourse again, and she said no, that she had to get to school. He let her go.

The offender makes use of the young person's curiosity, unsureness, ambivalence, and powerlessness. In addition, he may begin the encounter in a nonsexual way, and the child may be unaware that sexual activity is to follow. Three young boys described their experience with a 30-year-old man:

"We were playing ball in the playground. This guy came over and joined us. Then he said he had some great pictures to show us if we came with him. We went one at a time, and he showed us pictures of naked people. Then he had us suck him, and he did it to us."

In this example, the offender began his approach nonsexually. This type of offender is described in the literature. McCaghy cites one type of encounter between an adult and a child as nonsexual in approach. The molesting, according to McCaghy, occurs in the course of nonsexual interaction with the child.[1]

Material Rewards

Children are likely to be offered some type of material goods, such as money, candy, or toys. For example, in one offender's apartment—where he would take his victims—there was an elaborate toy room that included model trains, cars, and toys that little boys would especially enjoy. The children would be enticed by the toys, as well as candy and money.

Social Activities

In some situations, the children are enticed by fun activities. In one situation involving many children, the offender, who was known both to the school officials and to the families, would take children to the race track or out for dinner. Sometimes he would take several children to his house to watch television, eat supper, and play cards. The child who lost the game would have to take his or her clothes off. The situation would advance to where the offender would take the children separately for sexual activities after their clothes were removed.

Adult Approval

Children are taught from an early age to be obedient to adults. They learn that if they do what the adult tells them to do, they will be rewarded by gaining the adult's approval. Not to obey an adult may result in punishment. Therefore, it is not surprising that offenders can pressure children into sexual activity by telling them that it is "okay to do." As one victim said, "If an adult tells you to do something, you do it." In the case of a 30-year-old boyfriend of the mother who lived with the family, the six-year-old daughter was told, "Good girls do what their Daddy tells them to do." The reward in this situation, for over a six-year period, was the gain of the father-surrogate's approval.

Need for Human Contact

There are people—typically children or adolescents, but sometimes adults—who are almost desperate for human contact. They are socially or geographically isolated and without strong ties to a social network. For example, in one case, a woman in her late twenties came into a hospital giving various versions of a rape to staff and police. Most striking was her emotional estrangement from people and her history of a drifting lifestyle, dating back to age 13, when her emotional problems became obvious ("I overdosed and had to go to a hospital to have my stomach pumped out"). She emphasized that she had no place to go, that no one cared about her, that she did not wish to return to her parents' home, and that she had been drifting from place to place and guy to guy. No elements of force or intimidation could be determined ("I got dumped tonight. I was with two guys I lived with . . . but they left . . . I fell and was put in a car by three to four guys"). When asked about forced sex, she talked of her feelings in general about sex ("I get no enjoyment from sex . . . really feel guilty when I have sex"). It appeared that what the victim obtained from the bargaining in this situation was human contact.

Type of Sexual Activity and the Victim's Reaction

The type of sexual activity of the offender ranges from hand-genital contact, to oral-genital contact, to attempted penetration, to penetration. In some cases, there is no physical touching, only visual or verbal contact.

Children usually describe the experience in terms of whether it was physically painful or pleasurable. The following example of an 8-year-old girl whose assailant was her grandfather illustrates the painful aspect of the assault.

"He had me lay down . . . and then he showed me his penis, and I remember his talking to me and telling me where he was going to put that inside of me, and he showed me where he was going to put it and made me touch myself, and he made me touch him. That's when I decided that there was no way. I looked at this thing and I looked at me and thought "no way." And I got upset, and I tried to get away from him, but he said, "Oh, everything is going to be all right." . . .

*And he kept telling me that. Then he started to enter me, and I can just re-
member the pain."*

Sometimes the activity will be pleasurable. Such situations tend to be hand-
genital experiences rather than sexual penetration. One 19-year-old woman re-
counted her childhood experience with her grandfather.

*"He would sit me in his lap with my legs slightly spread apart and stroke my
inner thighs, labia, and genital area . . . . I found it very pleasurable. I would have
my back against his torso, my head on his chest, and sometimes fall asleep. He
was also so warm and gentle, and he would tell me stories."*

Pressing for Secrecy

If the offender is successful with his victim, he may try to conceal the deviate
behavior from others. The child may not necessarily be aware that the behavior
should be concealed, especially if the act is gentle and pleasurable and the child
does not believe it is wrong. But in many cases, the offender will try to pledge
the victim to secrecy in several ways. The offender may say this is something
secret between them, or, in some cases, he may threaten harm to the child if
she does tell.

In most of these situations, the burden of the pressure to keep the secret is
experienced psychologically as fear. Children and adolescents spontaneously
have described the following fears, which they said bound them to the secret.

Fear of Punishment

The child often fears punishment if she or he tells. In one situation involving an
8-year-old and her 9-year-old brother, the offender said to them, "If you tell
anyone, I'll ruin your summer. If you tell your mother and father, they won't
believe you." This offender not only threatened punishment, but said their
statement would not be credible. The sister wanted to tell, but the brother was
influential in maintaining the secret, saying that the parents would not believe
them.

Fear of Not Being Believed

As in the preceding example, some children do not think they will be believed.
As one 23-year-old woman said, in reflecting on why she did not tell her parents, "You know, to this day, I don't think they [parents] would have believed
me."

Fear of Being Blamed

Some children never tell because they fear the reaction the outside person will have to the disclosure. One victim said she just knew her parents "never would have acted right." Or the child may fear being blamed for the activity. One person said, "I think I never told because father [offender] might have said I was lying or I was a bad child, and no one would like me again." In some situations, the children, in fact, are blamed after the disclosure, or discredited in some way. One 19-year-old male said, "Mother made us feel we were the cause of her brother being bad and wouldn't let us talk to our cousins." In another situation, an assistant district attorney, preparing his prosecution of a man charged with multiple counts of sexual assault on many young girls and boys said, "Those kids are street wise—real 'cutesee.' . . . They did it to have fun."

Fear of Abandonment or Rejection

Children may fear that revealing the secret will cause catastrophic results. As one young person said,

"I thought it would be terrible to be separated from the family. I thought something terrible would happen if I told. . . . The fear of rejection was really great as a child."

Dominant-Subordinate Role

Children are in a subordinate role vis-á-vis authority figures in almost all situations except peer-related activities. Children are prime targets because many of the same qualities that make a child a "good" child also make him or her an "easy" victim. As one woman said, in recounting her childhood experience with her father,

"I think the reason why a lot of kids don't do anything, don't tell anybody, is because an adult is an authority figure, and somehow they have been forced to do something wrong by an authority, and therefore it must have been right."

Communication Barrier

Children sometimes have difficulty putting a description of the activity into words, and frequently the child tells another companion, who in turn tells an outside person. Children may not know the adult words. One person describes the difficulty of saying what happened:

" . . . that's extremely rare where a kid would really be able to waltz up to Mom and say, "Guess what? Guess what your father did to me? Is it wrong for Grandpa to stick his thing into me? I mean, can you just imagine?"

Disclosure of the Secret

A secret disclosed without both parties' consent may be termed betrayal. Thus, there is the ever-present tension that the secret may be broken unilaterally. Georg Simmel, a sociologist, states "The secret is surrounded by the possibility and temptation of betrayal; and the external danger of being discovered is interwoven with the internal danger, . . . of giving oneself away."[2] In many accessory-to-sex cases the secret is broken, and this is a critical turning point.

Disclosure of Sexual Activity

The disclosure of the activity becomes a key clinical factor. The emotional reaction of the victim is greatly influenced by how and when the secret is disclosed and by the subsequent reaction on the part of the outside person. There are several ways in which the secret may be disclosed.

Direct Confrontation. Sometimes the act will be observed by others, and direct confrontation will occur. In the case of a 12-year-old mentally retarded girl who was seen being led into a neighbor's house, the police were notified and, upon entering the room of the man, found the offender in the act of intercourse with the girl. Sometimes the child is confronted with the fact that someone has found out about the sexual activity. One 19-year-old woman recounts her childhood experience in which her mother confronted her as follows:

"One time when I came back from a weekend with my grandparents, my mother wouldn't talk to me. . . . She finally said she was disgusted with me and that she knew what my grandfather and I were doing and that I would have to tell a priest in confession. . . . I knew what she meant because no one else did what he did. . . . She wouldn't talk to me for days, and I was upset and mad at her. It was her father, and he told me to, and I was supposed to obey elders, and I didn't think it was wrong. So why was she mad at me? Why wasn't she mad at him?"

Victim Tells Someone. Some victims are able to tell a parent or outside person directly about the sexual activity. For example, one 9-year-old girl was able to tell her mother that her stepfather had been "fooling" with her.

The Clue. Visible clues are provided by many victims who are unable to tell someone directly. Such clues included walking home without clothes, staying out all night, or pregnancy. Some more subtle clues were an unexplained accumulation of nickels and dimes or new clothes. In another case, the children were observed eating lollipops all the time, and when the mother asked why, she was told "Uncle Jimmy gave it to me and told me not to tell you." Or the child may draw a picture or write a note. One mother told how she discovered the situation:

"My daughter half hinted at it, and I had a funny feeling something was wrong so I pumped her. We were sitting at the table having coffee when my husband asked her to do something, and she said no. I asked her to do something, and she did it. Later she asked me if I knew why she did things for me and not for my husband. I said no. And she said she would tell me some other time—it was grown up stuff. Well, I got this awful feeling, and I knew I had to find out, so I asked her. She said she couldn't tell me but would draw it. . . . I took one look at what she drew on the paper and went kookey."

Signs and Symptoms. If the sexual activity continues over time, signs and symptoms often develop, and these may be brought to the attention of a professional. Some parents observe such signs as the child staying inside more frequently, not wanting to go to school, crying with no provocation, taking an excessive number of baths, or sudden onsets of bedwetting, and they become suspicious and seek professional help. The following illustrates this.

The mother of a 15-year-old girl stated to the nurse, "Mary is taking baths constantly and keeps complaining of stomach aches. She gets very upset when one of our neighbors comes around. She used to like going riding with him, and he took her for cokes and donuts. . . . I am suspicious of what might be going on."

It was learned that the 35-year-old neighbor has been pressuring the girl into sexual activity, and this was producing somatic and behavioral symptoms.

A variety of symptoms may be described by the child, whereupon the parent or the professional decodes the message. The symptom may be gastrointestinal, where the child vomits or complains of stomach aches, or the child may develop a urinary tract infection or a medical condition such as pneumonia or mononucleosis. The following case material taken from a hospital record illustrates how a silent reaction was missed during the first hospitalization but picked up the next time by the mother, the physician, and the nurse.

Eleven-year-old girl admitted with two-day history of right lower quadrant pain that is absent now; sharp and intermittent without exacerbation or worsening over a two-day period; no vomiting or diarrhea. Sore throat for one day. No other remarkable findings except that one year ago she was admitted to another hospital and was hospitalized five days and diagnosed to have pelvic inflammation. A careful history obtained from the patient and the mother separately revealed the following.

Patient told mother last evening that she was sexually assaulted by her father four times. Parents are now separated, divorce proceedings in progress. The child states that six months ago she and her four siblings were staying alone with their father (mother had left the house for four weeks following parental argument). Father would either put the other children to bed early or send them on errands and then tell the patient to go to his bed. She would do so. He would then ask her to pull down her pants and he would do likewise. He would put "vaseline on his pickle" and would "put it into her." She did not look, she turned her head and screamed. She thought it went "into her bum." She was lying on her back each time. This scene happened two times previously, approximately one year ago when the mother was absent from the home. The patient told her two siblings that her father told her if she ever told anyone he would kill her, so she never told anyone else till last evening. The mother was questioning her about ordinary games played when she stayed with her father, and the patient then related the "dirty game" story. Mother became disturbed and brought the child to the clinic, wanting to press charges against her husband.

Trauma Impact and Assessment

We have just presented the key issues to cover during an interview regarding the sexual activity between the young person and the offender. Now it is important to identify how to determine impact on the child and to predict areas that might be difficult for the child to resolve.

Victimizing Issue

Identifying the motivation of the offender helps to focus on how the young person has been victimized. Is the child a victim of a sex-pressure offense and the offender's need to dominate through the use of his or her authority via enticement or entrapment? Or is the child a victim of a sex-force offense and the offender's need for power and control through intimidation and aggression via exploitation and sadism. Such information may help in sorting out some of the counseling issues to address in the follow-up phase. In all these assaults—whether sex-pressure or sex-force—there may be the following questions to raise:

1. Was the child introduced into sexual activity prematurely, and what impact will this have on the young person's adult sexual life?
2. Was the child told not to tell about the sexual activity, and what impact will being bound to secrecy through threats and/or intimidation have on the young person's adult life?
3. How does the child feel about the pressure and/or force used by the offender?

Observing Symptoms Over Time

Parents need to be instructed about the possible physical and behavioral symptoms that can develop in the child from being pressured to engage in sex. They also need to be informed about the normal range of reactions.

The following case illustrates a typical account of an accessory situation. The medical examination may reveal little or no trauma. However, the behavior changes can easily be noted in the days following the assault.

The mother brought her 5-year-old daughter Leah to the hospital clinic and stated that the child had been playing outside the family apartment and was taken from the area by a 9-year-old girl and her 12-year-old brother. They kept Leah for about three hours near the railroad tracks, under a bridge. Leah told her mother that the boy pulled down her pants and was scared away when a man yelled, "What's going on down there?" Leah was examined with the report as follows.

Medical report: *Leah is a 5-year-old, white female who was brought to the clinic by her parents for suspected molestation. Two children, aged 9 and 12, took her away from her home today, and when she was returned, she had some bruises on her ankles, and her mother was concerned that she had been molested. Her mother says that she is a shy girl, and Leah has no complaints at this time.*

Physical examination: *Well-developed, well-nourished 5-year-old, somewhat shy, but cooperative and in no acute distress. Skin revealed a few bruises on her ankles and lower legs. Rest of physical exam, including the external genitalia, was completely within normal limits.*

Lab: *Vaginal culture was taken to rule out gonococcal disease. Blood sample was also taken for Hinton to rule out syphilis.*

Follow-up report: *The nurse-counselor, in making a routine follow-up telephone call, received the following information from Leah's mother. "Leah is refusing to go to school. She is playing by herself and states that she likes to be alone. She cries out in her sleep, 'I don't want to be under the bridge. Don't touch me.' and also holds her pubic area. She is not eating and refuses to go outside to play saying, 'Bad things happen out there.'" It was also learned that Leah only eats when her mother feeds her and only falls asleep when mother holds her. At night when the child got up to go to the bathroom, she would go into the mother's bedroom to wake her up and have her take her to the bathroom. Also a 17-year-old male friend of the child's brother came to visit and the child ran and hid under her bed until the boy left. The mother said, "The dog now sleeps on Leah's bed—maybe he knows something is wrong."*

Minor phobic symptoms may be reported when the child sees or hears the offender's name or sees him. One 12-year-old mentally retarded girl who was unable to verbalize her concerns would run into the house whenever she would see the offender in the neighborhood. Another victim assaulted near a bathroom described her own change in behavior, "Afterwards I just wanted to get away from him. I was afraid to go where he was after that. Didn't like visiting there any more in the summer. I stayed in the house a lot . . . used the chamber pot under the bed rather than using the bathroom."

Changes in sleep patterns may be noted as well as the occurrence of dreams and nightmares. One victim described a recurrent dream that she had around the age of 8 that reveals her feeling of being trapped in the situation.

"Round disk figures were making me do things. Like in one instance I was in a safety pin race with elephants and I was walking so slowly; I couldn't walk fast and the elephants would beat me. I remember feeling this terror that something terrible would happen if they beat me, and each time I would wake up before the end of the race. . . . I couldn't do what I wanted to do. . . . I couldn't move fast enough."

When threats have been used to silence a child as a way to maintain sexual activity over time, two reactions may occur: (1) the victim emotionally and socially withdraws from family and friends; and/or (2) the victim runs away from the conflicting environment.

In addition, some other symptoms and behaviors we have observed over time with children who have experienced an accessory-to-sex situation are as follows: early prostitution in mid-adolescence or before, early access to drugs or alcohol, poor school performance, decrease in physical health status, apathy or listlessness, and sexual dysfunction, i.e. sexual aversion or nonorgasmic response when an adult. Symptoms are not necessarily restricted to those listed, but the ones described are the ones we have seen. In some cases, a direct link can be observed between the assault and the symptoms.

Silent Reaction to Accessory-to-Sex Syndrome: Keeping the Secret

We defined silent reaction to accessory-to-sex activity as one in which the child has kept the burden of the secret within herself. This secret creates considerable tension, and victims can have several reactions to having to keep the secret.

Coconspiracy Dyad. Two victims of the same offender agreed that they did not feel guilty about the sexual experience, but rather about the fact that they had kept it hidden from a parent. In this situation, when the secret was disclosed, a split occurred in the family, and this was equally upsetting to the victims.

In another silent reaction, the victim said:

"It's the lying and the hiding and the not talking about it that is bad. It has to be put in perspective—need to talk about it rather than make it such a hideous thing."

Resistance Techniques. There are techniques that children will use to avoid the sexual activity. They do not betray the secret, and they do not disobey the pledge of secrecy, but they do play a game. One victim said:

"He said I would get another silver dollar if I did it [again]. And I said I did not want to do it right then, but that I would do it some other time. And for the seven years I played that little game, 'Well, I can't do it now, I have to do this for my mother.' I was never so diligent for my mother except when we were visiting [him]."

In a situation involving a father and two daughters, one victim described how her sister managed to avoid the father:

"My sister said my father was doing the same thing [to her] ... but she wasn't afraid to talk back—be aggressive about it and he left her alone. .... She would get emotionally sick now that I think back. She would throw up her food when she was upset. She cried a lot and had nightmares—that would be when he was after her, and this kept him away from her."

Symptom Formation. Symptoms will develop as the victim is pressured to keep the secret over time; these symptoms are related to the tension inherent in the fear of disclosure. Fears become exaggerated, as in the following case.

"I felt anxiety, frustration, and constant fear—a real paranoia that someone would find out. It affected my relationships with my peers. I lived in a shell and escaped by reading. ... I was always afraid of people and thought something terrible would happen if people found out."

The fear may be exaggerated to the degree that, as an adult, the victim feels a sexual partner will know about the activity. Victims may even fear blackmail. One victim said, "I was afraid if I ever told a man or anyone that I might be blackmailed." The fear may be expressed through recurrent dreams, as in the following:

"I am riding on my father's shoulders down the main street of the town where we lived. I am naked from the waist down. As we walk, my father has oral sex with me and everyone sees us."

The symptom of flashback during subsequent sexual experiences may be reported. One victim describes this in the following manner.

"Sometimes when I'm not quite ready to have sex and [my partner] starts to enter me, I just black into that. I just think of that, the pain; it is a similar pain. . . I can't deal with it at all."

Reporting the Silent Reaction. What triggers the person to reveal the incident to another person is clinically important. It may be a timely question; it may be an association to a conversation; or it may be the concern of the interviewer. One victim said the first person she told was a close friend over the telephone when they were both drunk. Another victim could not tell until the significant parties involved were dead.

One notable feature when the silence is broken is the unresolved issue phenomenon. In this phenomenon, the incident has been encapsulated within the psychic structure for so long that when the person finally discloses the secret, the emotional effect can be quite strong, as in the following case.

"I am going to get hysterical in a minute and that's really terrible. I always giggle when I get very upset. I'm sorry. . . . You know he was wearing green work pants with a metal zipper. I never thought of that before either. I never really sat down and discussed it in detail. He unbuttoned his shirt, God . . . all of a sudden I just have this feeling of this hairy chest on my chest . . . like remembering him rubbing my chest . . . with his chest. . . ."

When a silent reaction to a sexual trauma is diagnosed, the details of the incident should be fully discussed in order to start the process of resolution in motion.

Discussion

In research articles on the subject of the psychological components of the reactions of child victims to sexual offenses, the issues of victim participation and the child's personality structure are stressed. Abraham discusses sexual trauma as a form of infantile sexual activity that is often desired by the child unconsciously.[3] Bender and Blau, in their report on 16 cases in children between the ages of 5 and 12, state that there is evidence that the child derived some emotional satisfaction from the experience and, in some cases, was the initiator or seducer.[4] In the follow-up of this group, Bender and Grugett described how children use charm in their roles of seducer.[5] Weiss *et al.* report on the personality of the child who favored the occurrence of the sexual activity.[6] In contrast to these positions, Melanie Klein states that the experience of a seduction or rape by an adult may have serious effects on a child.[7]

In reviewing our data on child and adolescent victims, we have tried to not be bound by traditional ways of viewing the problem, and instead to describe, from the victim's point of view, the dynamics involved between offender and victim in terms of inability to consent, adaptive behavior, secrecy, and disclosure of the secret.

Our data match that of Gagnon and Simon, regarding the importance of social network reactions. They state that the network's response may further complicate the child's reaction to disclosing the sexual activity.[8] Our data clearly indicate that a symptom reaction syndrome is one result of the pressure to keep the activity secret, and of the reaction of others to the disclosure of the secret. However, we believe that the child does react in some way to being involved in the sexual activity itself.

It may be speculated that there are many children with silent reactions to sexual trauma. The child who responds to the pressure to go along with the sexual activity with an adult may be viewed as showing an adaptive response for survival in the environment. Case finding for this type of sexual child abuse will not be easy.

One can speculate on reasons in addition to those already discussed for victims maintaining the secrecy of the sexual activity. When the offender is known, and maintains a relationship to the child as in assault by a family member, the offender can engage in surveillance in order to supervise what the victim does and to whom the victim talks. Surveillance by the offender may correlate with the victim maintaining the secret. This may explain, in some situations, why the victim refuses to tell, or, if a statement is made, retracts the statement at a later point. Some children also may feel a sense of loyalty to the offender as described in Chapter 7.

The study raises many questions. If the victim goes along with the sexual activity and thus adapts to the situation, are there trauma effects? If so, is it the sexual component that is traumatizing to the developing personality or is it the threat of adult aggression and fear of disclosure and punishment? What are the psychodynamic consequences when the sexual incident is not dealt with? Will the victim develop neurotic and personality defects? Will there be a lack of social controls or lack of adult identification? What does happen if the child is deprived of childhood experiences and overstimulated with fears, sexual activity, and aggression? What implications are there for the development of a concept of sexuality?

Only long-term study can begin to look at some of these areas. It is our hope that these data may encourage further indepth exploration of the effects of the repetition of sexual trauma on the developing personality of the child and the rights of children to their own sexual development.

References

1. Charles H. McCaghy, "Child Molesters: A Study of Their Careers as Deviants," in *Criminal Behavior Systems: A Typology,* eds., Marshall B. Clinard and Richard Quinney (New York: Holt, Rinehart and Winston, 1967) p. 81.

2. Georg Simmel, "Secrecy" in *The Sociology of Georg Simmel* ed. and trans. Kurt H. Wolff, (New York: Free Press of Glencoe, 1964), p. 334. (Published 1908 *Soziologie*).

3. Karl Abraham. *The Experiencing of Sexual Trauma as a Form of Sexual Activity,* 1907, Selected Papers, trans. D. Byron and A. Strachey (London: Hogarth Press, 1927), p. 47.

4. Lauretta Bender and Abram Blau. "The Reaction of Children to Sexual Relations with Adults," *American Journal of Orthopsychiatry* 7 (October 1937):500-18.

5. Lauretta Bender and Alvin Elderidge Grugett Jr., "A Follow-up Report on Children Who had Atypical Sexual Experience." *American Journal of Orthopsychiatry* 22 (1952):825-37.

6. Joseph Weiss, Estelle Rogers, Miriam Darwin, and Charles Dutton, "Study of Girl Sex Victims," *Psychiatric Quarterly* 29 (January 1955):1-27.

7. Melanie Klein, *The Psychoanalysis of Children* (London: Hogarth Press, 1932).

8. John Gagnon and William Simon. "The Child Molester: Surprising Advice for Worried Parents," *Redbook*, February 1969.

Sex-Stress Situation
Ann Wolbert Burgess and
Lynda Lytle Holmstrom

The third type of sexual trauma that we have encountered is a type of victimization we call *sex-stress situation.* Here both parties initially agree to have sexual contact, but then something drastically "goes wrong." Cases of this type then come to the attention of authorities through a variety of routes. It is important to understand sex-stress cases, because they constitute an implicit conflict between staff and client over what constitutes an appropriate case.

A service institution is likely to receive cases that are not related to its primary goal. Hospital emergency wards are a classic example; many patients that arrive in emergency rooms are not in need of emergency care. In most emergency services studied by Roth, for example, trauma cases were in the minority and few cases were defined as urgent.[1]

Our experience has been that rape programs, rape centers, and emergency services whose goal is to handle rape cases likewise receive cases, such as sex-stress ones, that are not directly related to that goal. This pattern of utilization is important for two reasons. First, sex-stress cases greatly influence how the institution deals with rape. Hospital emergency room personnel, police, and child protective staff know that some "rape cases" are in fact cases in which the parties consented to sex. This fact looms large in staff perceptions of all rape cases. Staff tend to become obsessed with trying to determine whether a case is a "real rape" rather than asking what kind of victimization has occurred. A great deal of staff time and energy goes into labeling and culling "less worthy patients," rather than into identifying the nature of the young person's distress and her or his request for services. Secondly, in sex-stress cases, the young person and the family have been through some type of upsetting sexual experience, and they deserve to be offered counseling to help them sort out the issues that are disturbing them. Rather than simply downgrading their need for help, staff might be better advised to acquire those skills which would be useful in dealing with such cases.

Types of Sex-Stress Situations

Sex-stress situation is an anxiety reaction that occurs as a result of a consensual sexual situation that has subsequently "gone wrong." The person for whom the sexual situation produces the greatest anxiety is usually the one who brings the matter to the attention of the hospital staff or police. There are two main types of sex-stress situations: mutual agreement and contracting for sex.

Mutual Agreement

In this sex-stress situation, both parties have agreed to have sexual relations, but later either (1) parents become anxious, (2) one of the sexual partners becomes anxious, or (3) officials in authority positions intervene.

Parental Anxiety. Parents may become anxious when they *discover* the child is sexually active, or when they *suspect* the child is sexually active.

In the discovery type, the parents are aware that their child is seeing or dating someone, but are not aware of any sexual activity. Discovery of such activity comes as a big surprise. In one case, for example, a 12-year-old girl and a 35-year-old man had been seeing each other. He was a very supportive figure in her life, especially following the death of her oldest brother in an automobile accident. One night, the girl's father, upon learning that his daughter was probably with the man, called the police who subsequently found the couple in bed. The man was an influential leader in the community, to which the family had recently moved, and had befriended the new family. The parents had never suspected any erotic involvement between their daughter and this man. The parents pressed charges against him. At the probable cause hearing it was learned that "love letters" had been exchanged between the two, and that the girl had gone willingly with the man to a cousin's home. The father said:

"I'd like to kill him. What he did is much more serious in our country than it is here. . . . He couldn't say he did it because he was ignorant of the laws or because that kind of thing went on in our country."

In the suspicion type a parent is uncertain as to what activities the adolescent is engaging in, and brings the child in for an examination to determine if the child is sexually active. For example, in one case, a 13-year-old girl was brought to the hospital by her parents who wished her to be examined for possible rape. The girl was supposedly taken from her house at about 7:30 P.M. by a married neighbor. The parents were away from the home at the time, and the girl left her house without permission of the relative who was babysitting. The girl denied having sex both to her parents and to the hospital staff. But the father's request to hospital staff was very explicit: he wanted to know if his daughter had had sex that evening.

Partner Anxiety. In this sex-stress situation, one of the sexual partners, usually the female, becomes anxious over the relationship or the activity. She then brings the matter to the attention of an authority. As one example, an adolescent after her first sexual experience may become anxious over becoming pregnant and will attempt to obtain morning-after contraception by stating she had been raped. She may well ask that her parents not be notified.

The important point is that the presenting *complaint* in these cases is rape, but the real issue is something else. The task for staff is to identify the underlying issue. The case of a 12-year-old girl who told her mother that a neighbor raped her illustrates how careful interviewing was needed to identify the real request. In this case, the girl was becoming increasingly upset over her mother spending so much time with a male neighbor. A brief family history revealed the father had died three years previously and the grandmother—to whom the girl felt the closest—had died the previous year. The mother would ask the daughter's opinion of the neighbor ("Isn't he nice, like your father?"). Rather than feeling positively toward the man, the girl felt ambivalent. He was not nice like her father. The man had enticed her into sexual activity. Since the girl was feeling conflicted, she told her mother that the man had raped her. The mother believed her daughter and asked to make a complaint at district court. Three hearings on the issuing of a complaint were held. However, the clerk of court refused to issue a complaint for two reasons: (1) there was some testimony about the girl's sexual activity with age-mates; and (2) she made a statement at one point that she made up the story. This court action did not resolve the matter. The mother became more upset. The girl essentially missed a whole grading period in school. Crisis counseling was advised through the district court's witness assistance program. In counseling, the issues of greatest concern to her were the deaths of her grandmother and father as well as the sexual situation. The clerk's decision did not resolve the accused neighbor's situation either. The man subsequently lost his job as a jail attendant as a result of propositioning a nurse and attempting to rape her.

Contracting for Sex

In some situations, there will be a contractual agreement for sex, but then something goes wrong. Prostitutes may be victimized in a sex-stress situation through nonpayment, perversion, robbery, and violence.[2] In one case, for example, an adolescent came into a hospital stating that she had been raped by two men who forced her into a car after she asked directions. The men took her back to an apartment, stole all her money, and each had sex with her. The police later learned that this adolescent was a runaway from a detention center in another state. The current home address she gave belonged to a man in his fifties who took in runaway girls. The police speculated that the adolescent was probably robbed and would have to account for her lack of earnings to the man who was the pimp for the houseful of girls. If she claimed rape, the man might not beat her.

Intervention in Sex-Stress Situations

Given our society's current ambivalence about sexuality, it is important that agencies be prepared to deal with the anxiety or stress generated from many sexual situations. It is apparent that police, hospital staff, and other helping agencies will continue to receive distress complaints and requests for help from people experiencing stressful sexual situations even though it is not the primary goal of the agency. If staff are prepared to deal with such issues, they will be less anxious themselves and more in a position to help.

There are two main areas of therapeutic skill useful to staff working with people in sexually stressful situations. First, staff personnel need to be aware of those techniques which decrease their own anxiety over listening to sexual accounts and thereby increase their therapeutic effectiveness. Second, they can improve their interviewing skills that specifically aid a person in distress. The skills useful for staff personnel to develop in themselves are: (1) the ability to deal with sexual issues, (2) the ability to adhere to protocol, and (3) the ability to observe verbal associations.

Dealing with Sexual Issues

A crucial factor in the treatment of sex-stress situations is the staff person's own attitude toward the child and how this is conveyed to the child. If you find yourself judging the person rather than trying to understand the situation, all therapeutic leverage will be lost. It is important to come to grips with your own feelings about sex. Being comfortable with one's own sexuality reduces the possibility of projecting values and prejudices onto the child, adolescent, or situation. Adolescence is a developmental time of life that is heavily focused on sexual development and identity, and personnel dealing with young people should not compare their own childhood and adolescent experiences with those of the client. A warning sign that you are projecting should sound when you hear yourself saying, "I never would have done that as a kid," or "That never went on in our community when I was growing up."

Adhering to Protocol

Staff members may wonder what to ask or what to say to a child or adolescent who makes a complaint about a sexual situation that seems hard to believe or understand. One can never be faulted for sticking to the rules or playing it straight. It is important that each person with a complaint may have the opportunity to tell their whole story and to be asked all the routine questions normally asked in a sexual trauma interview. Adhering to the protocol will often provide enough information to allow you to determine the actual issue, obtain the request, and then try to negotiate something that will be useful to the child.

In one case, for example, parents brought their 14-year-old daughter to the emergency department saying that she had been acting different—sleeping all day and not talking when she was up. The mother finally asked the daughter if she had been raped, and the girl answered yes. The police interview was done in the hospital. The officer prefaced his interrogation as follows: "Now, I have heard these kinds of cases for many years. And I know the area you were in because I worked there for 12 years. I want you to just tell me what happened and not be embarrassed." The officer played it straight and asked all the usual questions, such as the specific place where the incident occurred, the streets involved, what happened, how the men held her down, and their names, ages, and any other identification. Because the parents realized that consensual sex was involved, a few days later, they made the decision not to press charges and decided to handle the issue as a family matter.

Adhering to protocol provided respectful attention to the adolescent and her family. The stress and anxiety of the situation decreased and the family was able to deal with the situation. In the next case, involving a prostitute, the value of playing it straight is indicated by the eventual determination of the real stress issues.

Observing Verbal Associations

An *association* is the mental connection between one idea and another. In usual circumstances, when asking a question, you expect the respondent to answer your question with a statement that relates to the question. When this does not occur, you find the interview becoming confused and departing from the issue. There may be several reasons why this occurs. First, people may have many thoughts coming into their minds that they talk about in rapid succession. Second, people may have difficulty understanding the questions, either because of age, comprehension level, use of drugs or alcohol, of the presence of a psychiatric disorder, and thus may have many unrelated thoughts. Third, people may not have the answer to your question and, rather than admitting that, will attempt to make up an answer to satisfy you. Or, fourth, people do not want to answer.

The following example illustrates some unusual associations to routine questions. The case also shows the value of playing it straight as a way of monitoring verbal associations. The young woman, age 19, slightly older than the adolescent age range, is presented because she so clearly described her ambivalence regarding prostitution. The associations reveal a rape at age 14, as well as her ambivalence over her work. It was speculated that this woman had difficulty with some of the questions because of drugs, either prescribed for nervous tension or self-selected.

Counselor: *"How are you feeling?"*

Vivian: *(slight laugh) "I'm sore. Feel OK, well, I have a headache. I am nervous . . . my head is pounding. I am seeing a psychiatrist. Had what you would* call a nervous breakdown last month. I'm seeing Dr. Jones. I'll give him a call."

Counselor: *"Maybe you could just start telling us what happened. That would be helpful for us."*

Vivian: *"I was grabbed from behind. I was in the North project. Then I went to my girl friend's. I have to go back there. She will be concerned."*

Counselor: *"You went to your girl friend's after this happened?"*

Vivian: *"I changed clothes."*

Counselor: *"When did all this happen?"*

Vivian: *"About 4 or 5 P.M. I was going to my girl friend's apartment. They pushed me into someone's apartment. The guy wasn't home. He works. Don't know how they got the door open. It has a safety lock."*

Counselor: *"Did you see the men?"*

Vivian: *"I think I'd recognize them if I saw them again."* (shaking head very slowly)

Counselor: *"How many? Were they white or black?"*

Vivian: *"There were two . . . about 22 to 25 years old and black. They could be junkies. They took $150. It was in my bra and fell out as they grabbed me."*

Counselor: *"Did they talk to you?"*

Vivian: *(laughs)* *"It was two against one. Not much I could do."*

Counselor: *"No, I can imagine."*

Vivian: *"One held me. One put his elbow on my chest (rubs area) . . . it still hurts."*

Counselor: *"How were you feeling at the time?"*

Vivian: *"I was trying to fight. They held me down. Then after they were finished, they put me out in the hall."*

Counselor: *"What kind of sex did they have with you?"*

Vivian: *"Oh, they were sucking my breasts . . . the usual way of carrying on. At least they didn't try it the back way."*

Counselor: *"How did it make you feel?"*

Vivian: *"I try not to let things get me down . . . that's the way I try to keep from getting depressed. The psychiatrist does me a lot of good. What made me do it was I got in an argument with my mother. Tried to take pills to calm me down. Not on pills now. Took them all at once. Nerves went so bad that I just went looking for any pill I could find. But I'm doing fairly well now."* (This association followed discussion of the sexual part of the assault. Also indicates *she argued with her mother over something sexual and that one way she handles her feelings about sex is to take pills.)*

At this point, the gynecologist talked with Vivian about protection from venereal disease. After he left, Vivian hinted about some decisions she was facing. She also talked about whether to tell her mother about the assault and decided not to since her mother currently had medical problems facing her. Then the interview continued regarding what Vivian did after the assault.

Counselor: *"How did it go with the police?"*

Vivian: *"Fairly good. I was nervous, not sure of the apartment."*

Counselor: *"Did they give you a hard time?"*

Vivian: *(laughs) "I was glad to get away." (Her association is not to the police, as the question implied, but to the assailants.)*

Counselor: *"No, I meant the police." (refers back to question)*

Vivian: *"Oh no, they were fine."*

Counselor: *"Would you press charges?"*

Vivian: *(avoided the issue) "If they were found, but I don't know their names."*

Counselor: *"How do you think this will affect you?"*

Vivian: *"Well, I will be a little more cautious. I'm edgy now. My nerves bad. Don't have anything to calm me down. Get these awful sinus headaches. Will have to be more careful where I keep my money. I'm not going to let this worry me about where I go. I never had any fear of going by myself. Guess I'll go home and go to bed."*

When asked about her reactions to coming to the hospital and her feelings about the pelvic examination, Vivian told us that she goes regularly for her VD checks and her birth control prescription, which later matched with her statements regarding her "being in the life." When asked whether she had ever been sexually assaulted before, she said,

"A couple of years ago . . . my mother's cousin. It didn't go to court because my mother talked to his mother. Guess that was five years ago. We were blood relatives."

Counselor: *"How did you feel about his getting off?"*

Vivian: *"Didn't feel too good. Just wanted him to get off me." (Her association was to the assailant rather than the court implied in the question)*

Counselor: *"I mean about getting off of jail."*

Vivian: *"Oh, I wish he went to jail. He bolted the door and had a knife and held my mouth. (Association to circumstances of the first assault)*

Counselor: *"How long did it take to get over it?"*

Vivian: *"Couple of weeks."*

Counselor: *"Did you talk to people about it?"*

Vivian: *"Yes. Then I forgot it."*

The interview was long due to the young woman's extreme lethargy and difficulty in thinking and talking very fast. But it was clear that she did want to talk. Her request was for ventilation—that is, she preferred talking and following her own associations, rather than trying to make any connections between what she was feeling and what she was saying. The interview continued, and it revealed her ambivalence over being a prostitute. Two of her main conflicts were: (1) her mother's firm stand against such work ("My mother said if I went into *that,* she might as well forget that she had a daughter. She said if she died, not to come to her funeral"). And (2) the custody of her own daughter ("I wanted my daughter to live with me but my mother kept her. She said my daughter would understand things"). The positive aspects of "going to the streets and taking up the profession" were stated as financial ("I can have the things I want. I'm getting a new apartment Friday.... It has rugs and marble. And I can help my mother"). She also took pride in her work ("I do it well"). She denied being hurt by any customers, although she admitted there were times when she had not been paid ("When that happens, you don't fight it"). By the end of the interview, she was still ambivalent ("I don't think I'll go out tonight, although it's still early"). She thought she would try it for a while to see if it "makes me too depressed. It's not too hard, but it's not too easy."

The alert interviewer will analyze the verbal associations, seeing if the answers match the questions. If the answers do not relate, he or she will then check to see if the person understood the questions. Also, the interviewer should try to determine why the person has unusual associations since this information could be important for referral.

There are three main therapeutic interventions useful in sex-stress situations: (1) identify the issue, (2) elicit the request; and (3) provide resources or referrals.

Identify the Issue

If the child or adolescent states that she or he has been raped and you suspect there is more to the story, how do you determine what the real issue is and why the young person has come to you?

In the following case, an aunt brings her 15-year-old niece to the pediatric clinic stating that the niece was raped two days ago. It turned out that the girl was not raped but that the aunt—who had raised the niece and her brother since they were 3 and 5 years old—was concerned that the girl was having sex voluntarily and wanted her examined. The gynecologist stated that the girl had rights to privacy and that he wouldn't examine her to determine virginity.[3] The following verbatim interview with the aunt illustrates some interviewing techniques that can be used when the issues of a case are not clear.

(Prior to starting the interview, the nurse introduced us to the aunt with the following words, "They are skilled in helping mothers and daughters work through sexual problems.")

Counselor: *"Can you start by telling us some of your concerns about your niece?"*

Aunt: *"I don't feel a 15-year-old girl should be giving her body to these good for nothing boys. But the doctor sees nothing wrong with it."*

Counselor: *"What does your daughter say about it?"*

Aunt: *"She doesn't talk with me. She knows I'm strictly against it. The boys want just one thing. She knows my views. I'd rather give her up than have her bring in something like that. I have problems of my own. I have five children. I have a sick husband. He's been in the state hospital. And a son 17. She loves the streets. She changed a few weeks ago. She'll say she's been baby sitting, but won't have any money. She'll come home at 2 A.M. Someone will telephone her and say 'this is her man.'"*

Counselor: *"How do you handle it with her?"*

Aunt: *"I told her I don't think she should have him call and say, 'this is your man.'"*

Counselor: *"Her reaction is to be quiet?"*

Aunt: *"She stays out. And she's having trouble learning, and this is a change. She's supposed to be in the 10th grade and is still in the 9th."*

Counselor: *"Has her behavior changed?"*

Aunt: *"She just shut up."*

Counselor: *"Do you have any evidence of sexual activity?"*

Aunt: *"Well, I don't know what else she's doing if she's out till 2 A.M. I haven't seen any sign of her period for about two months. She's always been a good liar—she's lied on a Bible."*

Counselor: *"How do you handle her menstrual period?"*

Aunt: *"I explained the consequences of it."*

Counselor: *"Your 17-year-old son—has he noticed changes in her too?"*

Aunt: *"That's her brother, but they don't get along."*

Counselor: *"Who is she close to?"*

Aunt: *"Closer to me than anybody. She might talk to her friends."*

Counselor: *"Do you talk to her?"*

Aunt: *"One boy came to the house, and oh God, the most ignorant guy in the world. I said, 'you wait until you're older; get your education; then you're on your own. Until then, give yourself respect.'"*

Counselor: *"Does she understand?"*

Aunt: *"She understands."*

Counselor: *"What does she understand about being here tonight?"*

Aunt: *"She understands that I want to get her examined to see if anything is wrong and she has a bad cough. She said she'd been to the hospital—but she'd never been there. My husband has his spells, and the neighbors say he would have sex with her but I know it's not true because he doesn't have the time because I'm almost always there. I'm not concerned about my husband, I know him."*

Counselor: *"What's the nature of your husband's problems?"*

Aunt: *"He has moods . . . gets depressed and feels someone is trying to outslick him. And the neighbors get down on him. And if the child gets pregnant, the neighbors will say it's his fault."*

Counselor: *"So you want to know if she is pregnant."*

Aunt: *"But the doctor is on her side. Like she's the adult, and I'm the child."*

Counselor: *"Did you tell the doctor your concern about pregnancy?"*

Aunt: *"No . . . I've given up on him."*

Counselor: *"How can we be helpful?"*

Aunt: *"I don't know. Right now I can't take the responsibility."*

Counselor: *"What is the relationship between you and her?"*

Aunt: *"She's my niece, but I've had her since she was 3."*

Counselor: *"Are you her legal guardian?"*

Aunt: *"I'm her legal guardian. . . . She was my sister's child."*

Counselor: *"Where is your sister?"*

Aunt: *"Who knows. She left when she was 3."*

Counselor: *"Have you had trouble with the boy?"*

Aunt: *"No. He can't mess himself up because he's a boy."*

Counselor: *"So there are two different views—yours and your niece's."*

Aunt: *"We have two different views, and so it doesn't make sense to take care of her. I can't afford this. I have a sick husband."*

Counselor: *"Does she understand your problems?"*

Aunt: *"No, she doesn't understand. Plus I'm expecting again. Due in October. I'm having my tubes tied after this one."*

Counselor: *"You took care of her before you were married?"*

Aunt: *"I raised those kids before marriage. I wasted a lot of years of my young life on those kids."*

Counselor: *"What alternatives are open to you; what choices?"*

Aunt: *"Don't know what I can do . . . doctor didn't help."*

Counselor: *"What did the doctor say?"*

Aunt: *"He thinks she has her rights."*

Counselor: *"How do you feel about birth control in general?"*

Aunt: *"It's something to entice a young girl and nothing will happen to her."*

Counselor: *"How did birth control pills come up?"*

Aunt: *"I said if she's done something she should be on birth control pills."*

Counselor: *"Are you concerned about who would take care of a baby if she had one?"*

Aunt: *"Well, who would?"*

To summarize, some of the important themes raised by the aunt are as follows.

1. Sexuality of the niece. The aunt believes that proper girls do not have sex before marriage, and that birth control pills "entice" a girl to be sexually active. The aunt makes a comparison between her niece and nephew, and her thinking here is not completely logical. She says she does not have trouble with her nephew because boys "can't mess themselves up." Logically,

therefore, the aunt should favor birth control for the girl because if she were on the pill she could not mess herself up. It becomes clear that the issue is the girl's sexuality, not just a question of whether the niece will become pregnant.

2. Her own sexuality. The aunt has had five babies in six years and is pregnant with her sixth baby. She is having a tubal ligation after this baby is born.

3. Concerns about her husband. He has been hospitalized for psychiatric problems. She says the neighbors are talking about him and suspected sexual activity with the niece. She strongly denied the possibility of such activity because she says she stays home quite a bit of the time and would have noted any irregularities.

4. Lack of recognition. The aunt feels she has given the best years of her life to her sister's children, and the girl is disrespectful and not appreciative of her sacrifice.

This case illustrates several issues, each of which needs additional discussion and exploration. The woman's request is twofold: (1) for ventilation—to tell some-one about her life and her family, and (2) to gain an ally for support as she deals with some of the above problems. Clearly, a referral for supportive counseling is indicated and might best be arranged through the obstetrical clinic where she has routine prenatal appointments. One issue will be her sterilization. It will be important for the counselor to go over each issue one by one, moving on to subsequent issues as each one is successfully handled. The woman could be encouraged to seek out counseling services on her own or could be provided with alternate resources in her neighborhood.

After identifying the issues for the aunt, it was important to determine if the girl had any requests for services. When asked how we might be helpful to her, the girl said she could not think of any way. The girl did not want to talk with her aunt present ("She will have enough to say to me on the way home. I don't have anything to say to her"). The physician asked the girl if she wanted birth control pills. She said no ("I'm not into anything yet"). She said she might want them later ("To get my aunt off my back"). She did have a request for information regarding how to obtain contraceptive materials, and this was explained during the interview. The girl also had a chance to vent some of her frustrations over how her aunt was reacting to her:

"She doesn't think I'm old enough to have a boyfriend. But I have a job, and if I'm old enough to have a job, I'm old enough to have a boyfriend. I have my own time card, and I have my own ID to cash my check."

The niece wanted more independence and was having difficulty negotiating this with the aunt ("She makes be babysit and stay home, and it's no fun").

Identifying the issue may take time. It takes patient interviewing and listening to identify the real reason underlying such a rape complaint. When you suspect there is more to the story than you are hearing, a good guide is to ask open-ended questions such as: Do you know why you are here? How are you feeling? Such questions can be used with any client to get a sense of what the issue is. If the person seeking services realizes you are interested and willing to listen, the issue(s) usually becomes explicit.

Eliciting the Request

Once you have identified the issue, the next step is to determine how best to help. The request is what the young person wishes you to do to reduce his or her distress. In sex-stress situations, it may take extensive interviewing for people to trust you enough to be able to say what is really troubling them.

After the problem is agreed upon (e.g., "It seems you are very concerned about your daughter's dating"), you then might ask, "How can we (the agency) be most helpful to you with this problem?" The person may need some help defining the method of help, and thus you may have to suggest some possibilities such as, "Would talking over this problem help?"

The case presented in the beginning of this chapter, of the runaway adolescent, may be used again to illustrate the request concept. The girl found herself in a very frightening situation and sought out the police with the implicit request for protection.

"The guys left the apartment. I got dressed . . . then heard a car door slam and men talking. I was very frightened and went out a door to the street. I saw a car coming and a house with a light. I knocked on the door. A man answered through the door . . . would not let me in but said he would call the police, which he did."

When the girl arrived at the hospital, after talking with the police and stating that she had been raped and robbed, her opening statement to the counselor contained many ideas. The problem in the initial interview was to help the girl focus on her difficulty and then to identify the request for help. The girl's opening complaint was as follows.

"I don't know if I can get over this one. I have just finished seeing a psychiatrist. This happened three years ago. I am dating a black man now, and I don't know if I will be able to keep seeing him. This has really hit me. I just don't know."

This statement contains four issues: the current victimization, her psychiatric history, a previous rape, and her current boyfriend. The counselor adhered to protocol and inquired about the current rape. The girl was able to give the details of the assault and did not associate away from the current rape until the counselor asked about the previous rape.

"It was my fault. I was hitchhiking for the summer with two other girls . . . three years ago. A guy picked us up; took us to the movies and then back to his apartment. He had sex with all three of us. The other two wanted it, but I didn't. . . . It was my first sexual experience. I had a nervous breakdown following it.

It became clear that the request was for psychiatric referral. The girl needed to talk about the issues raised in the beginning of the interview as well as the current stressful situation. The complicating factor was that it was difficult for her to be in touch with anyone since she was illegally in the state and wanted as a runaway in another state. Attempts were made to do follow up work but she could not be located. Had there not been such complications, she would have been referred to a mental health clinic.

Referrals

Once you have identified the real issue and determined how to help, the final question is: Where can one get the services requested? People who experience sexually stressful situations should have access to counseling or other services if they so request them. The person may be able to ventilate sufficiently in one interview to settle the anxiety over the current situation. In other cases, however, there are complicating factors; in such cases, a mental health referral should be considered. We recommend that all agencies working with young people have listings of agencies for referrals. If you make a referral, it is important that you do a follow-up to see if both the client and the agency followed through with their intent. First, it is sometimes very difficult for people to seek mental health services; and second, the mental health services may have a heavy caseload and the victim may get lost in the bureaucracy. By checking back with the victim or parents to see how they are doing you get an answer to their success in obtaining services as well as conveying to them your concern that they received all the help they could.

The following sex-stress case, in which a mother discovered the sexual relationship between her 15-year-old daughter and a 23-year-old man, illustrates how valuable keeping in touch with the family, at least by telephone, is for them to receive essential services.

The mother pressed charges of statutory rape, knowing that the daughter had consented to go to the apartment and to have sex. The court hearing for probable cause was postponed three times. One week before the fourth scheduled date, and two months after the couple was discovered, the daughter ran away with the defendant. The mother notified the police and filed a warrant for a runaway child. Three months later, the mother received a letter from her daughter in Puerto Rico. The letter read as follows:

"I am with José in a small village out from San Juan. He beats me, beats me badly, when I say I want to come home. He comes home drunk and beats me. One night he beat me and I tried to run away. I fell down and started bleeding. He took me to a hospital. I had a miscarriage. I want to come home. I want you to come and get me."

The mother spent the next several weeks contacting all the officials necessary to get her daughter back to her home state, which included calling Puerto Rico, the attorney general's office, and the FBI. The daughter was returned to the mother. Because we were still following the case, the probation officer, assigned to the daughter when she returned, called for our opinion on the case. We sent a copy of our records to the probation department, with the mother's permission, and made the following recommendation:

"The daughter was seen by the Victim Counseling Service, following being examined and treated for 'alleged rape' and drug overdose. The central issue at that time was her relationship with a 23-year-old man and the resulting conflicts between herself and her family. . . . Prior to the disruptive events in her life, Theresa had shown many strengths, such as achievements in school, creative talents in sewing, cooking, and peer friendships. However, her conflict in interpersonal matters, such as dealing with her family, resulted in serious action-oriented behavior of drug overdosing and running away from home. Rather than define Theresa's current difficulties as psychological in origin, we recommend the crisis be defined as problematic to the whole family unit. Family therapy would be a treatment model of choice. If the family therapy does not repair family ties and relationships and Theresa continues to act out under stress, individual psychotherapy should undoubtedly be considered."

Theresa was pregnant again by the boyfriend when she returned home. This added a complicating factor to her recovery from the victimization process. Referral to family services was successful. Family therapy was initiated and careful attention paid to the victim, her relationships with her family, and her reintegration, along with her new child, into the family.[4]

References

1. Julius A. Roth. "Utilization of the Hospital Emergency Department," *Journal of Health and Social Behavior* 12 (December 1971):312-320.

2. Ann Wolbert Burgess and Lynda Lytle Homstrom, *Rape: Victims of Crisis* (Bowie, Md.: Robert J. Brady, 1974), pp. 286–297.

3. The confidentiality aspect of this case is discussed in Lynda Lytle Holmstrom and Ann Wolbert Burgess, *The Victim of Rape: Institutional Reactions* (New York: Wiley-Interscience, forthcoming) Chapter 4.

4. Hospital staff reaction to this victim is discussed in Lynda Lytle Holmstrom and Ann Wolbert Burgess, *The Victim of Rape: Institutional Reactions* (New York: Wiley-Interscience, forthcoming) Chapter 4.

Divided Loyalty in Incest Cases
Ann Wolbert Burgess, Lynda Lytle Holmstrom, and Maureen P. McCausland

The knowledge that a child or adolescent has been sexually assaulted by a family member is usually an upsetting event for a family. The decision whether to report the event to an outside authority such as the police or a hospital may depend on a number of variables such as the family relationship of the perpetrator and child, the amount of physical trauma that resulted, the ages of the people involved, and the family and/or community view of sexual activity between family members.

This chapter looks at the social pressure and the psychological stress involved in making a decision about where to place one's loyalty after sexual assault by a family member. Important aspects in the two cases that are described include: *family structure* (nuclear family), *type of victimization* (pressured sex and secrecy), *relationship of victim and offender* (father-daughter), and *age of victim and offender*.

Divided Loyalty

The issue of family loyalty is very important in sexual assault cases in which the assailant is a family member. The question that the family must face is: Should we be loyal to our child and react to the offender as we would react to any perpetrator basing this decision on our duty as community members to bring such a person to the attention of the law? The alternative to this choice is to make an exception for the family member perpetrator and be loyal to the family ties rather than bring him to an outside group's attention. The family must choose one of the two courses of action. It is important to note: are the criteria on which they base their decision independent of the particular social relationship they have to the offender or do they apply by virtue of that relationship?[1]

Decision making involves a cognitive thought process. It may also involve an emotional reaction to completing the process. When a person must decide whether to side with one of two family members over an issue, the psychological reaction may be experienced as a sense of divided loyalty.

The issue of where family loyalty is placed has been described by clinicians and social scientists.[2] In reporting on clinical case studies of 15 victims of father-daughter incest, therapists Herman and Hirschman describe patterns of family relationships. They cite the almost uniform estrangement of the mother and daughter as a pattern that preceded the occurrence of overt incest. The message transmitted to the daughters by the mothers was as follows:

"Your father first, you second. It is dangerous to fight back for if I lose him I lose everything. For my own survival I must leave you to your own devices. I cannot defend you, and if necessary I will sacrifice you to your father.[3]

The pressure over family loyalty that confronts the young victim of incest may often be seen during the court process. A project report on child victims of sexual assault conducted by the Queen's Bench Foundation states this conflict as follows:

In cases where the offender is a parent or relative, the victim is often pressured by other family members to retract his/her statement. Even if s/he does testify, the child is an ambivalent witness, at best, because of his/her natural affinity for the offender.[4]

Two clinical cases follow to illustrate: (1) a family's reaction to the disclosure of an incest situation and the divided loyalty issue; and (2) the result of the divided loyalty issue in an incest situation that was unresolved for twenty years. In both cases, the victimization is pressured-sex incest. Please refer to Chapter 12 for case discussion of rape incest.

Divided Loyalty in the Nuclear Family: Clinical Case 1

Family members may face the issue of divided loyalty within the nuclear family unit. The following case is of incest within a nuclear family. It illustrates the divided loyalty issue experienced by one mother following the discovery of her husband's incestuous behavior with her daughter. The type of victimization was pressure for sex, sexual activity and pledge to secrecy. The age difference and family relationsip was an 11-year-old stepdaughter and a 35-year-old stepfather.

The Assault

The mother walked into her daughter's room at night and saw her husband jump up from one of the beds. Her 11-year-old daughter pulled the covers over her head. When asked what he was doing, the husband replied, "I didn't do anything." The mother asked the daughter if he had "bothered her," to which the girl answered "yes." The mother ordered her husband out of the house and told him not to come back.

This situation triggered a crisis reaction for the mother. She found she was unable to continue in her work ("I'd be at work, get thinking about it, break down and cry and have to come home"); had emotional disruption ("My nerves are shot and I feel so lost"); and family disruption ("My 11-year-old daughter just cries all the time and my 4-year-old daughter is having such bad dreams she comes to sleep with me").

The mother made four initial decisions:

1. To be loyal to her daughter ("I feel betrayed. I'll never have him back. I could deal with him and another woman, but not my daughter").
2. To threaten the husband but not press charges ("I hate to drag her into court, although I did tell him I'd take him to court. I don't think I could go through it").
3. To tell others and not maintain a family secret ("I called his mother and told her what happened. . . . I called his employer and told him he shouldn't be employed doing what he does").
4. To seek crisis counseling ("I don't know which way to turn. I love him, but I'm hurt. I don't know what to do. It's tearing me apart").

Crisis counseling included mother and daughters. The counselor suggested that the husband be included, but he declined ("People only get psychiatric help if they are crazy"). The mother was seen first, to provide a detailed account of her thoughts, feelings, and reactions to the crisis. While the two daughters were waiting, the victim was given crayons and paper to draw her reaction to several questions stated on the paper. She was also told the questions would be talked about in counseling. The victim's sister played with toys from the playroom in an unstructured setting. After the mother was seen, the victim was seen individually to go over her artwork and feelings about the crisis. Then both mother and daughter met with the counselor together to make decisions about family issues and counseling.

Issues Identified by the Mother in Counseling. The following issues were of primary concern to the mother in her individual sessions.

1. Missing her daughter's clues that something was wrong. ("My daughter had changed from a happy child to a troubled child this year. She has been having trouble in school—her grades have dropped from honor roll standing. I told my mother something was wrong and I was going to take her to a psychiatrist. She has been complaining of stomach pains and soreness in her genitals. She told me she had blood in her pants. I thought she was beginning to menstruate and told her the facts of life, and she sat there and cried. She told me she was having nightmares and that someone was trying to kill me.")

2. Blaming self. ("I have kicked him out before—for other things like his drinking and smoking. But he has always held a good job, and we did have good times.")
3. Sexual relationship with husband. ("Our [sexual] relationship was not good. A while back I was angry at him and told him no sex. I found a motel ticket in his pocket, but he denied everything. Then a week before all this happened, he told me he had pain while urinating. I told him to go to a doctor. The doctor told him it was an inflammation of the urethra.")
4. Concerns about daughter's behavior. ("I am concerned about her behavior. My youngest daughter said once her sister took her pants off and climbed on top of her while she was in bed. . . . She talks a lot on the phone to boys and wants to know why she can't have a boyfriend. . . . She wants to be an adult so much.")

Issues of Concern to the Victim. In the combined play and counseling session, the victim discussed her concerns:

1. Description of the activity. ("It started when we lived in the other house. He told me not to tell. Just before my tenth brithday. . . . He would do it when mother was out of the house working. My sister and I sleep in the same room. We'd watch television at night and my sister would fall asleep and then I would. He would come in around 10:30 P.M. and turn off the TV. He said he was playing a game. Then he'd do it, and after he'd leave, I couldn't go to sleep. Then we moved, and he did it more. I wanted to tell my mother . . . . but I was scared she'd send me away to an orphans' home.")
2. Feelings about the activity. The counselor first wrote the questions on separate pieces of paper. While the mother was in a counseling session, the daughter used her time to write her answers to the questions on the papers.

What did he do? "He got on top of me and did what he did. Put vaseline on me . . . . it hurt."

How did you feel about it? "I felt sad when it happened."

How do you feel about your Daddy? "I feel happy and sad. Happy because it is all over. Sad because he is gone."

What is the worse thing that could happen if you told? "He might try to *kill* me."

How do you want to feel? "I want to feel happy. . . like I used to."

The last question was aimed at establishing an alliance and some trust for the beginning therapeutic relationship. The child's request—to feel happy again—was taken as the starting point. The counselor defined the goal of counseling in terms of her request: to help her feel good again about herself and her family, as she once did.

The disruption in the victim's life after disclosure was noted in her dreams ("I dreamt I got kidnapped and he killed me"); her concentration and resulting poor performance in school ("I try to keep my mind off it, but I can't"); her thoughts ("Why did he keep doing it?").

One crisis has the potential for triggering additional crises. In this case, the victim learned new information about her father that created another upsetting situation. She had believed her father was her natural father when indeed he was not. In fact, the mother began seeing her husband after she was pregnant with her daughter and they decided not to tell the child this history. The news was learned by the victim at the time of disclosure of the incest. She said to her mother, "I thought he was my father." The mother said, "If he was, he'd never do such a thing to you."

Additional sessions with the mother and daughter dealt with the following issues.

Tactics by the Husband. The mother reported that the husband was asking for a second chance ("He is in tears . . . he calls crying. I want to kill him. . . . He tried to deny it, and then said, 'What can I say; I'm sorry' "). The mother-in-law called collect from another state to say her son said he did not do it. The husband told his mother that he and his wife had had sex. He put a towel around himself and went in to tuck the girls in bed. The wife got mad and accused him. He said his wife was trying to scandalize his name. The mother-in-law kept asking when they were going to get back together.

The victim reported that her father kept coming to school to try to talk with her. He wanted to know what she said he was doing and what else she had told her mother. He said she didn't have to say that. Then he said, "Come here, baby, and let me give you a kiss."

Confrontation with the Husband. The wife confronted her husband with two specific issues raised by the disclosure of sexual activity:

1. Laboratory confirmation that both the victim and the wife had gonorrhea. This disclosure led to the husband admitting that he had been at a motel with a prostitute.
2. Motivation for the incest. The husband said, "She comes into my room and flirts with me. I was afraid to tell you, but I did talk with a minister who said pray to the Lord and He would help me." The wife said, "Even if she did behave as you said, why didn't you correct her? Fathers are supposed to do that. If she came into your room and stole money from your dresser, you would correct her. You should have told her that was no way to behave, if she really did that."

Six Weeks Later

Prior to the disclosure of the incest, the family had made plans to move to another state. The mother decided to keep that plan despite the crisis. She took her daughters to look for a house. The husband, knowing where she would be staying, went ahead and was there when she arrived. He asked if he could talk with her. He said he was wrong and asked if they could start over again.

The wife listened to him and said she would ask her daughters. She asked if they wanted to be a family again. The victim said, "Yes, but not as before." The father then talked with her and said he was sorry, and would she forgive him, and that he wanted them to be a family again. The mother decided on a three-month trial period with the following conditions imposed on the father:

1. No sexual activity with the daughters.
2. Act like a responsible family member.
3. Stop drinking, smoking, and arguing.

At the same time, the mother instituted regular talking sessions with her daughter twice weekly. She wanted to establish a pattern so her daughter would feel comfortable bringing up her concerns. She emphasized that her daughter keep no secrets about her father's behavior. The mother said emphatically: "This has been such a bad blow. I want to do my best. I want to be sure I have tried everything before making any decision to break up the family." The victim was asked her feelings about the decision, and she said she felt comfortable with the decision. The mother agreed to seek counseling in her new location should some stress become evident. The victim counselor also agreed to stay in contact via long-distance telephone for support as well as evaluation of the plan.

Case Discussion

This case illustrates the disruptive nature of a two-year incest situation. The pressured, and secret sexual situation resulted in the subtle symptoms exhibited by the victim prior to disclosure, as well as the explicit symptoms in all the family members once the event was disclosed. The mother decided immediately not to enter the legal system, but even so, the loyalty issue took six weeks to resolve.

In this case, various pressures helped maintain the nuclear family as a unit. The mother initially was shocked and upset, but clearly loyal to her daughter. But, as the crisis period settled, pressure by the husband and his family succeeded in restoring the nuclear family on a trial basis. The mother and daughter were able to use crisis counseling as a supportive service in terms of sorting out issues and clearly defining the limits in establishing a new family relationship. It was most important that the child was not blamed for the event, that she have clear communication access to her mother, that she realize her mother's loyalty to her, that she be reassured that clear limits would be put on the father's sexual activity with her and that the issue was made explicit to the three involved.

In conclusion, this crisis intervention model is useful for families who wish to preserve the family unit. This model sets limits on the father's behavior; provides a monitor for his behavior; and elicits the wishes of the victim and other family members. It gives families immediate access to crisis counseling and intensive support as they are settling the family loyalty issue and strengthening the protective element for the children. A treatment model useful for families who do enter the legal system is described in Chapter 14.

Unresolved Divided Loyalty and Incest: Clinical Case 2

We have discussed one case where the divided loyalty and incest issue was made explicit and counseling facilitated some settlement of feelings and reactions. In cases where the incest is not disclosed, this psychological process of resolving feelings fails to occur. The emotional issues and feelings continue to be experienced and may intensify into feelings of contempt, hatred and alienation. The second case we wish to present illustrates an unresolved incest situation. The family structure and age relationship was a 10-year-old daughter and 45-year-old natural father. In this case the victim, twenty years later, describes her feelings of divided loyalty at the time of the incest. Her conflict was: Should she be loyal to her father and thus keep the secret to protect him, his professional reputation, and his family? If one reads between the lines of her letter, one has the impression that this young woman chose to keep the secret to avoid disruption of family unity. We see her reexperience the agony of this decision a second time when she learns of her father's pressing for sexual activity with his step-daughter. After she visits with her father and his second family, correspondence begins and it is through the exchange of correspondence they they "disown each other." The father wrote that he had discussed both the problem and his letter with his therapist and his lawyer. In his letter, he announced that he was severing all family ties with her (". . . Do not come out here again; we will neither have you in our home or have anything to do with you.") In an earlier part of the letter the father made the following remarks about his daughter: ("During these years you have become either a great big two-faced hypocrite or you have become so utterly self-centered in your own hateful vicious thoughts as to approach being irrational. All your life, even as a little girl, you have always vastly overdramatized everything that happened to you, fabricating small molehills of happenings into great big emotional mountains having little resemblance to actual events.")

Following are excerpts of the reply from Courtney to her father.[5]

Dear Mark,

Do not feel too badly about telling me not to come visit you again. At my last visit I had already decided not to subject myself to any more visits, and to write you and let you know that; so it turns out we both had the same unpleasant letter to write. We have not come to a parting of the ways now. We came to a parting of the ways when I was 10 years old. . . .

. . . . .

You mention in your letter that you wished I had been put out of the family when I was sixteen. Is that because I was not properly acting the way a daughter should, and if so, does it not follow that someone should have put you out of the house for not acting the way a father properly should (i.e. molesting/raping his own 10 or 11 year old daughter for a year or so)??. . .

. . . . .

Another thing that never occurred to you: did you ever think that at least part of the reason I wanted to get out of the house was because I was very screwed up over having been raped/molested by my very own father? Did you ever realize that part of the problems in my relationship with my mother arose from the conflict I felt over having been sexually compromised by her own husband, my own father, one and the same person? Think a minute. Don't you think that could wreak havoc on the mind and relationships of a young child or adolescent? What moved you, a man nearly 45 years old, to use a child for your adult sexual needs? As your daughter, you were in charge of protecting me, nurturing me, overseeing my development toward adulthood.

Instead I find myself an adult of 31 years old, still trying to come to grips with the devastating effect that has had on my life. It makes me quite bitter to think that that is what you are probably referring to when you write, "All of your life, even as a little girl, you have always vastly overdramatized everything that happened to you fabricating small molehills of happenings into great big emotional mountains having little resemblance to actual events." Is that the veiled message in that sentence? That the molestation/rape by my father when I was 10-11 years old a "small molehill" in my life. . . . The fact that I had to live with my own mother with the hypocrisy and deception that I had to keep a secret about her own husband, and her own daughter, from her—is that a "small molehill" in my life? Is it so impossible for you to admit to yourself that you did something vastly evil, that you have to call it a "small molehill" in my life? How do you know what it is in my life? Can't you admit to yourself or to me that you have done anything wrong in all this? Is the only way for you to cope with it to say that I overdramatize? That I fabricate? Because for 20 years I have never confronted you with it, you allow yourself to decide it is a "small molehill" in my life, that I "fabricate" and "overdramatize." Do you have any idea how insulting that is? How would you feel if mother performed fellatio on my brother when he was 10 years old. . . How would you feel if your mother performed fellatio on you whenever your father left the house? Would that be a "small molehill?" . . .

As I said, about this "little molehill" as you have insultingly belittled the most devastating tragedy that has occurred in my life (and it is my place, not yours, to decide what has been tragic in my life: you don't know because I have never told you, and I have never told you because I have never been close to you, and I have never been close to you because you have wronged me as a 10/11 year old), this "little molehill" of an experience is why I have had too much psychological and sexual difficulty to get married although one day I would like to. I am not doing all this research into rape because I enjoy it. Part of the time my heart pounds and my hands shake and I feel revulsed as I read or listen to a lecture on child sexual assault--but I have been waiting for this problem to "go away" and I finally decided that it wasn't going to just go away, and before my entire adulthood passed away, I had better do something active about it, no matter how unpleasant it is. I can just read your mind now, saying to yourself how I have always dramatized, and that I must be fabricating. Well, I'm not. I know better than anyone else what I have gone through on this. . . .

Let's speak of deceit and hypocrisy. Yes, I have a long history of deceit--since I was a little 10 year old child I had to deceive all the world and my mother, that my father took sexual interest in me and initiated sexual activities with me. Remember how you taught me the art of deceit? First you put me in a situation that had to be kept secret (for your protection) and then you pledged me to secrecy and I remember you telling me not to tell people about these goings on, and especially not to tell mother, because "she wouldn't understand." As a 10 year old child, what was I supposed to do? You are an intelligent man— you figure out the options available to a 10 year old child in that position. What does a child of that age know about society, and about morality, and about deceit, and about handling adult sexual relationships, much less illicit adult relationships. What does a 10 year old child know of those things? Well, first of all, she does not know the facts of life (by the way, you beat mother at telling me about intercourse, she waited till I was 11 years old, but since you had at 10 already showed me, I had to pretend (i.e. deceit, hypocrisy) I didn't know what mother was talking about, I had deceived her with my ignorance about sex, the option was to be honest and tell her that daddy had already showed *me), but even though she does not know the facts of life, she does know that something terribly wrong and terribly bad is going on. As a 10 year old she is still in the process of learning what societal morality is, so everything is not quite clear to her as it would have been to her mother or to another adult, but she does know something terrible and bad is going on and that she is a part of it. So she certainly does already know something about deceit already, she has had to learn about that to survive in the position she is in as best as she can understand it. What does the child of that age know about handling adult sexual relationships? Not a damn thing. Maybe if you had approached her when she was a little older, a little further along in her moral development, maybe if you had approached her after her mother had told her the facts of life at age 11, and after her mother told her she should not let boys (of course never suspecting her adult husband) do those things to her, maybe then she would have known enough about handling adult sexual relationships, much less illicit ones, to have said "no" immediately when her father approached her for sex. But she was only 10 years old, and it took her approximately a year till she was 11, to put an end to her sexual abuse. . . .*

And that brings me to the last point in this long letter. Why did all this arise now? Why is it at this particular point in time, instead of some other time during the last 20 years of the "big secret," that the final breach occurs? Why after years of silence, did I finally choose to confront you with the ugliness of your past, instead of allowing it to lie "at rest" (although as this whole letter has explained, the sordid affair was never at rest in my head, but was ever actively twisting my psycho-sexual development) as it had for so long?

The very obvious answer, of course, which I explained carefully to you . . . was because I had arrived for a visit only to be struck incredulous that my father was making sexual advances toward Jane, his 17-year-old step-daughter . . . Incredulous, but of course I only knew too well how true it had to be. And my response was, and continues to be, that I would and will do whatever necessary to stand between Jane (or any other child or adolescent) and any sexual abuse from you. . . .

And as for your "reputation," I was willing to leave your reputation alone, little as you deserved it, until you threatened Jane. Just remember that, Dad: until you began improper sexual advances toward your step-daughter I left your reputation alone. When you started to harass Jane sexually, then I began to apprise them of what your "reputation" had ought to be. Until then I had continued in the decit and hypocrisy in order to protect you, and your marriage, which was always in my power to destroy. And another thing for you to remember, Dad, I still haven't let the "big secret" out, again out of protection for you. Put yourself in my shoes and imagine things from my position: can you understand how ironic it is being in my position, where I kept my mouth shut *about your sexual abuse* of me *to* protect you *from destruction of one family—your first family—and here I am 20 years later, keeping my* mouth shut *about your sexual abuse* of me *to* protect you *from the destruction of a second family. . .*

The daughter that never was,
Courtney

This case illustrates the dimensions of an unresolved incest and divided loyalty situation. The incest was never revealed to an outside party until years after the victim, herself, was successful in stopping her father's behavior. The young girl, at the time, chose to protect her father and not disclose the incest, thus maintaining the family unity. The victim, as a young adult, sought counseling as a way to gain relief from sequela symptoms of the incest. Twenty years following her own experience with her father, she learns of his incestuous behavior with another family member and she is faced again with a loyalty issue: should she now disclose his behavior; The father takes action to prevent the disclosure of the original incest by severing ties with his daughter. However, the daughter, in agreeing to this, also emphasizes that she will disclose the situation should she hear that her father has not stopped his sexual activity with young people.

One model of intervention in unresolved sexual trauma is victim therapy which is a short-term psychotherapy model. The focus of treatment is for the person to experience the feelings and thoughts about the sexual activity that were initially avoided and not discussed with anyone. During treatment, the person is likely to express feelings more openly, to have more detailed recollections of the sexual activity, to dream more actively of the assault and related life experiences. This process often is complete in 8 to 12 sessions. After successful resolution of the trauma, victims feel increased self esteem, in more control of their life, and may resume less conflictual life patterns.

In summary, this chapter has discussed the concept of divided loyalty as seen in incest cases. The model of intervention in disclosed incest cases may respond well to crisis intervention and crisis counseling. Unresolved cases of incest may respond best to victim therapy.

References

1. Talcott Parsons. "The Professions and Social Structure," *Social Forces* 17 (1939):462.

2. Albert D. Biderman, "Victimology and Victimization Surveys," in *Victimology: A New Focus,* Vol. III, *Crimes, Victims, and Justice,* eds. Israel Drapkin and Emilio Viano (Lexington, Mass.: Lexington Books, D. C. Heath Co.,

1975), p. 155; Regina Davis. "Survival Strategies of Minority Women: The Continuing Struggle against Racial and Sexual Oppression" (Paper presented at the Eastern Sociological Society Annual Meeting, Session sponsored by Minority Sociologists and Sociologists for Women in Society, New York, New York, March 18-20, 1977); Joseph Peters. "The Philadelphia Rape Victim Study," in *Victimology: A New Focus,* Vol. III, *Crimes, Victims, and Justice,* eds. Israel Drapkin and Emilio Viano (Lexington, Mass.: Lexington Books, D. C. Heath Co., 1975), p. 189.

3. Judith Herman and Lisa Hirschman, "Father-Daughter Incest," *Signs: Journal of Women in Culture and Society,* 2 no. 4 (Summer 1977):745–746.

4. Queen's Bench Foundation, *Sexual Abuse of Children* (San Francisco, Calif.), September, 1976, p. 20.

5. We are indebted to Courtney for granting us permission to excerpt sections from a copy of an 11-page letter written to her father.

Part III Services

The sexual assault of children has been recognized as a social problem for some time by law enforcement and child welfare agencies. It is a problem of increasing concern to health service providers and other professionals whose work brings them into contact with victims and families. The subject of child sexual assault raises many questions. How may such incidents be detected? How should they be investigated? What effect will they have on the victims? What should be done to minimize the negative consequences of such assaults on the victims? This part of the book deals with services that can be provided to victims and their families.

Child Sexual Assault: Some Guidelines for Intervention and Assessment

Suzanne M. Sgroi

A frequent response to child sexual assault is "refer it to the experts." Unfortunately, few communities can boast of having a sufficient number of skilled professionals equipped and willing to handle these disturbing cases. At the same time, child sexual assault has become an increasingly visible problem, with more and more cases reported each year.[1]

Who receives these reports? The person who has primary contact with the child victim and his or her family will most often be a teacher, school guidance counselor, social worker, health or child care professional, or perhaps even a police officer or child protective service worker. As yet there is no "specialty" for child sexual assault, no professional discipline that provides comprehensive clinical training to deal effectively with all phases of this complex biopsychosocial phenomenon. Most disciplines fall far short of offering even basic information to guide the professional who finds himself or herself in the role of initial investigator by virtue of being first on the scene, or the person to whom the victim or family has appealed for help. Thus it is sobering for front-line personnel to realize that they are frequently perceived to be "experts" on child sexual assault by the communities they serve.

Obviously, it is neither feasible nor desirable to attempt to train a large cadre of "experts" on child sexual assault. On the other hand, members of the helping professions who deal with children must become more knowledgeable about the basic approach to investigating and assessing these cases. As they learn more about the dynamics involved, front-line professionals can better assist child victims and their families to receive the multiple diagnostic and therapeutic services that may be required. In the end, the informed front-line professional may be the most effective "broker" of such services for families in which sexual assault of a child has occurred.

What are the most important considerations in the basic approach to sexual abuse of children and adolescents?

Frequency

First, the frequency of the problem must be considered. We are now aware that sexual assault of children, especially very young children, is much more common than previously recognized. A number of factors have combined to make cases of child sexual assault more visible.

1. Freer discussion of sexuality in general among lay people and professionals
2. Greater concern about rape victims and the promotion of more "victim-oriented" sexual assault legislation in many states
3. More emphasis on child abuse and neglect, with inclusion of sexual molestation as an entity to be reported under child abuse reporting statutes in many states

As a consequence, the former trickle of cases handled by police and child protective service units, family and children's service agencies, schools and child guidance clinics, and, especially, hospital emergency rooms, is rapidly assuming flood proportions.

Spectrum

With increased reporting, a broader spectrum of child sexual assault is emerging. Until recently, both the professional and lay communities have placed major emphasis on sexual assault of children by outside perpetrators while at the same time deemphasizing the frequency of incest in Western society. Conventional wisdom taught that most child sexual assaults were perpetrated by pedophiles— persons (usually male) with an exclusive preference for prepubertal children as objects of sexual gratification. This is unfortunate because true pedophiles are probably responsible for a small proportion of all sexual abuse of children. However, gross underreporting of intrafamily cases in the past has skewed public opinion toward a belief that most child sexual assault is perpetrated by individuals who are outside the family circle. This is not surprising since the barriers to recognition and reporting of incest are so pervasive and problematic. Nevertheless, a larger number of intrafamily child sexual assaults are being identified each year. A profile of the perpetrator as a man who has sexual contact with children *in addition to* engaging in and maintaining adult heterosexual relationships is now emerging from newer clinical data.[2,3,4] A trend toward a spectrum of child sexual assault encompassing a majority of intrafamily cases perpetrated by heterosexuals who are not pedophiles and a minority of extrafamily cases perpetrated by outsiders, pedophiles, or homosexuals can now be discerned. This emerging picture is viewed with little enthusiasm by those who are already aware that child protection from subsequent assaults is almost invariably easier to achieve in cases involving outside perpetrators and far more difficult in incest cases.

Mechanics

The mechanics of the sexual assault situation, i.e., the type of sexual contact actually involved between adult and child, is one of the least understood aspects of the problem. Within the context of the broader spectrum of child sexual assault just described, the mechanics are less perplexing. Most people imagine that sexual assault of a child by an adult will be a brutal and violent act involving physical trauma to the child by forcible penetration of the vagina, rectum, or mouth. Although this may occur, and occasionally does occur, most often the sexual assault will be nonviolent and without forcible penetration.[5,6] The types of sexual contact may include mutual stroking, fondling, and masturbating behavior by adult and child, in addition to disrobing and inspection and handling of the genitals.[7] Frequently the perpetrator (usually male) will limit himself to penetration of the child's vagina and/or rectum with his fingers instead of attempting penetration of these structures with his penis. Since the child's mouth may well be the largest orifice that can be penetrated, the scenario often includes genital-oral contact (fellatio or cunnilingus). Variations of this behavior include contact between victim's mouth and perpetrator's genitals and vice versa.[8,9] In many cases, the perpetrator may masturbate against the child's abdomen or perineum culminating in an ejaculation against the child's genital or rectal region without any attempt at forcible penetration. The frequent occurrence of vaginal and/or rectal gonorrhea infections in child victims in the absence of trauma or evidence of penetration of vagina or rectum can be explained by this behavior.

Dynamics

To describe most of the foregoing types of sexual contact as "nonviolent" implies a degree of cooperation by the child victim. In other words, the mechanics of the sexual contact between adult and child depend heavily on the dynamics involved. Chapter 5 describes in great detail the usual nonviolent methods used by adults to pressure children into sexual activity over time without disclosing the "secret" of the relationship to others. These include offering material rewards, exploiting the child's traditional societal role of acquiescence to adult demands, and misrepresenting moral standards.[10] Suffice to say that these dynamics certainly play an integral part in most child sexual assault situations that occur over time. There is also evidence to suggest that many pedophiles, unlike sexual offenders against adults, are more likely to be motivated by impulses other than aggression toward their child victims.[11] Thus a nonviolent enlistment of the child victim's cooperation (sex enticement or entrapment) may be more gratifying for the perpetrator. In any case, the total spectrum of child sexual assault encompasses a preponderance of cases where the perpetrator, whether outside the family or intrafamily, utilizes nonviolent methods to enlist the child's mutual cooperation and continued silence, thereby enabling repeated sexual contacts over time. Accordingly, most child victims are the subjects of a continuum of exposure to sexual abuse, usually by the same perpetrator.

Outside Perpetrator

As a general rule, child sexual assault by a perpetrator who is outside the family circle and/or household generates far less emotional trauma for everyone concerned, even though the likelihood of physical trauma to the child resulting from a one-time-only attack is somewhat greater. Even if the child's parents or caretakers have contributed to the situation by an act of omission, such as inadequate supervision or an unfortunate choice of babysitter, there is likely to be less threat to family integrity. It is not uncommon for the outside perpetrator still to be someone who normally has access to the child, e.g., the school bus driver, janitor, or a neighbor. The victim may be male or female, and more than one child may be involved. Practically every phase of the situation is easier for the family and helping professionals to handle. Exceptions to this general rule include examination and interviewing of the child victim and dealing with the child's awareness of sexuality following the incident.

Intrafamily Perpetrator (Nonparent)

This grouping of perpetrators includes family members who occupy nonparental roles in relation to the child victim and nonspousal roles in relation to the child's mother. (Since assault by female relatives is rarely reported, this discussion will be limited to assault by male relatives.) The relatives most often involved are grandfathers, uncles, cousins, and brothers. Older perpetrators are far more likely to be nonviolent and to engage the child in repeated sexual activity over time. Younger perpetrators are more likely to cause physical injury to the child victim and may be less adept at manipulating him or her into a long-term sexual relationship. Victims may be either male or female, and there may be some tendency in the case of an older perpetrator to victimize one child at a time, although multiple children in the family may become targets over time.

Family reaction to child sexual assault by a nonparental family member varies greatly with the identity of the perpetrator and his degree of integration into the family unit. In general, greater family disruption can be expected than when an outside perpetrator is involved because of the complicating effects of relationships, degree of trust, and amount of economic and emotional interdependence between the perpetrator and other family members. The net effect of this increased family disruption can be expected to result in more severe emotional trauma for the child involved.

The situation of sexual contact between siblings is included in this grouping. Although technically classified by law as incestuous, family reactions to sexual contact between siblings are highly variable depending on the relative ages of the children, type of sexual contact involved, and direct consequences. In general, nonviolent sexual contact between young siblings who are approximately the same age is tolerated relatively well by other family members, even (or especially) if the children are of the same sex.[12] Our society tends to regard this type of sexual contact as within the context of "normal" sexual development, particularly when the circumstances suggest that the behavior is of short duration and exploratory in nature. Sexual contact between adolescent siblings or between siblings where there is significant age disparity tends to be regarded with more alarm, especially if trauma, infection, or pregnancy result. The degree of visibility of sexual contact between siblings may also influence the family's response. A relationship that has become visible to outsiders may well precipitate violent response by other family members.

The variant situation where friends of a child's older sibling assault the younger child with or without the participation of the older sibling should also be cited here. This variation may well be reported by the child victim himself or herself. When discovered, parents usually move quickly to curtail such behavior, limit the perpetrator's access to the child, and, frequently, proceed against the perpetrator.

Although usually reluctant to acknowledge an incestuous relationship between siblings, the parents or caretaking adults usually (but not always) will take firm steps to stop the sexual relationship once convinced that indeed it exists. Extreme denial that this type of intrafamily child sexual assault is taking place, despite strong supporting evidence that such activity has occurred, should alert professionals to the possibility of more severe family pathology, possibly even child sexual assault by a parent.

Intrafamily Perpetrator (Parent Figure)

Child sexual assault by a father or father-figure represents perhaps the most difficult diagnostic and therapeutic challenge in clinical practice. Underreporting and failure to identify this situation are so widespread that there is growing conviction among clinicians that a father or a father-figure is, in fact, the most common perpetrator by far. The child victim may be male or female; usually only one child is involved at a time, although multiple children may be victimized over time. In his monograph "Protecting the Child Victim of Sex Crimes Committed by Adults," Dr. Vincent DeFrancis presented a devastating profile of the mother in situations of long-term father-daughter incest that has since been corroborated by others.[13, 14] The mother's role always involves some degree of denial (usually a great deal), and the sexual relationship between father and mother is usually disturbed and frequently nonexistent at the time of the father-child sexual relationship. Sometimes the mother takes an active role in transferring the responsibility of gratifying the father's sexual needs to a child in the family. In case after case, the pattern of the father initiating a sexual relationship with one of his children at the time that the mother is pregnant with the youngest child and continuing child sexual relationships thereafter can be documented. We are beginning only dimly to appreciate the causal role played by alcohol when the perpetrator of child sexual assault is the father or a father-figure.

Similar dynamics occur when the perpetrator is the child's stepfather. However, it has been this author's experience that the father-daughter incest taboo is so great in our society that professionals and lay people within the community tend to view child sexual assault by a stepfather who is not a blood relative with far less alarm and discomfort than when the natural father is the perpetrator. When the perpetrator is the mother's boyfriend, a wide range of responses are possible. On the one hand, the mother may value her relationship with the boyfriend so highly as to deny the situation altogether. On the other hand, the mother's response may be to terminate her relationship with the boyfriend immediately.

In any case, sexual assault by a father-figure, especially of long-term duration, implies a high degree of disturbance for all family roles. It follows that identification and pursuit of the problem will involve a high degree of family disruption. In many cases, the child will have no functioning adult ally in the household. Dealing with the emotional disturbance and family disruption, for the most part formerly thought to be irreversible and incurable, is now being attempted in a few centers with encouraging results. The alternatives of voluntary or forcible separation of perpetrator and victim, sometimes achieved by criminal prosecution and conviction of the perpetrator, are still the only coping methods available in most communities. Few treatment facilities currently exist for convicted perpetrators. At the present time, we are desperately in need of treatment modalities that can treat the family as a unit, instead of focusing solely on the perpetrator or the victim. Such treatment modalities may be enhanced by the capacity to deal both with families where the perpetrator has been convicted of a sexual assault and families in which the perpetrator has not been convicted.

However, this author is not familiar with any successful treatment program for incestuous families where an authoritative incentive for rehabilitation is lacking. In other words, there is little chance that an incestuous father and his family will become engaged in treatment at all unless that treatment is recommended by a law enforcement or child protective services agency or mandated by the court. Recidivism is high for the relatively small number of incestuous families that do become engaged in a treatment program in the absence of such sanctions.[15]

Child's Reaction

A number of variables may operate in determining the child's reaction to a sexual assault situation. The identity of the perpetrator is a key factor. In general, the greater the emotional distance between child and perpetrator, the less emotional trauma can be expected. Thus an outside perpetrator who is a total stranger will probably have less impact than an outside perpetrator who is known to the child. With an intrafamily perpetrator, the degree of emotional impact will probably vary with the closeness of the relationship.

The number of incidents and the length of time over which incidents of sexual assault occurred are also important. In general, a single incident, although disruptive, may be easier for a child to integrate than a series of incidents occurring over time.

Obviously the degree of force or violence used by the perpetrator will be an important determinant of the child's reaction. By the same token, the degree of fear and/or shame invoked in the child by his or her participation will affect how he or she reacts. The more violence, fear, and shame involved, the more emotional trauma to the child can be expected. The degree of gratification and secondary gain for the child as a result of the sexual relationship must also be assessed. In many cases, the sexual relationship may have been a positive one for the child, or at least a neutral experience on balance. Termination of such a special relationship may well result in a sense of loss for the victim, especially if the perpetrator was a relative or even a parent. The child's feelings of grief or loss may be aggravated by temporary or permanent physical separation from the perpetrator. In certain situations, the child may literally never see the perpetrator again. The degree of trauma to the child can be expected to be directly related to the degree of disruption produced by the separation in such cases.

Some children may feel very guilty about their role in such a sexual relationship. An important factor here is the child's age and developmental level, as well as the expressed reaction of parents and "significant others" (e.g., siblings, peers, teachers, etc). The child whose parents react by "blaming the victim" (see the next section) may be made to feel extremely guilty on many levels. In any case, the child can be expected to be acutely sensitive to the expressed reactions of those around her or him and react accordingly.

Misinterpretation of behavioral signs is an extremely common error made by personnel who are trying to determine if sexual assault of a child actually occurred. Children can exhibit the entire gamut of behaviors in response to a sexual assault, ranging from the negative to the positive. Unsophisticated observers may note calm and unconcerned behavior or outright denial of the situation or positive response by the child to the suspected perpetrator (all these behaviors have frequently been observed in child victims where sexual assault has been proved) and mistakenly conclude that no sexual assault could have occurred because of the child's reaction. It is essential that helping professionals who come in contact with these children be knowledgeable about the wide range of possible reactions that may be exhibited. Negative reactions in child victims may include physical symptomatology, sleep and eating disturbances, and school phobias.[16]

Family's Reactions

The reactions of family members when a child has been the victim of sexual assault are similarly affected by many of the same variables that affect the child's reactions, i.e., identity of the perpetrator, number of incidents, length of the sexual relationship over time, and degree of force or violence involved. Depending on the identity of the perpetrator, a gain-loss assessment may come into play for both parents (in the case of an outside perpetrator or family member other than father) or for mother (in the case of a relationship between child and father or boyfriend). In the latter situation, the "gain" of acting in the child's best interests by terminating the sexual relationship, possibly terminating all family contact, with the perpetrator or perhaps bringing criminal charges against the perpetrator are weighed against the possible "loss" that may ensue as a result of any of these actions. In many instances, the potential loss of relationship with the perpetrator or economic loss (when the perpetrator is the father who may be convicted of sexual assault and go to jail) may well outweigh the mother's concern for the child. Family members' perception of "what other people will think" is frequently a related factor. For many adults in our society, sexuality is still such a guilt-ridden topic that fear of the public knowledge of the situation that will almost certainly ensue if the case is investigated by the police and prosecuted is frequently strong enough to deter parents from cooperating with law enforcement officials.

For many families, the need to blame someone for the incident is the primary reaction. The need to affix blame can take the form of blaming the victim (in this case the child), blaming the assailant, or even blaming themselves (usually for failure adequately to protect the child from assault).[17] In all families, the need to deal directly with the child's sexuality following the incident is frequently a painful issue that must be faced.

As mentioned in the preceding section on child's reactions, family members may demonstrate a variety of expressed and unexpressed reactions to child sexual assault. These may include job disruption, physical illness, eating and sleep disturbances, as well as sexual problems between parents.

A potential family reaction that deserves special mention is that of extreme violence. Child sexual assault situations are exceedingly volatile, with the potential for violence directed on the one hand toward both the perpetrator and child (in the case of an outside perpetrator), or toward the mother, affected child, and all family members in the case of incest by father or father-figure. Although difficult to prove, it may be hypothesized that a probable scenario for the sensational family mass murder incidents so frequently reported in the newspapers (usually father shoots his wife and children and then turns the gun on himself) is that previously undiscovered incest by a father is suddenly brought out into the open (and perhaps into consciousness) in a challenging manner. In any event, it is exceedingly dangerous to "set up" confrontation situations where incest by a father is suspected, particularly when the accusation is made by a child involved. Another method frequently used by unsophisticated professionals to assess the validity of a sexual assault complaint by a child is to confront the parent with the child's unsupported accusation to see if the parent reacts in a manner compatible with the investigator's perception of an "innocent" man's response. This method is not only extremely dangerous for the entire family (especially the child who is thereby placed in the role of the accuser) but also is based on the erroneous supposition that direct confrontation by a child's accusation is an effective method of affixing blame or eliciting a confession of wrongdoing from an adult in any type of child maltreatment situation. As David Copperfield and Oliver Twist well knew, it is not. In child sexual assault situations, professionals should always avoid setting up such direct confrontation situations unless they are certain that it will be possible to separate the suspected perpetrator and the target child (preferably the mother and other children as well) immediately thereafter via arrest of the suspected perpetrator or temporary orders of custody for the child or children involved.

Investigative Interviewing of Children

Every community needs to have a few professionals available who are both skilled and experienced in interviewing child victims of sexual assault for investigative purposes. In many cases, especially where the perpetrator is not a parent, investigative and therapeutic interviewing can, in effect, be done simultaneously, so long as the interviewer is prepared to utilize standard crisis intervention theory. This includes observing the child's emotional style, establishing interviewer credibility, developing and then proceeding with the "request concept," and assisting and supporting the child in remembering facts and details that will aid the prosecution to establish a case against the perpetrator.[18] Establishing an alliance with the child and use of media to help the child "open up" and enhance recollection are extremely important. There is evidence to suggest that this process can be extremely helpful in assisting children to integrate and resolve the sexual assault incident as well.

Since it is neither feasible nor desirable for all professionals who deal with children to develop extensive interviewing skills and experience in this area, it would be well to concentrate on developing a few such "specialists" in each community. Such individuals could conceivably originate from a variety of disciplines, e.g., social work, nursing, psychology, medicine, law enforcement, but the need for both specialized training and experience is obvious. They should be professionals, however, adding specialized interviewing skills and experience to a preexisting knowledge base acquired in pursuit of a professional degree. The credibility of the interviewer as an "expert witness" in court, and his or her ability to make recommendations and provide consultation for other practitioners, would thereby be greatly enhanced.

The time and circumstances of the investigative interview should be carefully considered. This type of interviewing takes time and frequently requires multiple contacts. The success achieved may well be influenced by the degree of preparation for the interview and the number of times the child has been interviewed before in addition to the number of blocks intrinsic to the sexual assault situation itself.

Medical Evaluation

Every child has a right to a complete medical examination if sexual assault is suspected.[19] It is difficult to overemphasize the need to check for venereal disease, especially to obtain special cultures for gonorrhea from throat, rectum, urethra, and vagina on male and female children, as well as to check for genital trauma. The mechanics of sexual contact between adult and child, as well as our current gonorrhea epidemic (over one million cases reported in civilians and military personnel in the United States in calendar year 1976) absolutely demand that this be done. The antiquated notion that pharyngeal, rectal, and genital gonorrhea infections in children are acquired by nonsexual contact has also been challenged.[20] It is so absurd to postulate that these gonorrhea infections in children are transmitted via contaminated bathwater, clothing, towels, and bedsheets that, to paraphrase Jane Austen, such theories scarcely deserve the compliment of rational opposition.

The potentially ominous significance of the presence of foreign bodies in a little girl's vagina or, for that matter, in the urethra or rectum of a male or female child, is consistently downplayed by health professionals. This is partially because the public is convinced that placing foreign objects in certain orifices such as the ears or nose (e.g., the refrain of a popular song of the 1950s relates that "our mommy said not to put beans in our ears") is a developmental rite of passage for every child. Be that as it may, it is incumbent upon responsible health professionals always to question *how* a foreign object found its way into a child's body. Insertion of foreign bodies into children by adults has long been a recognized variant of the battered child syndrome. Much greater concern should be aroused when a child manifests a foreign body in the rectum or genitourinary system. It has been the author's experience that these cases are frequently dismissed by the examining physician, who assumes without question that it was the child himself or herself who inserted a pin or a nail or a bottle cap into his or her own urethra, rectum, or vagina. Even repeated examples of this phenomenon in the same child or family tend to be minimized or ignored. Sometimes the children *are* themselves responsible. However, an older child or an adult may well be the perpetrator.

Genitourinary or rectal foreign objects in children should *always* be considered as possible indicators that the affected child has been the victim of sexual assault and evaluated accordingly. The novel *Sybil* and the movie by the same name both contain vivid portrayals of a psychotic mother who tortures her little girl over time by repeatedly using an enema tip to fill her bladder with cold water and by inserting a variety of objects (including a buttonhook) into the child's vagina and rectum. The portrayal is all the more chilling because it is based on a true and fully documented case history.[21] Sybil's childhood physician never questioned how the child got a bead stuck in her nose (the mother had inserted it), and he treated the little girl's recurrent urinary problems without inquiring into their origin. Lack of acceptance by health professionals that this type of sexual abuse of children can and does occur is surely the reason why it is so infrequently recognized and reported. It is thus essential that nonmedical professionals who work with child victims of sexual assault become highly knowledgeable consumers of the health care system on behalf of their clients.

Therapeutic Intervention

The type of therapeutic intervention required for child victims of sexual assault will depend greatly on the character of the multiple variables described in the sections on Child's Reaction and Family's Reaction. In general, the less complicated cases (outside perpetrator, nonviolent assault, short duration) may be expected to show good response with standard crisis intervention techniques aimed at the child and family members, especially if properly modified for the sexual assault situation.[22] Cases of child sexual assault by a family member (other than a parent or parent figure) tend to generate more complex issues that must be resolved by the victim and the rest of the family.[23,24] Such cases, however, are still within the realm of relatively short-term therapeutic intervention.

Incest cases where the perpetrator is the child's father or a father-figure represent, in general, an unexplored area, both investigatively and therapeutically. It is highly unusual for clinicians to be willing or able to confront the key issues of future child protection (both of the acknowledged victim and of other target children) and offender punishment in addition to addressing the complex task of total family rehabilitation. It is certain that therapeutic intervention aimed solely at victim or offender has little chance of achieving the goal of family reintegration. Child victims of incest by a parent-figure must be helped to address issues of achieving more mature psychosexual development and proceeding with normal developmental tasks.[25] Fathers who are perpetrators of incest must receive intervention that will assist them to achieve maturity in a variety of areas (e.g., improved impulse control, greater assumption of responsibility for their own actions, an increased awareness of the effect of their actions on others, more appropriate outlets for anger and frustration, and more effective and appropriate means of achieving gratification). Mothers and other family members must be helped to acknowledge their own contribution toward the incest situation with awareness of the secondary gain to themselves in permitting the behavior to continue. Mothers, in particular, need to confront their own behavior vis-à-vis father (including but not restricted to their sexual relationship).

Given that the father-child incest situation has been discovered, that an authoritative incentive to engage in rehabilitation is present, that an accessible treatment program exists, and that family members express interest in rehabilitating and reuniting the family at a "healthy" psychosexual level of functioning, what are the chances of success?

Although decried as unworkable in the past, there are a few programs for incestuous families that report success. One of these is the Child Sexual Abuse Treatment Program in San Jose, California, directed by Henry Giarretto.[26] (See also Chapter 14.) The San Jose program was initiated under the auspices of the Santa Clara County Department of Juvenile Probation and initially was aimed only at families in which the father had been convicted of child sexual assault. The authoritative incentive to participate is thus intrinsic. Intervention is aimed at offenders, victims, and families.

Irresolution

Last, but not least, professionals who investigate cases of child sexual assault should be forewarned that many cases will not be resolved conclusively. Despite the most vigorous, knowledgeable, and coordinated efforts, the total facts elicited by investigation frequently will neither prove nor disprove the allegation. Accordingly, every professional who is called upon to assist child victims of sexual assault must learn to live with irresolution of many cases. It is unfortunate that the natural human tendency to force closure on any anxiety-ridden issue tends to work against children in such cases. In other words, absence of conclusive proof that sexual abuse has occurred will be eagerly regarded by many investigators as grounds to assert that child sexual abuse did *not* occur. This tendency to force closure shuts many families (and their child victims) out of the helping system.

It might better serve child sexual assault victims to borrow and apply the concept of a "not proved" verdict from the Scottish system of justice. A verdict of "not proved" is brought in by Scottish jurors who believe that the evidence presented by the state does not suffice to establish a verdict of "guilty" or "not guilty." To describe a child sexual abuse case as "not proved" rather than "unfounded" might prevent premature closure by child protective services. It would also tend to put society's responsibility for child protection in "not proved" cases into better perspective.

Summary

Comprehensive evaluation of cases of child sexual assault requires expertise from many professional disciplines. A broader spectrum of child sexual assault

141

is emerging, with a greater number of intrafamily cases perpetrated by individuals who are not pedophiles. The mechanics of sexual contact between children and adults are poorly understood and, for the most part, involve nonviolent interaction. The dynamics of the sexual assault situation are strongly influenced by the identity of the perpetrator and the perpetrator's relationship to the child. Reaction of the child victim and his or her family may be highly variable. Professionals must guard against misinterpreting behavioral signs when trying to determine if child sexual assault has actually occurred. Individuals with specialized skills for investigative and therapeutic interviewing of child victims are needed in each community. Complete medical evaluation of all child victims, including tests for venereal disease and documentation of foreign objects, is essential. Genitourinary or rectal foreign objects in children should always be considered possible indicators that sexual assault has occurred. Gonorrhea infections of the throat, genitals, or rectum in children are also acquired by sexual contact. Intrafamily cases tend to be most disruptive and most difficult to resolve. The success of therapeutic intervention in cases of intrafamily sexual abuse of children is largely dependent on the presence of authoritative incentive to participate in rehabilitative programs. Irresolution of cases for lack of conclusive evidence should be anticipated, and professionals should avoid characterizing unproved cases as unfounded.

References

1. Suzanne M. Sgroi, "Child Sexual Molestation: The Last Frontier in Child Abuse," *Children Today* (May–June 1975):18-21, 44.
2. "Sexual Abuse: Dispelling the Myths," *Child Abuse and Neglect Newsletter,* Children's Hospital National Medical Center, March 1976, p. 3.
3. Henry Giarretto, "Humanistic Treatment of Father-Daughter Incest" in *Child Abuse and Neglect: The Family and the Community,* eds. R. E. Helfer and C. H. Kempe (Michigan State University, Bellanger Publications, 1976).
4. Elva Poznanski and Peter Blos, "Incest," *Medical Aspects of Human Sexuality* (October 1975):46-76.
5. Charles H. McCaghy, "Child Molesting," *Sexual Behavior* (August 1971): 16-24.
6. Leroy G. Schultz, "The Child Sex Victim: Social, Psychological and Legal Perspectives," *Child Welfare* (March 1973):147-157.
7. Arthur C. Jaffe, Lucille Dynneson, and Robert W. ten Bensel, "Sexual Abuse of Children: An Epidemiological Study," *American Journal of Diseases of Children* (1975):689-92.
8. D. W. Swanson, "Adult Sexual Abuse of Children (The Man and Circumstances)," *Diseases of the Nervous System* (1968):677.
9. J. McGeorge, "Sexual Assaults on Children," *Medical Science and Law* (1964):245.

10. Ann Wolbert Burgess and Lynda Lytle Holmstrom, "Sexual Trauma of Children and Adolescents: Pressure, Sex and Secrecy," *Nursing Clinics of North America* (September 1975):551–563.

11. A. Nicholas Groth and Ann W. Burgess, "Motivational Intent in the Sexual Assault of Children," *Criminal Justice and Behavior* (Fall 1977).

12. Poznanski and Blos, "Incest."

13. Vincent DeFrancis, "Protecting the Child Victim of Sex Crimes, Committed by Adults," Children's Division, American Humane Association, Denver, Colorado, 1969.

14. Giarretto, "Father-Daughter Incest."

15. *Ibid.*

16. Ann Wolbert Burgess and Lynda Lytle Holmstrom, *Rape: Victims of Crisis* (Bowie, Md.: Robert J. Brady, 1974).

17. *Ibid.*

18. Ann W. Burgess and Anna T. Laszlo, "When the Prosecutrix is a Child," in *Victims and Society,* ed. E. Viano (Washington, D.C.: Visage Press, 1976).

19. Suzanne M. Sgroi, "Child Sexual Molestation."

20. *Ibid.*

21. Flora R. Schreiber, *Sybil* (New York, Warner Books, 1973).

22. Ann Wolbert Burgess and Lynda Lytle Holmstrom, *Rape: Victims of Crisis,* Chapter 16.

23. Ruth B. Weeks, "Counseling Parents of Sexually Abused Children," *Medical Aspects of Human Sexuality* (August 1976):43–44.

24. Ann W. Burgess, Lynda Lytle Holmstrom, Maureen P. McCausland, "Child Sexual Assault by a Family Member: Decisions Following Disclosure," *Victimology: An International Journal* 2, no. 2 (Fall 1977).

25. Poznanski and Blos, "Incest."

26. Giarretto, "Father-Daughter Incest."

**Comprehensive Examination
for Child Sexual Assault:
Diagnostic, Therapeutic, and
Child Protection Issues**
Suzanne M. Sgroi

Examination for child sexual assault is usually defined in its narrowest sense, i.e., physical examination of the target child for signs of genital trauma. It would be far more effective in most cases to define examination for child sexual assault in the broadest terms. The components for comprehensive examination, as broadly defined, would then include a complete medical evaluation of the target child, interviewing of the target child, medical evaluation and interviewing of siblings (or other children who are similarly situated), interviewing of the caretaking adults, interviewing of the suspected perpetrators, and careful observation of interaction between family members, especially vis-à-vis the target child. No single facility, be it a hospital, child protective services agency, police department, family services agency, or mental health center, is likely to be equipped to perform all these components.

Entry Point

How, then, is it possible to obtain comprehensive examinations for child sexual assault? Clearly, there must be good communication and linkages between the professional staff of the types of agencies cited above. A troubled family with a sexually abused child could come to the attention of, or seek help from, any of these sources. Thus the family's entry point into the helping/investigative services system may be variable. The way in which the situation is initially handled may well determine the eventual outcome of the case. If the agency that receives the complaint or first suspects child sexual assault begins the comprehensive examination effectively, with full awareness of all the components of this process, the changes for a successful outcome are enhanced.

Creative use of the sexually abused child's entry point into the helping/investigative services system is crucial. Professionals must be familiar with their community's resources as well as those of their own agency. Ideally, a community plan that identifies the resources and affixes responsibility for who shall be responsible for what services will be mutually agreed upon by all involved parties. Such plans evolve only when concerned individuals make a commitment to pool their resources in the common cause and set aside competitive and divisive defense of turf. Sexually abused children drop "through the cracks" with frightening frequency in most communities because planning and coordination of services are lacking.

What is meant by creative use of the entry point? Simply stated, no two cases of child sexual abuse are alike. All tend to present significant challenges, because sexual abuse of children is such a highly charged topic. In some cases, a health-identified professional will be able to establish rapport with the parties and obtain the greatest amount of accurate information about the situation. In other cases, a child protective services worker, law enforcement officer, or other helping professional will best be able to fill this role. Individuals who are perceived as threatening by the family may still be able to lay the groundwork for a different type of professional to offer assistance that "feels like help." However, if a family is badly handled or "turned off" at the entry point into the helping/investigative services system, it may be virtually impossible to obtain access thereafter.

Needless to say, the capacity for creative use of the child's entry point depends heavily on the individual's knowledge of the mechanics and dynamics of sexual abuse as well as his or her familiarity with the community's resources to handle the problem. The ideal scenario would feature a professional who was highly knowledgeable about the phenomenon and had already developed relationships with individuals in the other community agencies who have the capacity to perform some or all of the component parts of the comprehensive examination for child sexual assault. The next best situation would involve the child's entry into an agency with well-established conduits and linkages with the other agencies. The least desirable scenario features a professional who approaches child sexual abuse with an attitude of ignorance and denial and is ill-equipped to work cooperatively with others to establish a data base and serve the child. In the absence of a community "superagency" that is equipped to handle all aspects of child sexual assault, comprehensive examinations will occur only where a high level of expertise and cooperation exist among professionals of several different disciplines.

Collection of Evidence

Why bother to do comprehensive examinations for child sexual assault? These examinations usually constitute the only means by which corroborating evidence of sexual abuse can be collected. There is a national trend to eliminate the legal requirement for corroborating evidence of sexual assault against adults. However, it is unrealistic to suppose that the child victim's allegation of sexual abuse by an adult, in the absence of any corroborating evidence, will carry a great deal of weight. This is, of course, especially true for very young children. Accordingly, in most cases, the younger the child, the greater the need to corroborate his or her story

As a basic premise, every case of child sexual assault deserves a comprehensive examination. *Evidence collection should always proceed as if the case will be taken to court.* The existence of carefully documented supporting evidence that child sexual assault did, in fact, take place may constitute the most significant therapeutic leverage in working with a family. This is especially true of intrafamily child sexual assault if a parent or parent-figure is the suspected perpetrator.

The following information, if present, may be used as evidence of child sexual assault:

1. Sperm recovered from the vagina or genital/rectal region of a female child.
2. Pregnancy.
3. Genital or rectal trauma in children of both sexes.
4. Gonorrhea infection of the vagina in female children or the pharynx, urethra, and/or rectum in children of both sexes.
5. Foreign bodies in the vagina of female children or in the urethra or rectum of children of both sexes.
6. Statement of sexual assault by the target child.
7. Corroborating statements of sexual assault by others (these could be other children, including siblings).
8. Confession by the perpetrator.
9. Other physical evidence of trauma that supports the child's statement (e.g., bruises elsewhere on the body if the child described being beaten; marks at the wrists and ankles if the child was allegedly tied up, etc.).
10. Supporting material evidence (e.g., blood or semen stains on clothing).

Items 1 through 5 are weighted according to their strengths as evidence. Items 1 and 2 should be equally weighted; at minimum, they constitute evidence of statutory rape. Sperm in the vagina of a child under the age of 13 years will virtually always cast the child as a victim of sexual assault by a male who has reached the age of puberty. However, the presence of sperm in the vagina of an adolescent child may also be regarded as evidence that the girl is sexually active on her own initiative.

Pregnancy, by the same token, raises the question of possible consenting sexual activity by the victim, even if the child's age classifies the situation as statutory rape. However, it should be remembered that pregnancy can occur in very young female children who have acquired few of the secondary sexual characteristics of puberty. Pregnancy may also occur in young girls who have not yet begun to menstruate in a regular cycle. At the 1976 annual meeting of the American Academy of Pediatrics, an unsubstantiated report was made by a physician attending a seminar on adolescence that 900 eleven-year-old girls had become mothers in Chicago in 1975! If this information is correct, it is a powerful indicator of the frequency with which 10- and 11-year-old girls are having sexual contact. Most thoughtful observers would agree that children aged 10 and 11 years must be regarded as the victims of sexual assault, regardless of the circumstances under which they were impregnated!

Item 3, genital or rectal trauma in children of both sexes, may constitute compelling evidence of child sexual assault if it is present. Since most cases of child sexual assault are nonviolent and are not characterized by forcible penetration, the chances of obtaining evidence of genital/rectal trauma are relatively small. However, this type of evidence should be identified and documented whenever possible.

Item 4, gonorrhea infection of the vagina, pharynx, urethra, and/or rectum, is a frequently overlooked indicator that a child has been sexually assaulted.[1] Contrary to popular opinion, children do not acquire gonorrhea from inanimate objects such as toilet seats, bathwater, or bedsheets. Children *do* acquire gonorrhea from direct, rubbing, mucous membrane to mucous membrane contact with another individual who is already infected. The bacteria that cause these infections (*Neisseria gonorrhoeae*) are extremely fragile and live only within the human body. They do not survive heat, cold, or desiccation and cannot live free in nature or within other animal hosts. It is thus impossible to grow *Neisseria gonorrhoeae* except under carefully controlled laboratory conditions.

Consideration of the usual mechanics of child sexual assault (as described in Chapter 8) in relation to the infection site will assist in reconstructing the type of sexual contact most likely encountered by the child. For example, a child of either sex who has a gonorrhea infection of the pharynx has undoubtedly been subjected to fellatio (i.e., contact between the child's mouth and throat and the perpetrator's penis) by a male with a gonococcal infection of the urethra. A male child with a gonorrhea infection of the rectum has been subjected to sodomy (i.e., contact between the child's rectal opening and the perpetrator's penis) by an infected male with gonococcal urethritis. A female child with a gonorrhea infection of the rectum may have been subjected to sodomy or may have acquired the rectal infection at the same time she acquired a concurrent vulvo-vaginal infection. If the sexual contact involved rubbing of the perpetrator's genitals against the child's genital/rectal area with subsequent ejaculation by the perpetrator against the same region, infection of the urethra, vagina, or rectum could occur.

In 1965 Branch and Paxton reported on a combined interview and examination study of 180 consecutive cases of gonorrhea in children 0 to 14 years of age.[2] Their data constitute the most significant and compelling evidence yet reported that childhood gonorrhea is an indicator of sexual assault. Of 180 cases, 19 were limited to gonorrhea infection of the eyes, appearing in neonates and in children up to 11 months of age. All these eye infections, after careful interviewing, were believed to have been transmitted by nonsexual contamination to the victims, either via the birth canal or by finger-eye contact. Of 20 cases of genital gonorrhea infection in children aged 1 to 4 years, a history of adult-child sexual contact was obtained in 19 of the 20! In the 5- to 9-year age group, a history of adult-child sexual contact was obtained in 100 percent of the 25 cases studied! In the 10- to 14-year age group, all 116 infected children gave a history of sexual contact. Thus genital gonorrhea accounted for 161 of 180 cases studied in children, with 160 of 161 cases involving acknowledged sexual contact with the child victims.

Reporting cases of venereal disease in children to the health department is a statutory requirement in every state. In Connecticut, health professionals are also required to report cases of venereal disease in children under 13 years of age to child protective services as well.[3] In this way, a family investigation for sexual abuse is conected in addition to the health department's effort to treat and prevent communicable disease. Otherwise, this important source of sexual abuse referrals tends to be overlooked.

Item 5, the presence of foreign bodies in the vagina, urethra, or rectum, is another frequently overlooked indicator of child sexual assault. Misconceptions about the dynamics underlying this phenomenon (as described in Chapter 8) account for reluctance to identify and document these foreign bodies and present them as evidence. Although not weighted as heavily as the first four items, foreign bodies in the urethra, vagina, and/or rectum of a child should always be regarded as having been introduced by someone other than the child victim *unless proven otherwise.* Their presence may, in conjunction with other evidence, strengthen the case for child sexual assault.

All the types of evidence listed in items 1 through 5 must be gathered via medical examination. Item 6, statement of sexual assault by the target child, may also be elicited during the medical examination. It may, in fact, facilitate the evidence-collection process to combine investigative and therapeutic interviewing of the child victim with the medical examination process. Especially in incest cases, parents may find the hospital or medical setting less threatening for the interviewing process. Item 7, corroborating statements of sexual assault by others (including siblings), may also be elicited as part of the medical examination. Needless to say, more information is likely to be elicited if the total examination process is spread over several appointments so that family members have more time to develop rapport with the examiner(s). However, investigative interviewing of all parties can also be done separate from the medical examination. The sequence and setting of investigative interviewing in relation to the medical examination most often depends on the child's entry point into the helping/investigative services system. The key, once again, is for professionals to have enough flexibility and knowledge of the total investigative process to be able to manipulate its components skillfully with the goal of obtaining the greatest amount of information with the least trauma to participants.

Item 8, confession by the perpetrator, is most likely to be obtained via police investigation. Although unpredictable, confession sometimes may be forthcoming if the perpetrator is confronted by a well-documented array of evidence that supports the allegation of child sexual assault. The following case example is illustrative.

Clinical Case 1

Sharon, the fifth child in a family of eight children, first was enticed into sexual contact with her father when she was 7 years old. Her mother was pregnant with Sharon's youngest sister at the time of the first contact. Sharon enjoyed her special relationship with her father over the next eight years. Her mother, age 32 when Sharon's youngest sister was born, did not become pregnant again, although she did not practice birth control. Sharon's sexual relationship with her father progressed from fondling and fellatio to full vaginal intercourse. The father kept close track of her menstrual periods, according to Sharon, and was careful to time their sexual relations so that she would not become pregnant.

When she reached age 15 years, Sharon joined a fundamentalist religious group and became convinced that her sexual relationship with her father was sinful. She began to evade him, and he responded by pressuring her more and more heavily to resume sexual contact. In desperation, shortly after her sixteenth birthday, she appealed to two women in her religious group for help. They helped her to go to the police and swear out a statement. One of the women offered Sharon a home with her own family. When Sharon's father was arrested and confronted with his daughter's statement, he waived his right to legal counsel and made a full confession, acknowledging the truth of the allegations. Sharon's parents voluntarily permitted her to live in the friend's home thereafter. After six months in the new placement, she was doing well and her grades had improved dramatically.

Several aspects of this case example are noteworthy. First, Sharon's mother was probably fully aware of her husband's sexual relationship with their daughter. Second, the girl derived sufficient support from her religious group to complain effectively to the police. Third, Sharon was old enough to decide to leave her parents' home and accept an alternative placement with someone who made her feel secure and wanted. Fourth, Sharon's father was not confronted by her allegation of sexual assault until after the police had obtained a warrant for his arrest and the girl already had a safe place to stay. All these circumstances combined to make Sharon's position relatively safe regarding violent retribution by the perpetrator, in this case, her father.

However, it is highly unsafe to place a child in the position of being the unsupported accuser of a parent or parent-figure. The chances of obtaining a confession under these circumstances are very small. Instead the child may be endangered to a far greater degree by focusing attention on a situation that the perpetrator will almost surely deny and then leaving the child in the custody of the suspected perpetrator. Avoiding confrontation on this level is nearly always desirable (see Chapter 8).

Item 9, other physical evidence of trauma that supports the allegation, should, of course, be noted and documented in the medical examination. However, this evidence, if present, could and should be documented by color photographs. The photographs could be taken by police or child protective services investigators either within the hospital setting or outside it.

Item 10, supporting material evidence, is most appropriately collected by the police. Here again, however, the cooperation of medical professionals may be crucial in encouraging the child's caretakers to retain items such as blood- or semen-stained clothing and turn them over to the police.

Access to the Child Victim

Obtaining access to the child victim for investigative and examination purposes can be difficult. When the child victim has at least one parent who can function as an adult ally, there is usually no difficulty in obtaining access to the child and permission for examination. In cases of sexual assault by outside perpetrators, the parents' or caretakers' cooperation is virtually assured. Although most cases of intrafamily child sexual assault raises a divided loyalty issue among family members, it is nevertheless usually possible to obtain access to the child victim if the perpetrator is not a parent or parent-figure. However, in the case of incest by a parent or parent-figure, access to the child may be extremely difficult to obtain. This is especially true of situations that are brought to attention by history furnished by a preadolescent child victim. When such children present to school officials, day care personnel, child protective service workers, or health professionals, a knotty management problem can ensue. For example, the helping professional may be confronted by a child victim who begs him or her not to contact the parents. School authorities may be unwilling to permit law enforcement or protective services investigators to interview the child without parental consent. Likewise, hospital and health professionals will be reluctant to perform physical examinations on children without parental consent unless an immediately life-threatening situation exists.

Several alternatives exist for obtaining access to child victims in order to perform comprehensive examinations for sexual assault. First, it is sometimes possible to obtain voluntary consent from at least one caretaking adult. Second, the court of appropriate jurisdiction may be petitioned for a temporary order of custody of the child victim, thereby enabling the state to give consent for examination. Lastly, nearly every state in the United States has a statute that permits minors to give their own consent for examination and treatment for venereal disease. For example, Connecticut's Public Health Code prohibits health and medical care facilities from notifying parents while permitting minors to give their own consent for examination and treatment for venereal disease.[4]

Such statutes may enable a comprehensive examination for sexual assault to be performed without prior parental consent on the grounds that a child at risk for sexual assault is also at high risk for being infected with a venereal disease. Ideally, there should also be direct statutory authority for minors to give their own consent for comprehensive examination for sexual assault without prior parental permission.

Methodology for Medical Examination

Whenever possible, the medical examiner should be an attending physician who is capable of (and willing to) give evidence in court, if necessary. A physician who is skeptical about the phenomenon of child sexual assault will be unlikely to perform a complete medical examination. Accordingly, the services of a knowledgeable and sympathetic physician should be sought.

Genital examinations should be performed in the context of a complete physical examination. A complete medical history should be elicited and recorded, as well as a full account of the alleged sexual assault incident(s). There should be careful attention to, and documentation of, any signs of physical abuse or neglect. Children under 5 years of age should have a concomitant "battered child workup," including skeletal survey for previously healed fractures, if there are any signs of external physical trauma present. In addition, developmental examination should be done on children under 5 years of age on whom sexual abuse is suspected.

Genital examination should include careful inspection of the perineum. Any signs of trauma should be carefully recorded. The condition of the hymenal ring and the diameter of the hymenal opening should be noted and recorded. Examiners should avoid reporting "hymen intact" since this terminology often mistakenly conveys the impression that no hymenal opening (imperforate hymen) is present. The diameter of the vaginal opening (introitus) should also be recorded.

If genital trauma and evidence of forcible penetration of the vagina or rectum are present, the child should be admitted to the hospital for a complete pelvic examination. If no external genital trauma is present, the examination can be done on an outpatient basis. A speculum examination is indicated if the hymenal opening will permit the insertion of a pediatric speculum. An aspirate or swab of vaginal secretions should be examined for the presence of sperm.

Every child in whom sexual assault is suspected should have pharyngeal, urethral, vaginal, and rectal cultures obtained for gonorrhea regardless of the mechanics of sexual contact already elicited by the history. Since *Neisseria gonorrhoeae* requires meticulous technique in culturing specimens in order to recover the organisms, it is best to plate out cultures on specific media (Thayer-Martin or Transgrow) immediately and incubate at 37°C under carbon dioxide. The use of transport medium, with its inherent drawbacks of elapsed time prior to plating onto specific media and incubating in a carbon-dioxide-rich environment, is discouraged. A swab of the posterior pharynx and tonsils will obtain adequate material for pharyngeal culture. Likewise, a swab of the vulvo-vaginal secretions will obtain adequate material for vaginal culture. Direct confirmatory culture of urethral discharge should be obtained in male children who have urethral discharge present in addition to gram stain or a urethral smear. A urine culture for gonorrhea may also be obtained. Contrary to the "clean-catch" urine technique, there should be no prior cleansing of the urethra and perineum with soap, water, or disinfectant. Instead, the first 5 to 10 drops of a "dirty" urine specimen should be collected by an alert and knowledgeable assistant and immediately plated onto specific culture media and incubated. This technique enables one to collect urine from the urethra and yields a high rate of positive cultures in patients with gonococcal urethritis. If a larger amount of urine is collected by an unsupervised patient, the specimen will be useless unless it is centrifuged immediately and the sediment plated for culture.

Rectal cultures for gonorrhea should be obtained by inserting a moistened swab into the anus to a depth of 1.5 centimeters. Since gonococci inhabit the anal crypts, the swab should be rotated sideways in a gentle fashion and retained within the rectal orifice for 15 to 20 seconds. If gross fecal contamination of the swab is noted upon withdrawal, the swab should be discarded and another specimen obtained. Again, direct plating of the specimen onto specific media followed by immediate incubation in a carbon-dioxide-rich environment is essential for recovery of gonococci.

Medical examiners should bear in mind that gonococcal infections of pharynx, urethra, vagina, and rectum may be entirely asymptomatic and frequently are not accompanied by physical signs. Accordingly, cultures for gonorrhea should be obtained from all potential receptor sites regardless of symptom history or physical appearance.

If a definite history of contact with an individual who is known to have gonorrhea is obtained, the child should receive epidemiologic treatment for gonorrhea as soon as cultures from all sites are obtained, without waiting for laboratory results. Likewise, a culture that grows out gonococci is an indication for immediate treatment. The same dosage of antibiotics is recommended for epidemiologic treatment as is recommended for treatment of documented gonococcal infection, that is:

Aqueous procaine penicillin G, 100,000 units/kg by intramuscular injection (use divided doses) accompanied by probenecid, 25 mg/kg by mouth, or

Erythromycin, 40 mg/kg/day in four divided doses for seven days (for penicillin-allergic patients under 6 years of age), or

Tetracycline, 25 mg/kg as a loading dose followed by 60 mg/kg/day in four divided doses for seven days (for penicillin-allergic patients older than six years).[5]

The advantage of treatment with the intramuscular penicillin-probenecid regimen is that of single-dose therapy with a regimen that has proved to be effective in eradicating incubating syphilis. The disadvantage to this regimen is obvious: it is painful and likely to complicate future examinations.

Another effective single-dose treatment regimen has recently been recommended for use in children, namely, amoxicillin, 50 mg/kg by mouth, accompanied by probenecid, 25 mg/kg by mouth.[6]

The amoxicillin-suspension-probenecid regimen has the obvious advantage of being nontraumatic for the child. Its use should facilitate maintaining rapport with children who will require repeated examinations.

Some examiners may opt for prophylactic treatment for all children who are alleged victims of sexual assault. This course of action eliminates the necessity to perform a repeat examination and cultures for gonorrhea in four weeks if no prophylactic treatment was given. Uncomplicated gonorrhea infections can be treated on an outpatient basis as described above. Gonococcal ophthalmia and/or infections complicated by peritonitis or arthritis require hospitalization and treatment with intravenous antibiotics.

In addition to obtaining cultures from all sites for gonorrhea, a serologic test for syphilis should be performed in all children who are alleged to be victims of sexual assault. Since the incubation period for syphilis is 10 to 90 days, repeat serology at one month intervals, for three determinations should be performed unless prophylactic treatment is given.

The entire genital examination can be performed and all cultures obtained in less than 1 minute by a knowledgeable examiner if there is no physical trauma present. Cooperation by the child is, of course, very important. It is unconscionable to force a genital examination on a frightened, struggling child. Most of the time required to perform these examinations, therefore, will be expended in establishing rapport and gaining the child's confidence. My experience has been that this prior time investment is well worth the effort and usually successful. If the child refuses to be examined, a process of negotiation and bargaining sometimes results in acquiescence. Sedation or deferral of the examination to another visit are other alternatives, depending on the circumstances. Occasionally, none of these alternatives can be utilized successfully; these cases will require admission of the child to the hospital for examination under anesthesia.

Methodology for Investigative Interviewing

Chapter 11 is entirely devoted to techniques for interviewing child victims. In this context, it is appropriate to mention the need to avoid putting the child in the position of directly contradicting the caretaking adult's history of what transpired. It is therefore best to obtain history from adults separately, or at least separate from the children involved.

Careful observation of family interaction is nevertheless very important. A common misconception is to assume that a child victim of incest will behave negatively toward the suspected perpetrator. Observers should recall that disruption can be manifested by many different behavior patterns, depending on the circumstances of the sexual assault situation. The experience may have been a positive one for the child. If there has been temporary separation from the perpetrator, a child victim of incest may have experienced a sense of loss and abandonment. Accordingly, reunification with the perpetrator may well be a very happy event for the child victim. Eagerly affectionate interaction between the child victim and a suspected perpetrator should not be interpreted as evidence that sexual contact did not occur between them.

When interviewing children, always attempt to do the interviewing with the child alone. This is of extreme importance in incest cases. A high degree of bias can be expected if investigative interviewing of the child is done with a parent or parent-figure present.

An outline for comprehensive examination for child sexual assault may be summarized as follows.

Comprehensive Examination for Child Sexual Assault

I. *General Approach to Problem*
   A. *Keep An Open Mind.* "Recognition of sexual molestation in a child is entirely dependent on the individual's inherent willingness to entertain the possibility that the condition may exist."[7]
   B. *Keep Cool.* Sexual molestation of children is such an emotion-laden topic for most people that objectivity requires much effort and self-discipline. Nevertheless it is almost impossible to protect or help the child victim in the absence of a calm and professional approach.
   C. *Keep Awake.* Be aware that situations of child sexual assault are the most volatile and potentially dangerous of all social problems from the usual perspective of the family and community. Even as *you* are remaining calm and objective, remember the potential for violent reaction on the part of other participants.
II. *Approaches Toward Investigation*
   A. *Medical Examination.* This is essential in all cases regardless of the date of assault. If properly performed, this can usually be done with the child's cooperation on an outpatient basis. Hospital admission is rarely necessary unless severe physical trauma is involved or unless a temporary hospitalization will facilitate child protection.
      1. *The medical examiner* should be a physician who is:
         a. Knowledgeable about what is required.
         b. A credible witness in court (preferably an attending physician

or a physician in private practice rather than an intern or even a resident physician).

  c. Unafraid to participate (many physicians are unsure of their own competence in this area and are reluctant to become involved).

 2. *The medical examination* should include:

  a. A good overall medical history.

  b. Identification of all trauma, with emphasis on genital, rectal, and oral trauma.

  c. Careful description of genital anatomy, regardless of presence of trauma (e.g., condition of the hymenal ring and size of the vaginal opening in small children).

  d. Tests for presence of sperm in the vagina in female children and venereal disease in children of both sexes, including a blood test for syphilis and cultures for gonorrhea from the throat, urethra, urine, vagina, and rectum.

  e. Documentation of genitourinary or rectal foreign objects.

  f. A pregnancy test for adolescent girls.

 3. *The context* should be that of an overall general physical examination. If necessary, be prepared to make the examining physician aware of the need to do a complete physical examination in order to:

  a. Identify other physical signs of child abuse or neglect.

  b. Deemphasize the psychological impact of the genital examination upon the child.

B. *Interviewing for Facts.* This may precede the medical examination or else be initiated as part of the medical examination.

 1. *Circumstances of the Interview:*

  a. Try to interview the child alone.

  b. Try to obtain the child's version of what happened independent of the parents', caretakers', or suspected perpetrator's version. Especially try to avoid having the child present during the adult's description of what transpired.

 2. *Approach to the Child:*

  a. Try to convey a relaxed, unhurried attitude throughout. If you are anxious, uncomfortable, hurried, or ill at ease, the child will quickly pick this up and be affected accordingly.

  b. Establish a relationship with the child prior to discussing the alleged sexual assault. Avoid "zeroing-in" on the topic of the assault prior to establishing a relationship.

  c. Identify and establish the child's level of understanding of human anatomy. Find out what terminology he or she uses to identify organs and functions. Be prepared to use the child's own terminology if he or she is too young to use appropriate terms. If necessary use diagrams, pictures, or dolls to illustrate or act out what may have occurred.

    d. Don't dwell too heavily on the identity of the alleged perpetrator. Avoid a "whodunit" approach.

    e. Avoid being judgmental about information supplied by the victim. Don't presuppose the experience was bad or painful for the child—it may have been neutral or even pleasurable. Avoid projecting your own feelings or perceptions about the situation onto the victim.

    f. Don't presuppose guilt or anger in the child victim—neither may be present. Again, avoid projecting your own reactions upon the child.

C. *Interviewing for Therapeutic Purposes*

  1. *Child self-expression:* Encourage the child to talk, bearing in mind that family members may discourage children from verbalizing their reactions. Use of media (pictures, dolls, or puppets) may also assist a child to express reactions.

  2. *Child reassurance:* Be prepared to reassure the child about:

    a. Possible physical damage to himself or herself.

    b. Potential consequences to child because of his or her own role in the incident (children are likely to be fearful of punishment).

    c. Feelings of shame or guilt—these should be anticipated in *all* child victims, regardless of the degree of their cooperation with the sexual offender.

  3. *Parent reassurance:* Be prepared to reassure parents about potential consequences of the assault for the child.

  4. *Parent participation:* Enlist parents' aid in encouraging the child to express and "work through" reactions to the incident at home.

III. *Approach toward Child Protection*

A. *Reporting.* Be prepared to report *all* cases of child sexual assault to:

  1. Child protective services.

  2. The Sex Crimes Analysis Unit (even if the facts of the case do not warrant or permit prosecution, a report should be made for statistical purposes if such an investigative and research unit exists).

B. *Avoiding Confrontation.* Avoid confrontation between the child victim and the alleged perpetrator whenever the alleged perpetrator is a family member. *Never* confront the alleged perpetrator with the child's own accusation against him or her in an intrafamily situation *unless* you are certain that the child or alleged perpetrator *can* and *will* be removed from the home. To permit or initiate this type of confrontation in the absence of an effective plan to protect the child from possible retribution by the perpetrator is to risk serious bodily injury or even death of the victim.

C. *Offender-Child Relationship.* Don't presuppose that the relationship between the child and perpetrator following the alleged incident will be negative if sexual assault actually occurred. On the contrary, a warm, affectionate, and loving relationship may exist and continue between the child and an incestuous parent. Observable evidence of spontaneous, fearless, and affectionate behavior between the child and alleged perpetrator neither supports nor disproves the allegation of sexual assault and should not be cited or treated as such.

D. *Sex Bias Concerning Targets.* Because females are traditionally regarded as the most common targets of sexual assault, it is easy to harbor a built-in bias that the only *child* victims of sexual assault are little girls. Do not overlook the very real possibility that little boys may be targets of sexual assault as well in both intrafamily and extrafamily situations. All too often attention is focused on female children in a situation where male children are equally or perhaps at greater risk, depending on the circumstances. Whenever child sexual assault is being investigated, both male and female children should be considered possible targets and interviewed and examined accordingly.

E. *Continuum of Exposure.* In general, the incident of intrafamily child sexual assault that comes to community or professional attention is rarely the first incident that has occurred within the family. Be aware that the incest phenomenon usually proves to be a continuum of exposure to sexual contact experienced by the child victim over a long period of time. A continuum of exposure should therefore be presupposed by the investigator unless specifically proved otherwise and investigation and examinations proceed accordingly, regardless of how long ago the alleged incident is said to have occurred.

F. *Irresolution.* Every professional who is called upon to assist child victims of sexual assault must learn to live with irresolution of many cases. Frequently the total facts elicited by investigation will neither support nor disprove the allegation. Do not automatically regard all *unproved* cases as unfounded. Child victims of unproved cases are often more needy of professional support and assistance than are proved victims of child sexual assault.

References

1. Suzanne M. Sgroi, " 'Kids with Clap': Gonorrhea as an Indicator of Child Sexual Assault," *Victimology: An International Journal,* 2, no. 2 (Fall 1977).

2. Geraldine Branch and Ruth Paxton, "A Study of Gonococcal Infections among Infants and Children," *Public Health Reports* 80 (1965):347–352.

3. State of Connecticut, *General Statutes*, Section 19-89a, as amended by P. A. No. 73-205.

4. *Ibid.*

5. Center for Disease Control, Department of Health, Education and Welfare, *Recommended Treatment Schedules for Gonorrhea*, 1974.

6. John D. Nelson, Edgar Mohs, Adnan S. Dajani, and Stanley Plotkin, "Gonorrhea in Preschool and School-Aged Children," *Journal of the American Medical Association* 236 (1976):1359–1364.

7. Suzanne M. Sgroi, "Sexual Molestation of Children: The Last Frontier in Child Abuse," *Children Today* 4 (1975):18–21.

10 Police Investigation in Child Sexual Assault
Mary L. Keefe

During the first six months of 1977, as team leader of the Rape and Its Victims Workshop sponsored by the Law Enforcement Assistance Administration (LEAA), I traveled to the 10 federal regions in the United States delivering workshops based on the Rape and Its Victims Prescriptive Package.[1] The major thrust of the workshop was that coordinated services would lead to a more effective and efficient delivery of them and, ultimately, to more arrests and convictions of those charged. During the workshop, many participants expressed concern about child sexual assault and were interested in learning about any new programs or practices being developed. Concern about child sexual assault has just recently come to the forefront. Some programs are underway, but it is too soon to make a judgement as to their success. However, it is evident with these programs, as with the programs involving adult victims, that coordination of the services concerned with the child victim will lead to more arrests and a higher conviction rate for child victimizers.

Incidence Statistics

A major effort is underway by law enforcement and criminal justice staff to compile statistics on the incidence of sexual assault.[2-7] During 1975, in New York City, there was a total of 5068 sex crimes reported.[7] Of these, 27.2 percent were victims under 14 years of age; 20.8 percent were females; and 6.4 percent were males. Although fewer males reported sexual assault than females, there was an increase of males reporting to 9 percent in 1975, as compared to 7.6 percent in 1974. Police should be aware that more young boys are being raped and that, for them, it may be as traumatizing an event as it may be for a female victim.

Sex crimes laws differ from state to state which makes it difficult to obtain a uniform picture of the amount of sexual assault of children. For example, in New York there are several crimes in the sex offense category.[3] There are three degrees of rape, sodomy, and sexual abuse or nine counts in all. Seven of these nine charges are felonies while sexual abuse and second and third degree charges are misdemeanors. There is also a sexual misconduct section that is a misdemeanor. Rape relates to sexual intercourse; sodomy relates to deviate sexual intercourse; and sexual abuse relates to sexual contact such as touching the genitals. Sexual misconduct includes both sexual intercourse and deviate sexual intercourse. It is a catchall term for the charges not included in the sexual offense category. Incest is not in the sexual offense category but is contained in the section of the Penal Law of "offenses affecting marital relationships." It is also a felony and is defined as an act of marrying or engaging in "sexual intercourse with a person whom he knows to be related to him either legitimately or illegitimately as an ancestor, descendant, brother or sister or either the whole or the half blood, uncle, aunt, nephew, or niece."[3]

Table 10-1 represents a breakdown of the 1975 New York City report for crimes committed on children under age fifteen.[7] These figures represent only those crimes in the first degree category (rape, sodomy, and sexual abuse). Eight crimes including incest are not included.

The Polk County, Iowa, Rape/Sexual Assault Care Center's figures for the time period from October 1974 to October 1976 revealed that 14.8 percent of the victims they assisted were below the age of 15.[8] A report from Montgomery County, Maryland,[9] indicates that about 40 percent of the victims of forcible rape in 1974 were minors, but there was no percentage given by age group for those below the age of 15.

Until recently, few cases had gone to trial.[10, 11, 12] In those cases which reached the trial level, the children had difficulty testifying and undergoing cross-examination. Children are easily confused by the courtroom procedures and atmosphere.[13]

Because so few cases go to trial, many people are not aware of the magnitude of the problem. But now that more cases are being reported, more cases will go to trial. The records in child sexual assault cases admittedly are very sparse because of the way the crime is reported and recorded. And some of these crimes are not reported to the police department but to another agency, such as Social Services or a Child Abuse Center. If reported to the police department, the complaint might be filed with the juvenile division and not become part of the statistics. If reported to the patrol division, the crime might be recorded as incest, a family court case, or rape. If recorded as a rape, it might be included in the Federal Bureau of Investigation's Crime Reports.

Some cases reported to the police may be marked unfounded after an investigation. Unfounded cases are, by FBI standards, those cases that have been investigated and the investigating officer finds no evidence to indicate a crime has been committed.[6]

Table 10-1
Breakdown of 1975 New York City Sex Crime Figures for Young People Under Age 15

Group	Frequency	Percent of all Victims, This Age Group	Percent Female Victims	Percent Male Victims
1–4	74	1.4	1.1	.3
5–9	422	8.5	5.9	2.6
10–14	852	17.3	13.8	3.5

There also may be bias and subjectivity involved in dealing with sex crime cases. For example, at a regional conference, one prosecutor described an incest case involving a mother's boy friend and the mother's 12-year-old daughter. The prosecutor reported that the mother was in the process of terminating the relationship and that the defense lawyer cross examined the mother on the issue of revenge—that is, implying that this was the motive for making the complaint of incest. The prosecutor continued to summarize his opinion at the conference on such cases stating, "incest cases are garbage." His subjective attitude and analysis of the case focused completely on the adults' relationship and failed to understand the impact this entire situation might have on the 12-year-old girl, and on the fact that a crime had been committed regardless of the mother's relationship with the assailant.

Notwithstanding the method of reporting, we see enough in the statistics to cause alarm. We have looked at the statistics of New York City, Polk County in Iowa, and in Montgomery County in Maryland.[7, 8, 9] In a study done in Brooklyn, New York, the average amount of cases reported to the authorities was 1113. This figure includes misdemeanors as well as felonies. Using this figure as a base, the report says that we could estimate a total of 3068 cases for the five counties in New York City. And these are the figures for just one city. If we projected this figure for the whole nation, we see the problem in its true proportions, and so far, we have not even tapped the unreported cases. The number of reported cases is enough to concern us. We want to make sure that the way we handle the reported cases will encourage more reports.

It is evident from these statistics that the child sexual assault problem is not new. Unfortunately, there are too few programs that address it. The public has not really recognized it as a problem, nor have the police. There are many unreported sex crimes involving children, but little has been done to encourage the reporting of these crimes. Although there are still few avenues to assist or protect the child who reports, some communities are exploring the issue.[14, 15]

For many years, the solution to an incestuous situation was to remove the child from the home. In some communities, this is no longer done. The family is provided with family counseling and allowed to remain together. Preliminary reports indicate that the problem can be corrected by this type of therapy. But much more has to be done to alleviate this condition.

All agencies have to recognize their own responsibilities. They should inform others in the field of their capabilities, to avoid role conflict. Once we understand what services each agency can offer, we can detect gaps in those services and attempt to fill them. The goal is the physical and mental well-being of the child and not buck-passing to other agencies of jobs we do not want to do ourselves.

Since child sexual assault is being reported in greater numbers, police must look at their procedures for processing these cases in order to maximize the performance of the individual officer. More people are concerned about the outcome of these cases and, in particular, with the methods police use in the handling of them. Judianne Densen-Gerber of Odyssey House considers children the hope of tomorrow, provided they are given the opportunity to grow up "straight and strong." Odyssey House has been able to attribute some cases of drug addiction to sexual abuse committed against the child while living at home. One such story was reported in the New York press. It read that a woman had been sexually abused by her father when she was 5 years old. He continued this sexual abuse until she ran away from home at the age of 13. (According to Densen-Gerber, many runaways are this age, and they leave for the same reason.)[17] This runaway was so damaged that she felt life held nothing for her but misery. She was unable to sustain any lasting relationship and finally turned to drugs. Her involvement with drugs led to an arrest, which in turn led to a therapy program. She was in the program for three years and seemed to be making a recovery. Suddenly, she committed suicide. Her psychiatrist was reported to have said, "We took heroin away from her and couldn't replace it with health."

Police Reponse to a Complaint

The police bear a heavy responsibility in sexual assault cases because they are usually the first to respond to the scene. However, it is the responsibility of all agencies responding to make sure that the crime victim will receive the proper treatment and be referred to those agencies which can provide crisis intervention.

The American Humane Association Study[18] indicated that two-thirds of all sexually abused children had suffered some form of emotional disturbance and 14 percent had become severely disturbed. Therefore, the first officer at the scene should be aware that proper treatment and understanding of the child may affect him or her positively and may decrease the chances of long term psychological damage.

The initial function of the police officer is to establish rapport with the young victim. Children are known to respond in the manner the questioner considers appropriate in terms of gaining adult approval. Also, children, because of their personality development may be open to suggestion. The investigator should not try to lead the child but allow the child to tell the story at his or her own pace and in the child's own words. It is important not to substitute other terms with which the child is not familiar and to find out the meaning of the child's words. For example, one child referred to the penis as "pee-pee" and her vagina as the "wee-wee."

Interviewing children is a sensitive process but, if handled correctly, useful information can be gathered. Special care must be taken as to where, and when, and how the interview takes place. In an emergency situation, the interview can be conducted in a patrol car. However, the equipment in the car and the radio calls may distract a child to the point where the child is more intrigued by the equipment than the situation he or she is in. A schoolroom may be effective, or an office in a police headquarters building might be used. If the parents are supportive and cooperative, the interview may be at the child's home. Care should be taken to choose a place without traffic or where the possibility of interruption is minimal.

It is important for the police officer to try to solicit the cooperation of the parents of the child. Without their cooperation, there may be no arrest or prosecution so it is imperative that the investigator not alienate the parents.

The interviewer can be most instrumental in helping the parents realize that it is important that the child not misinterpret the reactions of adults. As one step to establish some control in the interviewing situation, the police officer can tell parents that three facts are important for their child to understand: (1) the parents are relieved that their child is all right; (2) whatever the child did was the right thing because he or she is alive; and (3) they do not blame the child for the perpetrator's behavior.

If parents have difficulty with their reactions to the offense, the investigator should be able to refer them for victim counseling to help them deal with their feelings. The officer should obtain permission from the parents as well as the child to interview the child privately or if requested, with an objective observer. Privacy and a minimum of interruptions from external sources is important.

Actions Taken by the Police Officer

In addition to responding to the needs of both victim and family, the police officer must take certain actions: (1) coordinating with the hospital and prosecutor's office regarding the situation; (2) determining whether a sex crime has been committed and the specific crime; (3) obtaining a description of the suspect; and (4) communicating certain information such as the crime or suspect description. Also if there is a special squad within the police department, this group must be notified. If a specialist is not available, the police officer shall:

1. Try to keep the victim from doing anything that might destroy evidence, such as going to the bathroom.
2. Ascertain the circumstances of the case, so that a determination can be made as to the crime committed.
3. Evaluate whether to take victim to the hospital or interview first.
4. Evaluate whether to notify parents or guardian depending on age and policy. This is important if the victim goes to the hospital. Many hospitals will not conduct an examination or treat a minor without parental consent.
5. Make sure the doctor conducts an examination and collects the necessary evidence. Not all sexual assault cases require an internal examination.

The officer should be aware of the circumstances of the incident before the victim goes into the examining room. If an internal examination is conducted, make sure the necessary specimens are collected.

6. Take any evidence to the police or other designated laboratory for analysis.
7. Note how the victim looks and record observations.
8. Think—is there evidence at the scene that has to be safeguarded? Search the scene.
9. What about clothing? Will any of it have to be taken for evidence?
10. Make sure evidence is properly collected, packaged and marked.
11. Check on witnesses. Were there any? Get names and addresses or descriptions. If child was accosted on the way home from school, a companion or neighbor may have noticed something that was not suspicious at the time. Remember the young are often attacked by the young—not always older people. It is better to ask a witness if he or she noticed anyone at the scene rather than asking about someone suspicious.
12. If the offender is not immediately arrested, get a more extensive description. Ask for more details on what was worn, any unusual marks, scars or tattoos.
13. If the offender is arrested soon after the crime, take clothes, underwear etc. as evidence if warranted.

Police investigators should assess the overall situation to determine if the prosecutor's office should be called. Some offices work only during the 9-5 o'clock time period while other offices have someone on duty through the night. If the investigator believes the case is one to present complications or one where public attention may be drawn to the case, the prosecutor's office should be informed immediately. Many police departments and prosecutor's offices are aware of the many problems that can develop in a case and thus have established a strong working relationship. Some prosecutor's offices have sex crime investigators assigned so that a specialist will be available to assist the investigator as soon as a report is received. Coordination between the prosecutor and police is vital to the successful outcome of the case.[1,2]

Some cases present difficulties, such as when the parents are not supportive of the child or where there is doubt as to the nature or degree of crime. In such situations, it is most useful for the police investigator to consult with the prosecutor.

Of equal importance to the coordination of police and prosecutor services is the coordination between police and hospital staff.[4] The police officer should inform the hospital as to the type of case he or she is bringing in to insure that the proper professionals be available. These professionals include a pediatrician/physician to examine the child and mental health, social service, or rape counselor to meet with the family and child when the child arrives at the hospital. Failure to notify the hospital staff may result in additional medical and psychological complications for the victim as failure to notify the prosecutor of a difficult case will result in the loss of important time and evidence collection.

The police officer should make sure he has as complete a report as possible in the event that an arrest is made soon after the incident. This is especially true with children because information takes a little longer to gather and because evidence is not always available. If the person accused is known in the community, an investigation to substantiate the allegation may be necessary before an arrest is made.

In one case involving a 5-year-old victim, a 24-year-old neighbor was charged with the crime of sexually assaulting her. A witness to the crime was the victim's 7-year-old brother. The victim was taken to the hospital but the doctor did not find clinical evidence of ejaculation in order to give a positive diagnosis of penetration. The police officer, at this point, did not feel that he had enough evidence to make an arrest and he was supported by the prosecutor. He expected to continue his investigation by developing leads and looking for additional information. The mother of the victim was very upset that an arrest had not been made and she managed to find another police officer who was not aware that the case was under investigation and persuaded him to make the arrest. The suspect was eventually released because there was insufficient evidence at that point in time to hold him. Because he was now aware of the charge and if he were guilty, it would be difficult to gather incriminating evidence. No subsequent arrest was made.

It is wise to remember that these cases are very difficult, and coordination of all efforts is of vital importance. Rapport should be established with hospital personnel in order that the police officer is made aware of the outcome of the hospital examination and the implications of these results. The previously cited case involving the 5-year-old victim demonstrates this point. Although the doctor was not able to give a diagnosis of positive recent penetration he was able to state that there was a tear in the hymen. The prosecutor's office should be contacted early in the case. He or she will be in a position to advise the investigator as to what evidence or additional steps should be taken to complete the investigation.

The police officer always should collect as much evidence as possible immediately after the report. Some officers tend to become lax after hearing the suspect admit to having sexual relations with the young person. They fail to collect evidence because they have a confession. At trial, the defense lawyer may present many arguments such as saying the victim was a willing participant. Therefore, the officer in order to support the victim's testimony should make sure he has collected all evidence available. If the officer waits too long, evidence collection at a later date may be considered contaminated and thus nonadmissible in court.

Types of Reports

In cities where there are alternatives to reporting the crime to the police, other agencies may be alerted. However, it is estimated that over 80 percent of the crimes are reported to the police department. The police handling of the crime often depends upon how the crime is reported. There are several ways these reports can be made to the police: (1) a direct report, (2) an indirect report, (3) a referral report, and (4) a proactive report.

Direct Report

A direct report is made by the victim. The child or adolescent might be a victim of a gang rape, a kidnap and rape and/or be badly injured. The victim usually is left alone, thrown out of the car or abandoned in an unfamiliar neighborhood and because of these circumstances, looks to the police for help. In this type of report, the child usually recognizes that something "bad" has happened. The child is looking for help and has turned to people he or she feels can be of help such as the police. The child is willing to give information, can talk about the incident, and may be able to lead officers to the scene (in cases of kidnap and rape). Parents are not on the scene but should be advised as soon as possible. This notification should be made personally by another police officer and not by telephone. Once on the scene, the parents should be seen privately by the officer handling the case and told of the incident. The officer should allow the parents to ventilate;—they may blame the child, they may want to kill the assailant, they may accuse the police officer of failing to do his job, or they may blame themselves. The officer should allay their fears as much as possible, tell them that the child needs their support and guidance, and get on with the interview of the victim. Problems will arise when parents are not at home. Every effort must be made to locate them. If the victim is seriously injured, the parents' consent is not needed and he or she can be treated as an emergency case. For those victims who are not seriously injured, an adult in the family who can stand in as the parent-surrogate can give permission for an examination.

It is worthwhile to conduct the interview as soon as possible in order to get all the necessary information while the incident is still fresh in the victim's mind. This is especially helpful when the victim has been gang-raped. The officer is given the opportunity to get the names and/or descriptions of the perpetrators and what specific acts each performed. One case we investigated involved a 10-year-old victim. One of her schoolmates had called to ask her to come to his house and help with the homework. When she got there, she discovered that he and three older friends were alone in the house. She claimed she was given something to drink after which, although she did not lose consciousness, she was unable to defend herself. After the assault, she was thrown out of the house. Since her mother was at work, she went to the police station and told her story. She accused the two older youths of rape and sodomy and two younger ones of sexual abuse. She did not use the word *sodomy* but rather said that "he put his thing in my hiney." The officer had her describe *thing* and *hiney* so that there would be no doubt as to what she meant. She was escorted to the hospital where the Sex Crimes investigator met them. The police officer told the investigator of the steps taken. The investigator helped her to tell her story chronologically and cite exactly what sex acts each youth perpetrated. This cooperation helped enormously when charging the assailants and testifying when the case went to trial.

Indirect Report

An indirect report most often is received from the parent or parent surrogate. The victim may or may not be injured but does not comprehend the nature of the act. An example of this victim reaction was the circumstance in one report where a young victim returned to the playground and continued to play with her friend after being molested.[16]

These reports are difficult to handle, since they are not reported immediately. Time has elapsed and the parents may have projected their feelings onto the child. It will take time to talk with the child and the parent. If the parents are upset, the officer may need to talk with them regarding how their behavior is affecting their child. It is important the parents and child are willing to cooperate with the police. The parents, who may have already heard the story, and the victim should be separated and the interview conducted. If the parents or the officer want someone else in the room during the interview, it may be considered to have an objective person present.

At the outset of the interview, the police officer will have to establish a relationship with the victim. He may have to explain to the victim why the parents are acting in such a strange way. In one case, the police were called from the hospital by the parents. When the officer arrived the father was in an hysterical state. His son had been sodomized. The father kept saying, "What have they done to my son—they've made him a fag!" Then he would turn around and yell at the child for going off with a stranger. He disobeyed his parents. He had been told never to do such a thing. The officer was able to take the father aside and tell him of the adverse effect he was having on the boy. It took awhile but the father was finally convinced. The officer had to explain to the boy that the father was upset because he was a victim of a crime, what the crime was, and why they were anxious to arrest the person responsible.

This case was difficult to solve since the boy was accosted on the street. He had agreed to help a man deliver boxes in the neighborhood. The man took the boy five blocks away from home into an abandoned building where he molested the boy. This man committed four more crimes in the same area until apprehended. The young victims were good at describing automobiles and certain articles of clothing but weight, height and age were much more difficult details to describe. To elicit such information it is useful to use a comparison. For example, select some person and compare the suspect to the person saying, is he as tall as X, is he shorter than X, is he heavier or older than X. When finally apprehended, the suspect resembled the composite made of him from the boys' descriptions. In addition the victims were able to pick the suspect out of a line up. Line ups are always conducted with the full cooperation of the prosecutor to insure their acceptability in court.

Referral Report

In a referral report, another agency representative makes the report. The referral person could be from a hospital or a school who becomes aware of the sexual assault while dealing with another problem.

These interviews are often difficult to conduct. Although an agency person has reported the offense, the representative rarely wants an interview between the police and the victim to occur on the agency's grounds. What the agency people fail to realize is that the child is a victim and not a suspect; there is no violation of rights involved here. Most of the time, these interviews are conducted by a youth or juvenile division officer. He or she gathers the information and makes the determination as to whether a crime has been committed. The child is usually willing to talk and can supply much information. The interviewer must remember to allow the child to speak in his or her own language and not to ask leading questions.

One school counselor reported a case involving two sisters and their step-brother. Even though the mother had divorced the father, she would still call upon the step-brother to babysit. When he came to her house, he would sodomize both sisters. As a result, one of the girls was not able to concentrate in class, her schoolwork went down, and her marks suffered. Her teacher arranged a visit with the school counselor. The counselor, hearing what was troubling the girl, sought assistance from the police but did not make a formal complaint. The case was referred to the Sex Crimes investigator. On interview, the investigator learned that the assailant threatened them with death if they ever told anyone. Since he had punched them a few times, they believed him. The mother was informed and was upset over the news. A summary arrest was made in the case since there was a corroborating witness—the sister. The case went to court and the step-brother was convicted. He was convicted of the two crimes since the sisters were able to testify for one another.

Such cases should be reported to the police department or another concerned agency. It is the victim we are concerned about and not the reputation of the agency that makes the report. Cases of sexual assault that are uncovered or happen on school grounds should be reported—there is no excuse for failing to do so. Unfortunately, all sex crimes cases are not easily charged. Unlike other crimes, the police need to know a crime took place before a complaint is entered. This condition should not exist, but because of the history of rape and the myths that surround it, there needs to be more than a complainant's word to have the complaint formally recorded. Having a corroborating witness is ideal but rarely happens. Hospital evidence is very important since it will sometimes indicate sexual intercourse occurred. This evidence is often enough in charging a sex crime involving a minor.

Proactive Report

A proactive report is one in which the police, usually an officer of the juvenile court, while investigating one complaint discovers that there is an incestuous relationship involving his client. The officer should pursue this complaint and obtain additional information. This action should not be too difficult since the child or adolescent has already established a relationship with the officer. Once it is determined that a crime has been committed, the officer should make an appointment with family court to have the people appear. Some states do not have a family court protocol. In these areas, summary arrests—immediate action without the formality of a written complaint prior to the arrest—should be made.

One case I investigated involved a 9-year-old child who was truant from school. I went to the home and spoke with the mother, who claimed she had no control over the child and all the children were "bad." She continued, "And why shouldn't they be? Anything they wanted he [father] would give them if they played with him." When further questioned, it developed this "playing" included rape and sodomy. I went to family court with the mother and an older sister. After hearing the story, the intake worker ordered a warrant for the father's arrest. The judge ordered family treatment for the child and parents.

In summary, the police officer should inform the prosecutor either for on-the-scene assistance or advice as soon as possible after responding to the call. Keeping the prosecutor informed and advised will decrease the number of interviews to which the victim is subjected and the prosecutor will be able to point out to the police officer other areas or leads for investigation. The police officer also notifies the hospital if the child is to be examined, this gives personnel the opportunity to set aside a quiet area and notify proper staff. This action will save time and possibly decrease the amount of stress for the victim and family. The police officer seeks the cooperation of the parents and gathers all available evidence. Complete family interviewing together with cooperating and coordination of services will increase the chances for successful prosecution.

References

1. Lisa Brodyaga et al. *Rape and Its Victims: A Report for Citizens, Health Facilities, and Criminal Justice Agencies.* NILECJ, LEAA, Washington, D.C.: U.S. Department of Justice, 1975.

2. *Forcible Rape: A National Survey of the Response by Prosecutors,* Vol. 1, NILECJ, LEAA, Washington, D.C.: U.S. Department of Justice, 1977.

3. New York State Penal Law, 1975.

4. Mary L. Keefe, and Henry T. O'Reilly. "The Plight of the Rape Victim in New York". In *Victims and Society.* ed. Emilio C. Viano. Lexington, Ma.: Lexington Books, D. C. Heath and Company, 1976:391-402.

5. *Criminal Victimization Surveys in the Nation's Five Largest Cities* Washington, D.C.: United States Department of Justice, LEAA, April, 1975.

6. *Crime in the United States* Washington, D.C.: Federal Bureau of Investigation, 1975.

7. *Annual Report,* Sex Crimes Analysis Unit, New York: New York City Police Department, 1975.

8. *A Community Response to Rape.* Des Moines, Iowa: Polk County Rape/ Sexual Assault Care Center, 1976.

9. *Report of Montgomery County Sexual Offenses Committee.* Montgomery County, Maryland, June 1975.

10. Criminal Justice Liaison Division Study, "Court Disposition of Rape Cases: January to June, 1972." New York: New York Police Department Report, 1973.

11. *Forcible Rape: A National Survey of the Response by Police,* Vol. 1, NILECJ, LEAA, Washington, D.C.: U. S. Department of Justice, 1977.

12. *D. C. Task Force Report.* Washington, D.C., 1974.

13. Nancy Gager and Kathleen Schurr. *Sexual Assault: Confronting Rape in America.* New York: Grosset and Dunlop, 1976.

14. *Dade County Rape Awareness Public Education Program Progress Report.* May 1976.

15. *A Training Manual.* Rape Crisis Council of Lehigh Valley, Lehigh Valley, Pa. 1977.

16. Morton Bard and Katherine Ellison. "Crisis Intervention and the Investigation of Forcible Rape." *Police Chief* (May 1974).

17. Helen Dudar. "America Discovers Child Pornography." *MS Magazine,* (August 1977).

18. Vincent DeFrancis. *Protecting the Child Victim of Sex Crimes.* Denver, Colorado: The American Humane Association, Children's Division. 1966.

11 Interviewing Young Victims
Ann Wolbert Burgess and
Lynda Lytle Holmstrom

The interview, from a therapeutic perspective, serves two important functions. First, it provides the interviewer with observations and data to assess the amount of psychological stress the child and family members are experiencing. Second, it provides pertinent information about the assault.

The Therapeutic Interview

Preinterview Considerations

In preparation for an interview with a child, three factors need to be assessed: information regarding the person who has reported the assault, when the assault occurred, and an analysis of the child's emotional style. Data in response to these questions provide you with a framework within which to direct your inquiry.

First, who has reported the sexual assault, and how has it come to your attention? Did the child report to a parent, or have neighbors complained to the police about behavior they suspect? Is the child willing to talk? Is she frightened over the disclosure of the situation? In the following case, it took considerable time to elicit this information from the father, who had brought his daughter into the hospital for an examination.

The counselor, when the child was being examined, asked the father what he had observed in his daughter; had he observed changes or ways she was upset. The father had a hard time answering. He said he hadn't noticed or observed anything. The counselor asked if the daughter was upset. Finally, the father said, "My wife found out. Friends told my wife, and my wife told me."

This information tells you that other people in the social network knew about the situation, and the parents were not reporting any behavioral changes.

Second, what is the timing of the assault in relation to the interview? If the assault has just happened and you are seeing the child immediately following the assault, the opportunity for crisis intervention and crisis counseling is apparent. Timing may affect the personality defense structure of the child. For example, in an acute crisis situation, the material should be more accessible to the child's memory, and the psychological defenses may be lower in terms

171

of blocking of the details of the assault. The child may or may not want to discuss it when she is upset and in a crisis state. If the assault has occurred over time, the child may have more difficulty talking about it because the material may be less accessible and dimly in memory. A coping pattern of dealing with the assault—such as suppression or denial—may have developed.

The third factor for consideration is the observation of the child's emotional style. Two styles are usually obvious: the expressive and the controlled style. In the *expressive style,* the child is able to show how he or she actually feels about the situation. For example, the child may cry or look upset and state that she feels disturbed or confused. In the *controlled style,* the child is quiet, nonverbal, and generally not showing any feelings. There may be no eye contact, and the interviewer may need to use special techniques to learn how the child really feels. In the following case, the counselor had to patiently wait for the opportunity to help the girl express her feelings. Not until a second upsetting event did the girl express herself.

A mother brought her 13-year-old daughter to the clinic for a gynecological examination. The exam and interview revealed that the girl was pregnant and that her father had impregnated her. Child protective services were notified. The mother decided to press charges, and the father was removed from the home pending a court hearing. A second decision was made that the girl would have an abortion, and a date was set.

However, on the preabortion examination, the physician determined that the girl was over 12 weeks pregnant and would have to have a second trimester abortion and would have to wait three weeks in order to safely induce labor.

At this point, the girl became quite upset. She had not shown any emotion until then, but rather had been quiet and expressionless. The counselor was able to utilize this change in affect to talk more about the girl's feelings regarding the incestuous relationship, being pregnant, and the scheduled abortion.

It became clear in observing the reaction of the girl and her mother to the news of the delay for an abortion, that for them the immediate crisis was the pregnancy. They marshalled their energies to cope with this event and great effort was required for them to endure the three-week delay. During this time, the counselor coordinated agency resources to provide some structure and support through diversional activities for the girl. Following the abortion, the victim, her mother, and her sister were able to express a great deal more of what they were feeling—specifically their anger at the father and their distress over the amount of disruption in their lives. The mother was able also, through counseling, to focus more on the issue of her child as a victim.

Initial Approach to the Child

The professional style of the interviewer is an important factor in the initial meeting with the child. *Professional style* means regard for clients and how this is transmitted, such as through the way you meet the child, the way you introduce yourself, and the subsequent dialogue. The child, as well as family members, will be watching to see if you are concerned, interested, and respect them as individuals. The child and family members need to know who you are and the agency or discipline you represent. The next task is related to professional competence and involves establishing credibility. You need to prove your expertise and somehow convey your experience to the child. You can establish that this is part of your work ("I talk with children who have had something like this happen," or "I talk with children regarding upsetting situations that have happened to them").

Establishing an Alliance

The main task now, assuming that the child has permitted the introductions and seems ready to proceed, is to get the child to trust you. First, try to establish how the child perceives you so that you can assess if some degree of trust is present ("How do you feel about talking with me about what happened?"). Find out what the child has been told about the interview ("What did your parents tell you about why you are here?").

If the child had no preparation for the visit, you should try to provide as much concrete explanation as gently as possible. However, if you determine, through asking the child, that he or she knows why he or she is seeing you, acknowledge that the child is correct and that the parents have explained the visit properly and continue with the interview.

Our work with adult victims, as well as children, has convinced us that using the "request" format—researched and described in detail by Lazare et al.[1]—helps children to see that there is something in this interview for them. To effectively use the request model, the interviewer asks the child, at some point in the interview, how the child hopes or wishes to be helped. In some situations, the request is something the interviewer can agree to do ("I want Daddy to stop it"). In such a situation, the interviewer can outline, with the child's help, the action that can be taken to be sure the father's incestuous behavior stops. Sometimes the child's request may not be reasonable to the professional ("I don't want you to tell anyone about this"). In such cases, the interviewer would have to spend time on the issue before proceeding ("The law says this behavior must be reported, but we can first work out the details of how this is to be done, who specifically will know, and what the results will be, and you will know exactly to whom you can go for protection"). Sometimes the child does not know how to tell you what she or he wants and asks you what you can do. You can respond, "I can first listen to you tell me what happened. Then we can talk about how else I can be helpful when I hear what other requests you have."

Lazare *et al.,* in another study, state that there is conflict in all relationships and that this dynamic particularly needs to be addressed before any therapeutic progress is started.[2] One way to deal with the conflict is to negotiate. This negotiation phase follows identifying the request and deciding how the interview can be helpful to the child. The child states his or her request, the interviewer states what services can be delivered, and then there is a compromise over what to do. The child essentially needs to understand that the interviewer is honest. Sometimes it is helpful for the interviewer to make this explicit—that you will not lie to the child—because deceit has been a past pattern of authority figures in the child's life. The child needs to perceive the interviewer wants to try to understand, that together you both have business to do and agree to that fact ("After you tell me what happened, we can talk about what you want to happen next"). In the case of a 5 year-old boy, the child's request was to draw pictures with the magic markers the counselor had brought to the session, and they negotiated that the boy could draw pictures while he talked with the counselor. The child also requested to take some papers and pencils home with him, which was agreed upon in exchange for his talking with the counselor.

Most often the child has been a victim of dominance—someone has had power and control over the child. A therapeutic task is to try to neutralize this psychological trauma and return some degree of power and control to the child. The interviewer can acknowledge those areas in which the child does have control and negotiate those in which the child's control would be unreasonable to professionals, but the interviewer should allow the child to still have some voice in the outcome. For example, children should have some input into decisions regarding the perpetrator. Children can be asked their opinions, told the outcome of any decisions, and told how the decision was made. Such a procedure is respectful to the child and indicates to the child that he or she is being taken seriously in efforts to deal with the entire situation.

Description of the Assault

Encourage the child to give a description of the assault. The aim of the interview is to get the child to tell the complete story. Let the child identify the problem in whatever language he or she wishes. Avoid stating your perception of the assault or what you have been told. Technical jargon often increases a child's anxiety, confusion, and distrust. If you have to, interrupt the child only for clarification or to encourage the child to continue. Interruptions interfere with the mood and environment of the interview. Verbal prefaces may help to facilitate the child's talking ("It is important for you to tell me so that I can help you"). Avoid direct questions that force a child to answer with a yes or no. Such tactics are not helpful in encouraging details and expression of feelings. By allowing a child to tell the story at his or her own pace, you will allow the child to have more control of the situation. The more control the child has, the more he or she will participate in the interview and talk.

Move from general to specific details of the assault. Ask questions pertaining to what the child was doing before the assault, why he or she was there, what else was going on at the scene help to set the time and situation of the assault. Try to reconstruct the child's day ("What were you doing that day? What was the weather? Were you playing inside or outside?"). Ask how the person entered the picture, and try to learn what he was doing. Was he in the situation because of some socially acceptable reason as babysitter or bus driver? Where were other family members, and was any protective adult around?

The use of age-related media, described in detail in the next chapter, may be most useful in encouraging the child to explain the event. Having the child draw pictures may bring about much information about the situation.

Identify the consequences of telling, as perceived by the child. It is important to remember that children are easily frightened and that intimidation is a tactic frequently used by perpetrators. Threats are an easy way for adults to keep children in line. Try to deal with the child's fear ("What has frightened you the most about this situation?"). Then try to decrease the child's anxiety ("It is good that you have been able to tell someone so that we can now try to do something to help").

Difficult Interviews

The interviewer may have to use special techniques to get young victims to talk. The following interview illustrates how the counselor tried many techniques—mostly to no avail—to encourage the girl to say something. The girl, a victim of a sex-stress situation, had been admitted to the emergency room three days previously. The nurse stated that the "emotional part" of the victimization had not been discussed. When the girl was readmitted three days later in a "mute state," the counselors were called. One counselor met with the mother, and the other counselor went into an examining room to talk with Theresa.[3]

Counselor: *"I hope that by talking I can better understand what is troubling you."*

Theresa: *"Why bother?"*

Counselor: *My work is to help people who are under stress or in an upsetting situation. The hospital staff is concerned about you and called my colleague and me to meet with you."*

Theresa: *(Remained silent, continued to stare at the floor)*

Counselor: *(Remained silent for a few minutes, realized that silence wasn't working)*

Counselor: *"Can you tell me how you are feeling?"*

Theresa: *(Silence, looking very sleepy)*

Counselor: *"Can you tell me what you are thinking?"*

Theresa: *(Silence)*

Counselor: *"I get the feeling you are upset over something you can't talk about."*

Theresa: *(Silence)*

Counselor: *"Can you tell me in your own words what happened between you and the young man?"*

Theresa: *"Why?"*

Counselor: *"It might help me understand the situation, and then I might be able to help out. I don't know why you are so sleepy and why your mother is upset about you."*

Theresa: *(Looks down at the floor)*

Counselor: *Would it be easier for you if I asked specific questions?"*

Theresa: *(Nods head yes; this was the first breakthrough in 10 minutes)*

Theresa's acknowledgement that she was willing to be asked questions was the negotiated component of the interview. She would answer questions but was not going to present the details of the situation in a spontaneous manner. During the interview, which followed the usual protocol of questions asked in a sexual trauma interview, the counselor learned that Theresa was sleepy because she had taken pills from her mother's medicine cabinet. The physical condition was the result of a drug overdose. Essentially, Theresa had agreed to have sex with this young man. The parents located them at the man's sister's home. Numerous problems developed, such as her embarrassment over being discovered, having to go to the hospital, having the situation reported to the police, and her fear that the news would spread through the school. After admitting all her reactions, Theresa told of taking the pills. Following this disclosure, both counselors met with the mother and daughter to help plan the next step.

Interviewing for Emotional State

Special attention to the young person's emotional state should be given in the following situations: (1) when a prior or current psychosocial problem is suspected or identified; (2) when a previous rape is reported; (3) when there is some concern about the amount of emotional control the person has over his or her impulses to hurt himself or herself.

The following case includes all the above criteria, and thus a careful assessment needs to be made. If you do not feel comfortable in making such an assessment, a referral to psychiatric services should be considered. This case involves a 16-year-old girl who accepted a ride from a man when she realized it was too late to take public transportation. On interview, it was observed that the girl had a scar under her jaw and two slash marks high up on her arm.

Counselor: *"How are you feeling now?"*

Robin: *"All right (pause) No, not really."*

Counselor: *"How did you feel during the rape?"*

Robin: *"I was scared, especially after he hit me. I didn't struggle. He hit me across the face. I was scared because I had had an operation and have a glass jaw."* (She showed the scar)

Counselor: *"Any other feelings?"*

Robin: *"I started getting mad as he was driving around. I was a sucker for trusting him. I always put myself in these positions. I was scared, especially after he hit me."*

Counselor: *"Was the assault painful?"*

Robin: *"Yes, it still is."*

Counselor: *"How were you feeling at the time?"*

Robin: *"I don't know. I wasn't thinking about how I was feeling. It kept reminding me of the other times when I was in New York and I got raped."*

Counselor: *"Recently?"*

Robin: *"No, last August. Then after that I got raped once seven months ago."*

Counselor: *"It happened twice before?"*

Robin: *"Ya, I don't know what's happening."*

Counselor: *"Is it the same kind of situation?"*

Robin: *"Sort of the same way, I guess."*

Counselor: *"How do you feel now?"*

Robin: *"I'm pissed off at myself. I always get into these situations. That's why my mother has me checked (psychiatrically)."*

Counselor: *"Tonight—what's the most painful part?"*

Robin: *"When he stopped the car and the sex part."*

Counselor: *"And now?"*

Robin: *"I'm feeling all right. Tired."*

Counselor: *"Where did you go before, after you were raped?"*

Robin: *"In New York to the hospital. The other—I was not examined. My father took me to the state hospital. He thinks I'm crazy . . . but he's the crazy one. I've been at the hospital for four months as inpatient and then for a long time on day care."*

Counselor: *"Who is your therapist?"*

Robin: *"Dr. Jones. I'm still in treatment there on day care."*

Counselor: *"How is it going there?"*

Robin: *"All right. They are thinking of a discharge date on the 20th of this month. He's not sure where my head is. A lot of things that are happening now— if they happened last year I'd be back in the hospital."*

Counselor: *"What happens when you are under stress—like now?"*

Robin: *"First time I took it out on myself. Second time—on myself. I cut myself. Tried to poison myself and hang myself."*

Counselor: *"How do you feel now?"*

Robin: *"I'm pissed off at myself. I always get into these situations. That's why my mother has me checked."*

Counselor: *"Does your mother believe you?"*

Robin: *"I don't know. I can't understand how I do it either. I do hurt myself."*

Counselor: *"Are you in control of yourself now?"*

Robin: *"Yes."*

Counselor: *"If you feel like hurting yourself, can you call someone?"*

Robin: *"If I really wanted to, why would I call? But, I'm OK."*

This part of the interview pointed out the previous rape as well as the girl's history of hurting herself when under stress. The counselors were not comfortable with the fact that Robin could not guarantee that she would call her therapist should she become overwhelmed with stress. Very careful follow-up was made to ensure that she would call her therapist and tell him what happened. Robin did call him promptly the next day. There were additional facts to complicate this case; an older sister, also raped as an adolescent, had been hospitalized for a depression and while in the mental hospital committed suicide. In the week following Robin's rape, two additional crises developed that had an impact on Robin. A man known to the family—a security guard at a hospital—murdered his entire family and a good male friend of Robin's from the hospital committed suicide. Thus, many of these issues were dealt with by her therapist in her therapy sessions. From a crisis counseling perspective, the counselor's focus was maintained on the rape and on monitoring her reactions and symptoms.

Assessing the Impact of the Sexual Assault

After the child has described, as best she or he can, the details of the assault, the interviewer should focus on any changes in lifestyle or other symptoms that have developed since the assault. Ask specifically about changes in eating and sleep patterns. Is the child having any bad dreams or nightmares, and if so, have the child describe them in detail. Can the child concentrate in school? How often does the thought of the assault come into his or her mind? Does the child think other people know about the assault, people she or he has not told? Does the child report any physical symptoms: stomach aches, difficulty urinating, listlessness, or restlessness? Has the child had any illness during the time of the assault or since the rape occurred, and did the child receive immediate attention? Is the child playing with friends and going to school and engaging in other activities?

How have family members reacted to the news of the assault and to the child? Have siblings been told? What have siblings said?—What have parents said? Parents may blame the child, blame the perpetrator, or blame themselves; what does this family do? If the perpetrator is a family member or known to the family, how is the divided loyalty issue handled? What family members have sided with whom?

These questions may be asked during the first interview or on follow-up sessions. The answers help the interviewer evaluate the degree of disruption in lifestyle, which in turn is helpful in determining victim counseling intervention.

In summary, the interview of young persons regarding a sexual trauma should have therapeutic purposes as well as the purpose of gathering information.

We know that many children, adolescents, and adults are hesitant to report a sexual trauma in a general interview session. Therefore, we suggest that clinicians should consider asking routinely during interviews if a person has ever been pressured or forced into a sexual situation. Similarly, for perpetrators, clinicians should also consider asking clients if they have ever pressured or forced anyone into a sexual situation. If a sexual trauma is uncovered, the exploration of the assault through the interview process is continued as described in this chapter.

References

1. Aaron Lazare, Sherman Eisenthal, and Linda Wasserman, "The Customer Approach to Patienthood," *Archives of General Psychiatry* 32, no. 32 (1975): 553–558.

2. Aaron Lazare, Sherman Eisenthal, and Arlene Frank, "The Interview as a Clinical Negotiation," in *Diagnosis and Treatment in Outpatient Psychiatry* (Baltimore, Md.: Williams and Wilkens, forthcoming).

3. This case is discussed in detail in Lynda Lytle Holmstrom and Ann Wolbert Burgess, *The Victim of Rape: Institutional Reactions* (New York: Wiley-Interscience, forthcoming).

12

**Counseling Young Victims
and Their Families**
*Ann Wolbert Burgess,
Lynda Lytle Holmstrom,* and
Maureen P. McCausland

Our work with adults who have unresolved sexual traumas from their child-hoods, has impressed upon us the importance and need to provide adequate counseling to the young person at the time of the sexual assault. This chapter contains techniques in counseling children and their families, a detailed case of counseling a child victim of an incest rape, and additional issues for counseling families—primary prevention of child sexual assault.

Victim Counseling

The two main techniques we suggest for settling sexual trauma at the time of disclosure are (1) encouraging the child to talk, and (2) the use of media and age-related toys.

If the child is encouraged to talk about the experience, there is a better chance (1) that the child will settle his or her feelings about the entire situation, (2) that the family will be able to deal more openly with their feelings, and (3) that the experience will be integrated as a life occurrence for the child.

Victim counseling is an issue-oriented model of crisis intervention. Four victim crisis concepts form the conceptual framework for victim counseling. These concepts are as follows.

1. Sexual assault may be experienced as an external crisis for the victim, family, and often the community. The main task in victim counseling is to help the victim and family return to the precrisis level of functioning.
2. The sexual assault, as an external crisis, interacts with the internal or develop-mental issues currently being faced by the victim.
3. Going to court recapitulates the original assault and can assume crisis proportions to the victim and family.
4. One external crisis has the potential for activating additional crisis situa-tions. One most obvious complicating factor is when the offender is a

Sections of this chapter are abridged from Ann Wolbert Burgess, Lynda Lytle Holmstrom, and Maureen P. McCausland, "Counseling the Child Rape Victim," *Issues in Comprehensive Pediatric Nursing* (Counseling Issues), (November–December 1976):45–57. Used with per-mission of the McGraw-Hill Publishing Company.

181

family member. In such a case, the issue of divided loyalty will be raised and needs to be dealt with as a family issue.

Assessment Areas

The counselor's task in counseling young victims is (1) to carefully assess the child in general terms as well as specific ones, and (2) to utilize techniques that are useful to children in talking about stressful events.

Developmental Baseline. The counselor needs a baseline on which to be able to monitor or evaluate changes—either positive or negative—in the child's behavior. The counselor also needs an assessment of the child's biopsychosocial assets and restrictions. This information can help to tell where the child is, developmentally. Some basic questions to be asked are: Is the child developmentally where other children his or her age are? Is the child in the age-related school grade; does he or she know as many words as the average child; can he or she answer questions readily and intelligently; is his or her intellect equal to the age group; is his or her physical, behavioral, and social growth compatible with his or her age group? If not, the areas should be noted.

Child's Response to Stress. It is essential to assess how the child normally handles an upsetting, stressful situation. Ask the child what other upsetting things have happened in his or her life that he or she remembers. Also ask the child about events that have been related by their parents. This question will help determine the type of situations the child finds upsetting and the language the child uses to describe these events. Then ask the child what he or she did or does about these situations. For example, does the child cry or refuse to go anywhere? Is there someone special the child talks to or feels understands him or her? Questions of this type help to provide a baseline on the child's thoughts, feelings, and actions in terms of stressful events.

Family Integrity. It is important to try to assess the integrity of the family in terms of family ties. The family is a potential resource to the child as well as a potential liability. The assessment tries to determine how much strength the family can offer the child or how rejecting they may be to the child. Questions to help in this area include: who is in the family; who is living in the family home; what activities occupy the family as a group (e.g., social activities, religious events, traditional events); what extended family members are important to the child and family; what family members are closest emotionally to each other; what members are carrying out their responsibilities; how do family members view the child who has been victimized?

Family Response to Stress. It would be important to know what type of crises the family has experienced in the past; how they handled those crises; are they currently encountering any crises; in what ways do family members decrease or increase the stress tolerance level in a family? What are the strengths in the family; who are the strong, supportive members? What good, happy events have happened; how do family members treat each other?

Impact of the Sexual Assault. After assessing the overall developmental level of the child and the strength of family ties, it is important to note the impact of the current situation on the child and family. In particular, note what words the child and family members use to describe what has happened; what emotional reaction does the family show in describing the event; what has the event made the family members feel like doing; and what have they done?

General Therapeutic Techniques

The most important technique is to encourage the child to talk about the incident. If the child does not bring the subject up in the session, the counselor should tell the child that it is important to discuss it. This action tells the child that it is all right to talk about the assault. Some children expect the counselor to bring it up. If the counselor fails to do so, the child may think one of two things: (1) that something must be wrong with him or with what has happened, or (2) that the counselor does not take the assault seriously.

The goal of counseling is to have the child and family come to grips psychologically with the assault. The counselor assists with the healing process by bearing the painful feelings with the child and demonstrating that the situation is something to be discussed and settled. The counselor brings it up gently ("Are you thinking much about the situation?"). Then the counselor takes the lead from the child. If the child denies that it is an issue, the counselor can then acknowledge this position ("OK if you don't want to talk now—but I want to hear about it when it is troublesome to you or when you are having any dreams or thoughts about it"). If the child talks, the counselor encourages discussion.

Play Sessions

The use of play sessions as a technique to facilitate the counseling process is well known in clinical work with children. The play session involves the use of nonstressful techniques that decrease the anxiety children may feel in having to talk to you. This technique is aimed at gaining the attention, interest, and trust of the child. There are important differences that distinguish a child from an adult when he or she is being introduced to a professional for any kind of counseling:

1. Generally, the child is *brought* to the play session. In a sense, the child is a reluctant consumer, at least for the first session. Always assess how the child has arrived at your office and how he or she feels about it.

2. The child is not always told the reason why he is going to see you. Adults may have misrepresented the situation to the child; the child may have been told he was going to a place different from where they were taken, and this may result in additional stress for the child.

3. The child does not always sense there is a "problem" that must be discussed. The child may not feel any distress, the child may deny any problem, or the child may believe the problem lies with another person.

The setting for the use of age-related media to facilitate counseling is important in establishing a nonstressful atmosphere. If an office is to be used, an area should be designated for an informal, unstructured meeting. The play materials should be in full view. Sometimes the toys are placed, by age level, on a bookshelf, or they may be in a big toybox. The availability of play materials offers the child an opportunity to reduce stress and to utilize a natural expression through play, the activity a child knows best. If the counselor is making a home visit, toys may be taken in a case and used there. Depending on the goals of the session, the play session may be one of two types: structured or unstructured.

Structured. In a structured play session the interviewer may focus the play on specific issues by providing a certain set of toys for that setting. For example, if you wish to explore a child's thoughts and feelings about a hospital experience, having a toy hospital would encourage access to that material through play.

Unstructured. In an unstructured or free play session, you provide a wide variety of toys for the child to choose.

Choice of Play Materials. Most interviewing rooms or offices should contain some of the following supplies, although it may be impractical or impossible for a practitioner to maintain such a variety of equipment:[1]

Some creative art material, such as paper, crayons, paint.

Toys for aggressive fantasy play, such as guns, soldiers, cars, trucks.

Action toys, such as ambulances or rescue teams with cars.

Puppets, dolls, or doll houses for depicting interaction and projection.

Table games to be used for interaction with the interviewer, such as dominoes or cards to permit evasion of or relief from emotion-laden activities.

Introducing Self. It is essential, as in an interview, to establish credibility with the child. This involves telling the child who you are, why you want to talk with her or him, and the reason that the session may involve play toys. It is important to tell the child that you talk with children who have experienced what he or she has; sometimes telling the child that your work is to talk with children is sufficient. Then the child needs to be told that you want to hear "his or her side" of what happened in order to better understand the situation. The objectives in a play session are to: engage the child in activity, observe, and initiate conversation when appropriate.

Age-Appropriate Toys. To facilitate the child's play and the interview, the counselor should understand what are "age-appropriate toys" for the different developmental stages: preschool, school-age, and junior high.

Preschool. The preschool child is easily engaged in such activities as doll play, puppets, the use of the play hospital or school, and fantasy play. He or she may also draw pictures or tell stories to the counselor.

School Age. The grammar school-aged child may begin to be more verbal, but play materials still have a place in the child's life. Dolls or puppets may be selected, but action toys, art supplies and table games are often first choice. A deck of cards, dominoes, and checkers become a counselor's major means of engaging the child.

Junior High. The junior high school-aged child or early adolescent may opt for a straight interview, but again table games often are chosen. More complicated or challenging games, such as Scrabble, Clue, or Monopoly are intriguing to the junior high schooler.

Case Illustrations

The following cases illustrate the use of play therapy and media in working with children who have been sexually assaulted.

Puppet Play. There are two ways that puppets, as well as other play media, may be used to help counsel the child. First, puppets may be used to facilitate gaining the trust of the child, and second, puppets may be used to facilitate direct conversation with the child.

The use of puppets to gain trust with the child is used when the child is very apprehensive about the counseling session and/or the counselor or when the child is very young. In the following case, a pre-school child was unable to participate with the counselor because of a severe trauma reaction to females, which resulted from the circumstances of being sexually assaulted. The counselor used the technique of puppet play first with the grandmother, who brought the child to the clinic.

A grandmother brought a 3-year-old girl to the pediatric walk-in clinic for examination. It was learned that the child's 18-year-old sister had been sexually assaulting the child over a period of time. At the hospital, the child screamed and effectively resisted any intervention by female staff—by either the physician or nursing staff.

The grandmother was receptive to victim counseling, offered through the hospital. The counselor began by playing puppets with the grandmother. The child in the first two sessions sat huddled in her grandmother's lap with her eyes tightly closed, refusing to talk or look at the counselor. At the third session she gradually opened her eyes and watched the puppets:

Counselor: *"Hello little girl. How are you today?"*

Grandmother: *"I'm fine, thank you. What's your name?"*

Counselor: *"My name is Billy. What's yours?"*

Grandmother: *"Nancy."*

Counselor: *"Gee, I wish Crissy would play with us. Wouldn't that be fun?"*

Grandmother: *"We're going to have a good time. Will we play with the dolls?"*

Counselor: *"Oh, I see Crissy. Would you like one of the puppets for your hand?"*

Child: *(Nods head yes—takes puppet)*

The child continued to watch the puppets and looked at hers and made some hand motions with it. At the end of the session, the counselor asked the child if she would play with them next time, and she agreed.

A second use of puppet play is to elicit specific information from the child during the course of the play time. The case that follows illustrates this direct technique in which important information about sexual assault by a family member was gathered.

Susan, an 8-year-old girl was brought to the Pediatric Walk-In Clinic by her stepmother, with the chief complaint being "spotting from the vagina". The victim counselor was notified and talked with the stepmother who appeared angry, saying, "I don't want to talk. I want her examined. We need to know what happened."

The stepmother reported changed behavior in Susan over three weeks. ("She cries when Joe's name (natural mother's second husband) is mentioned; she won't go out to play"). The girl's natural parents were divorced and each one had remarried.

The child cried and clung to her stepmother and refused a physical examination and tests. The stepmother, with directions from the nurse, was able to obtain a vaginal culture using a cotton tipped applicator.

Plans were made for the stepmother, daughter, and natural father to return the next day in order to talk further about the situation and attempt to do a physical examination with the child's consent.

At the second hospital visit, the next day, the medical procedures were completed and the girl and parents were visibly relaxed. Susan played tic-tac-toe in almost complete silence with the counselor for the entire session.

The third session with Susan began on a different note. When entering the office she immediately chose a pair of hand puppets, and the following dialogue ensued.

Susan: *"Which is the boy?"*

Counselor: *"This is the boy puppet."*

Susan: *"This is the girl?"*

Counselor: *"Yes."*

Susan: *"Boys kiss girls sometimes."*

Counselor: *"They do kiss sometimes?"*

Susan: *"They do other things, too."*

Counselor: *"What kind of things?"*

Susan: *"The puppet can't say what they do."*

Counselor: *"Why not?"*

Susan: *"Those are bad words, and Joe will kill the puppet."*

Counselor: *"It's OK to say any words here. Puppets are safe here."*

Susan: *"No." (puppet shakes head)*

Counselor: *"It's alright. No one can hurt the puppet here."*

Susan: *"Boy puppets touch girl puppets in the private parts."*

Counselor: *"What do they touch them with?"*

Susan: *"Their private parts when they're in bed."*

Counselor: *"How does that feel?"*

Susan: *"It hurts."*

Counselor: *"It hurts?"*

Susan: *"Yes and the puppet told her mother."*

Counselor: *"Then what happened?"*

Susan: *"The mother whopped her."*

Counselor: *"How did she feel when the mother whopped her?"*

Susan: *"Sad, she cried."*

Counselor: *"She cried because she felt sad?"*

Susan: *"She's not supposed to say that ever again."*

Counselor: *"Oh, she can't say that again?"*

Susan: *"Right. The puppet wanted to go away then."*

Counselor: *"Where did she go?"*

Susan: *"Boston."*

Counselor: *"She moved to Boston?"*

Susan: *"Yes. But the puppet has to go home now. Goodbye."*

Counselor: *"Goodbye. Would the puppet like to play again?"*

Susan: *"Yes."*

Later sessions focused on issues of sexual activity with the natural mother's second husband, Joe. Dreams and nightmares experienced by Susan were filled with "monsters eating up ladies—monsters are black with short curly hair—sometimes a vampire comes, eats ladies . . . he leaves them without eyeballs and ears."

Eight weeks after the initial contact with the hospital, Susan was brought to the hospital complaining of abdominal pains. The physical examination was negative. The physician called the counselor who discovered the family was scheduled for a court appearance. The counselor met with Susan who looked frightened and withdrawn. She remained silent during the sessions and then produced the following notes:

Dear Miss Maureen,

What if Mary and Joe tell lies on my daddy. Will you let them take me.

Answer: yes ☐ *no* ☐

Dear Miss Maureen,

I'm scared that Mary and Joe are going to take me. But I know you won't let them take me. Will you

Answer: yes ☐ *no* ☐

In this type of situation, the counselor is faced with an important reality conflict of not knowing how the legal decision will be determined and not wanting to offer false promises to the child. In this case, the child and counselor talked about what the child wanted (to stay with her natural father and stepmother) what the counselor hoped (that Susan would get her wish); and what the reality decision might be (the complicated process of determining parental input and the statutory law). It was important to qualify on the paper to Susan that her boxes represented her hopes and the counselor's hopes but that the legal decision was still to be made.

Block Toys. The following case illustrates a young male victim who selected block-type toys to play with as he talked of the sexual assault.

Barry, a 5-year-old boy, was brought to the clinic by his mother after it was learned that a 64-year-old male had sexually assaulted the three children in the family over a period of months.

In the first counseling session, Barry selected Legos, a plastic building toy. This session was the day prior to his court appearance for a probable cause hearing. The following dialogue occurred.

Barry: *"Oh boy, Legos. I'll play with these."*

Counselor: *"You would like to play with them. What will you make?"*

Barry: *"I don't know." (Takes all parts out of the box)*

Counselor: *"We could build lots of different things."*

Barry: *"I'm going to make a police car. Did you ever make a car before?"*

Counselor: *"No, I haven't. Maybe we can do it together."*

Barry: *"Where are the wheels?"*

Counselor: *"Here they are."*

Barry: *"Here's the policeman."*

Counselor: *"What do policemen do?"*

Barry: *"They get bad men and send them to the judge."*

Counselor: *"Then what happens?"*

Barry: *"Somebody goes to jail. The judge puts people in jail."*

Counselor: *"That's right. Sometimes judges send people to jail when they do something wrong."*

Barry: *"This car is going to get the bad men."*

Counselor: *"What did this bad man do?"*

Barry: *"He fooled around with a little boy. He was real bad. The policeman and the judge will send him away."*

Draw-a-Picture. The method of drawing pictures of what happened to ensure that the child is settling the experience has been used in clinical practice for many years. We began using it in our work after finding it useful with two sisters, ages 9 and 10, who had been molested by their stepfather. The sisters had seen the hospital child psychiatrist and later said to a victim counselor, "I was afraid he was going to ask me to draw a picture of what happened, but he didn't." Further in the conversation, one sister said, "I know what he was trying to get me to say. He was a psychiatrist and wanted to know my reaction." The sisters were quite amenable to using crayons to draw the scene, which included two stick figures lying side by side in a bed. This prompted further discussions of the actual details of the activity, and the children were quite content to talk about the details they had drawn on the paper. Encouraging the children to talk about their experiences is an open and healthy way to deal with the tensions that have been built up over the secrecy process (see Chapter 5).

Writing-an-account. The technique of writing on paper all the details of a sexual assault frequently is used with adult victims. Because it was so useful for the adult victim, we have used this writing technique with certain older children. For example, in preparation for a probable cause hearing, the nurse-counselor encouraged an 8-year-old victim to practice her memory of the event. When the child talked about writing in her diary during the counseling session, she was encouraged to write her memory of it. This recording served a twofold purpose: (1) the child had something concrete to refer to immediately before court appearances, and (2) the diary was viewed as a safe private place for such information. The victim said:

"I write it in my diary. It bothers me. I have to tell what happened. But no one can read my diary but me. . . . I wrote two pages of what happened. I did it last night so I would remember it in my mind."

Multiple Toys. During a play session, a child may select multiple toys to express thoughts and feelings. In the following case, a 9-year-old boy selected various toys to express (1) the feelings about the assault, (2) identification with the perpetrator, and (3) solution to the situation.

Joey was waiting for the counselor to return for the weekly play session. The counselor had been in court that morning. As the counselor entered the room, Joey was carrying a toy ferris wheel. He started the conversation.

Joey: *"Hi. Let's go to our room. I can take this with me. . . . I missed you. (Expresses positive feelings for the counselor)*

Counselor: *"I missed you too." (Reciprocates the feeling)*

Joey: *"I know where you were. . . . You were at the judge's." (Checking his perception)*

Counselor: *"Yes, I was." (Acknowledged Joey was correct)*

Joey: *"Oh, look at this car. Who made this?"*

Counselor: *"You're wondering if this was made by someone else. It's a car to play with . . . but this is your special time." (Reaffirms the special time of play therapy)*

Joey: *"He's coming to get the little boy. The little boy fell off." (Uses car to express feelings about the assault)*

Counselor: *"Is he hurt?"*

Joey: *"No. But he's getting in trouble. The daddy is going to whip him now. He fools around with little kids." (Identifying with the perpetrator)*

Counselor: *"Oh, so the daddy is going to punish him?" (Encourages the expression)*

Joey: *"Yup. His Dad. Where is something to whip him with?" (Sorting out good and bad behavior and punishment)*

Counselor: *(Gives Joey a straw)*

Joey: *(Beats the toy) "There he won't mess around anymore. Send him over there."*

Counselor: *"Those kids must have been scared when he messes around with them." (Tries to elicit feelings the victim had)*

Joey: *"Yes." (Stands up) "What are those?" (Changes subject—difficult to talk of own scary feelings)*

Counselor: *"Those are dolls."*

Joey: *"Oh, this is a girl."*

Counselor: *"What do you think?" (Encourages curiosity)*

Joey: *"It's not a girl."*

Counselor: *We could undress it and see." (Encourages curiosity)*

Joey: *(Takes off the clothes) "Oh, it's a boy baby. I'm going to give him a bottle."*

Counselor: *"Let's get some water for the bottle." (They go out to the water fountain and fill the baby bottle)*

Joey: *"Let's make the man pee." (Pushes stomach of the doll) (Acts out sexual thoughts)*

Counselor: *(Remains silent and observes the action and conversation)*

Joey: *"It's coming out. Oh no. It's bad. I'm going to beat him. He's bad. He fooled around with little boys." (Uses the doll to project feelings onto and talks of the assault.)*

Counselor: *"The man fooled around with little boys and something came out of his bone." (Uses Joey's word for penis to clarify the sexual activity)*

Joey: *(Still beating the doll with the straw). "Yes. Now he's in jail." (Expresses his solution to the situation)*

In this case, the use of anatomically correct dolls was most useful to encourage the child to describe some sexual scenes of the assault. It is often easier for the child to project the activity onto dolls and then to move from the external to talk about how it felt and what it meant to him internally. The dialogue indicates Joey is not ready to personalize the assault (as seen in the change of subject), but we would anticipate that later play sessions would move to the direct conversation about the assault.

Junior High. The junior high school aged child or early adolescent may opt for a straight interview, but again table games often are chosen. More complicated or challenging games, such as Scrabble, Clue, or Monopoly, are intriguing to the junior high schooler.

Roberta is a 13-year-old girl who was sexually assaulted by her mother's boyfriend while watching television. The counselor used the conversational method during the interview with the victim. During one session the girl abruptly stopped talking when some painful feelings were emerging ("I thought Freddy loved me . . .") and stated, "Oh, you have some checkers. Let's play a game. We never did that before." They played for a short while and the clinician pointed out the girl's difficulty talking about the assailant ("It's sometimes easier to play with a game than to talk about something that hurts us") the girl was able to acknowledge this difficulty ("I get really upset when I think about what Freddy did. He used to act like a father to me and Billy").

This is also a classic example of Erikson's play disruption theory.[2] Erikson states that play disruption occurs when you reach material that is upsetting to the child. The child may stop the dialogue and switch to another activity or request to leave the office for a drink of water. The counselor has two options: (1) let the child drop the activity and switch because the anxiety is high, or (2) point out to the child that you understand it is upsetting material and suggest she or he talk about it. In the case example, the counselor used the second approach, which yielded more material about the assault.

In addition, after the child has been engaged in the activity and is talking, it is important to quietly observe the child and how he or she utilizes the toy—what they say, what they do, how they interact with it and you. This period clearly indicates to the child that this is her or his time to express any thoughts, feelings or wishes. No verbal demands should be made on the child until she or he is settled into the play activity.

Victim Counseling in Rape Incest: A Case Illustration

On a Sunday evening at 7 P.M., a mother of five children left her home to visit a friend, leaving the care of four of her children to her common-law husband, who was also the father of the three youngest children. When the mother returned at 8 P.M. her husband left saying he needed to buy some groceries. The mother found her second oldest child Nancy, age 9, in bed earlier than usual and wrapped in a blanket with her head under the covers. The mother pulled back the covers and found blood on the sheets and saw that the child was bleeding from her genital area. Nancy said, "Daddy grabbed me, ripped off my panties, and did something that hurt." The mother immediately brought her daughter to the hospital.[3]

Victim counseling uses four conceptual models in the understanding and intervention into crisis problems: (1) the medical model, (2) the social network model, (3) the behavioral model, and (4) the psychological model. It is important for clinicians to be familiar with these models in order to plan and provide care to child victims of sexual assault.[4] We will discuss the general principles within each model and then relate the model to the case illustration.

Medical Model

The medical model of care deals with the physical condition of the human body and is influenced by biological and psychological concepts of the body.

Assessment of normal and abnormal conditions from physical trauma to the body are made by physical examination of the patient. Knowledge of the chemical composition of body fluids is necessary in the analysis of tests taken. Specifically, the sexual assault victim is examined for overall physical trauma, gynecological trauma, the presence of sperm, and other evidence of forcible rape.

Implementing the Medical Model. One of the major concerns of the family, the children, and the hospital staff is how much physical injury—specifically to the pelvic area—occurred. This phenomenon is observed in the analysis of parents' crisis requests for their children in which primarily medical concerns were stated.

The physical examination may be upsetting to the child, especially any invasive procedures. The meaning and psychological impact that the exam can have on the child should be carefully considered by parents and staff in the circumstances surrounding the crisis period. Parents as well as the child need to talk about their feelings about the examination. The gynecologist's and pediatrician's roles are especially crucial in dealing with the young rape victim.

Findings. To return to the case illustration, significant medical findings were: tenderness in both lower quadrants, blood on her legs, and a large blood clot protruding from between her labia. Her abdomen was painful when her legs were moved. Nancy was admitted to the hospital for two reasons: (1) to further assess and treat the physical trauma, and (2) to remove the child from the home environment until the situation could be assessed. Additional medical procedures had to be performed, such as blood tests and an intravenous infusion. These intrusive procedures further upset Nancy, who cried and clung to her mother. She asked to go to the bathroom. The nurses brought her a bedpan but she was unable to use it. A full internal examination was done that evening in the operating room under anesthesia and later in the recovery room, a catheterization for a distended bladder was attempted and proved unsuccessful. The next morning Nancy was afraid to void and said it hurt. The technique of clinical bargaining was tried by the nurses.[5] Nancy was offered the option of voiding in the bathroom and if successful, of having the intravenous removed as well as the reward of a cookie. She did void by herself, the IV was removed and she got the cookie.

Social Network Model

The focus of the social network model of care is the way in which the individual interacts and functions in relation to a specific group, such as her family, peers, and community. Observation of people who accompany the victim to the hospital is important in assessing the social network.

The treatment method is to make explicit use of the victim's social network. The goal of utilizing the social network of the victim is to strengthen his or her self-confidence to in turn facilitate resuming a normal lifestyle.

Implementing the Social Network Model. The strongest potential support system available to the child is usually the family. A major effort needs to be made on follow-up to assess how well the family has been able to deal with the rape.

Parent's Ability to Deal with the Issue. Parents have many feelings when learning that their child has been sexually assaulted. Sometimes the impact of the news makes it hard for them to talk with their child about the incident. Parents, like many people, may believe discussion is more upsetting to the child. As one parent said, "I never talk to her about it. I just want her to forget."

Many of the children spontaneously talked about the incident, although the family found it too difficult to discuss. The parents need to talk about how they are encouraging or discouraging the child to talk about it. One mother said, "She talks about it. I tell her to forget it. She gets nervous when his name is mentioned." Another mother said, "She has brought it up three times today. I try to ignore it so she won't think about it, but she keeps talking about it." In this situation, the mother was encouraged to talk about her feelings and told it was normal for the girl to talk about it, that when she had talked enough about it, she would probably stop. And she did.

In returning to the case example, Nancy's reaction to her family while in the hospital was clearly ambivalent. The day after admission, she kept the sheets over her head, frequently cried, and refused to eat or talk with anyone. When the mother visited, Nancy was very quiet. This behavior stressed the mother to the point that she experienced an anxiety reaction and fainted during one of the early visits. She was seen by the psychiatric nurse-clinician, who was able to talk with her about some of her feelings about the rape and her husband. The mother also gave the nurse a torn-up picture of the husband, which was later used by the police for identification. Later the nurse talked with Nancy and found out the child was angry with her mother for not protecting her.

The nursing intervention was to provide consistency in care to the child in order to promote and encourage trust. Within a short period of time, there was a dramatic change in Nancy's behavior; she began to talk with staff, let them touch her, and allowed them to care for her. This reversal in behavior coincided with Nancy saying, "My mother's mad—she's mad at my father because he hurt me." Clarification of the loyalty issue provided important support to the child. Nancy perceived her mother taking a stand by being angry at the father. It was important how her mother resolved the issue of her loyalty to the father versus Nancy. However, Nancy's ambivalence to family could be noted when relatives visited (grandparents, sister, mother) in that Nancy would elect to be with staff rather than family.

After discharge from the hospital, Nancy refused to return to school or to play with her friends. Several home visits were made by the nurse, who discovered that Nancy refused to attend school because she thought everyone knew what had happened. The nurse offered to contact the school to help coordinate plans for Nancy's return as an intervention technique, and the family agreed to this.

Contact was also made between nursing and the child welfare agency to determine the safety of the home and whether Nancy could remain there. Of interest was one of the child worker's comments, "How did a child of this age get herself into so much trouble?" The issue of who is blamed in child sexual abuse continues to be an issue that professional staff need to discuss. The nurse decided to deal with the issues by offering consultation to the agency on any of their sexual assault cases. Education of other staff to the multidimensional factors involved in child sexual assault is an important service of the victim counselor.

While Nancy was in the hospital, her father returned to the apartment and took stereo equipment, the television, and his 3-year-old son's clothing. This action contributed additional stress: (1) the family still was not safe from him, and (2) the family had to ask for financial assistance from the welfare agency for the child's clothing.

Behavioral Model

The behavioral model of care views mental health problems or distress as non-effective behavior, as behavior learned in a maladaptive way. A major emphasis of this model is to desensitize the victim to the phobias and fears which develop following a sexual assault.

The focus of care is to try to change the behavior pattern. A major aim is to neutralize some of the fear that results from the rape experience. A major therapeutic goal of the behavioral model is to deal with the symptoms the child reports, especially the phobic reactions. The child should be encouraged to resume a daily routine being careful to pace these activities. The longer the child avoids normal activities, such as attending school and other usual activities, the more difficult it will be to face up to the new fears.

Observing Symptoms over Time. Parents need to be instructed about the possible physical and behavioral symptoms that can develop in the child from the pressure of the situation and that are considered within the normal range for this reaction to a stress situation. Especially important to observe are changes in eating and sleeping patterns and development of fears.

In the case example, Nancy developed many fears. She refused to sleep alone and after coming home from the hospital, slept with her mother. She became very clinging to the mother and refused to venture out of the house. She had difficulty sleeping, and kept saying, "I'm afraid he is going to kill me." Nancy did not like living in the apartment and emphasized that she was afraid. One of the interventions was to investigate possible activities that Nancy could be referred to to help her resume some peer relationships. The victim counselor contacted summer camp programs to see which ones Nancy might be eligible for.

Implementing the Behavior Model. The counselor acted in a protective role on several home visits. Nancy described how fearful she was of playing outside, saying that the neighborhood children were terrorizing her. This report was very accurate. On one visit, the counselor sat with Nancy on her front door step and observed other children making very negative comments about her nationality (e.g., black children commenting on Nancy's Spanish origins) and her parents ("Your mother is a junkie and that's why your father raped you"). Nancy clung to the counselor after hearing these remarks with her eyes filling with tears. The counselor said, "We're OK, and we will just sit here till they go away." The children did go away but then came back making more remarks. The counselor decided it would be best to leave the situation and asked Nancy if she wanted to go for a ride in her car. This action proved to reduce the tension considerably. The counselor also acted as an advocate for the family in phoning and visiting the housing authorities to get the windows fixed that had been vandalized by neighborhood children.

Psychological Model

The psychological model of care views human interaction as a key determinant in helping people understand what has and is occurring in regard to the problem at hand. Talking helps people feel better, and encouraging the child to talk is therapeutic. The human mind works in priorities, and the way to help the child is to allow her or him to select the priorities and to try and follow her or his verbal lead.

The return hospital visit for follow-up may be an opportune time to encourage the child to talk about feelings and thoughts relevant to the rape. In the case example, Nancy's nonverbal behavior specific to being examined revealed her feelings about having to deal with a man again. She went into the examining room with the male physician, the nurse-counselor, and two other staff members and then into the bathroom where she was requested to change into a gown. After stalling tactics, she did put on the gown and showed the nurse her panties, which contained a small amount of bloody discharge. Nancy then would giggle and answer the physician's questions while sticking her head out of the bathroom door. As a resistance tactic she said that the physician was a policeman and she was not going to come out. Even though it was explained that he was not (she said he had a navy tie and shirt like the police detective), she would not come out of the bathroom. The physician and nurse decided the best strategy would be for everyone except the nurse to leave, the nurse doing a visual examination. This decision prompted a positive change in Nancy's behavior. She became verbal with the nurse, and there was direct eye contact for the remaining conversation.

The psychological model is essentially a verbal approach and hence, special attention should be given to the language used by the victim as well as the family. A child's language regarding body anatomy and the sexual assault more often than not will be what they have heard at home or with friends. In cooperating with the examination, Nancy said, "I want to know if my hole is alright because my father put his ugly thing up there and it hurt." When the child trusts the nurse, she may be able to mention her unanswered questions. For example, Nancy asked the nurse what happened to her when she was asleep under anesthesia saying, "Are my cuts fixed? Did they close up my hole?" Additional data may be revealed during the conversation. Nancy said, "My father put his thing there too," pointing to her rectum. Children will want to know what procedure they are receiving, and Nancy wanted to know what the nurse was going to do. The nurse explained the visual examination and showed her how she was examining her panties. Some basic education questions about anatomy and sex may occur. Nancy wanted to know "Did his thing go into my belly?" and "Do all girls have a hole and do all boys have those ugly things?" The nurse can use this time to honestly answer the child's questions, to perhaps find out what sex education there has been, and to plan for future sessions on such topics. If counselors can answer the child's questions comfortably, honestly, and simply, the child will probably be secure enough to ask additional questions later.

Discussion

This case will now be discussed using the conceptual framework of the four previously defined crisis concepts of victim counseling.

Rape: An External Crisis. The externally imposed crisis caused disruption in four lifestyle areas. The disruption in *physical* lifestyle was seen in the bruising and bleeding that occurred during the rape and the fact that Nancy had to be hospitalized for four days. It was necessary to do an internal examination while the child was under anesthesia to determine the extent of the trauma. Also there was disruption in the child's elimination system when she was not able to void. The disruption in Nancy's *emotional* lifestyle could be seen in her reaction to her family while in the hospital and her minor mood swings of crying and withdrawing, fluctuating with her dependence on the nursing staff. Nancy's major feeling was her ambivalence about her mother's part in protecting her from the assaultive behavior of the father. The school-aged child will show disruption in *social* lifestyle in the way she copes with formal organizations of school and the informal organizations of neighborhood and peer groups.[6] In this case, Nancy had difficulty returning to school, resuming relationships with her peers, and dealing with the brutal comments by neighborhood children.

Sexuality is an issue for a child victim even if it appears to be latent and not an obvious issue. The disruption in the *sexual life area* could be seen in Nancy's developing sexuality and continuity of this development. The issue of sexuality and raped children includes two parts: what is the sexual activity of the child, and what is the child's level of sex education. In this case, Nancy had no prior sexual activity with which to compare the assault, and she had limited knowledge of the basic facts regarding pregnancy and venereal disease. For example, Nancy had many questions relating to the understanding of her own anatomy and the sexual act.

Rape: Interaction of Internal and Developmental Issues. School-age children are working with a sense of industry and devote considerable energy to the mastering of tasks. Interruptions of these tasks by a sexual assault can threaten the degree of confidence a child feels in herself or himself. Also sexual assault during childhood registers with the child in terms of the area of the body that is the focus of the attack and his or her interpretation of the act as right or wrong because of the developing superego. In this case, Nancy was very persistent about the fact that "Daddy was wrong to hurt me," and very much needed the reassurance that mother also felt that way and would protect her from Daddy.

Court: Recapitulates the Crisis. In this case, the offender left town and was not apprehended. One year after the assault, a man was arrested by police who was thought to be the assailant and Nancy and her mother had to go to court to identify him, but he turned out to be the brother of the offender. Nancy was visibly upset as she looked at the defendant. She was quiet, cast her eyes downward most of the time, hunched her shoulders, and said, "They have the wrong one." Nancy clung to the nurse. When asked to draw the pictures of people she liked in the court—as a technique to encourage dialogue—Nancy drew the female victim specialist, the nurse, the police detective who had originally carried her from her home to the hospital, and the district attorney. Techniques aimed to reduce tension and fear for the child while waiting for the court hearing are an important aspect of dealing with the psychological distress of the court experience.

Rape: Potential for Additional Crises. This case points up the issue of divided loyalty. The child needed verification that her mother was going to protect her and not side with the offender. The fact that the offender left town immediately meant that the mother and the family did not have to deal with him on a day-to-day basis. However, the sudden loss of her male partner was a crisis for the mother and could be evidenced in her new inability to organize her household. She required considerable support from friends and family. The nurse noted the disorganization of the family and worked with the social service agency to provide extra money for the clothes that were stolen and the damage done by vandals to the home. A dramatic change was noted when the mother realigned herself with a new male partner. The companionship of a man was important to the mother and increased her ability to function. The nurse, on a home visit, observed that the furniture in the house had been totally rearranged, so that, in fact, it looked like a new home. This observation led to the news of a new male partner in the home. Although this helped the mother to function, it had the opposite effect on Nancy. She told the nurse that she "didn't like the new daddy" and the fact that she now had to sleep in her own room rather than with her mother.

In summary, we have discussed several techniques we have found useful in helping to relieve some of the distress and suffering experienced by child rape victims and their families. Assessment of the crisis level in the four areas of disruption will provide the crisis diagnosis. The intervention plan should include the medical, social, behavioral, and psychological treatment models of care. Evaluation of the return of the victim and her family to a precrisis level of health can be determined by telephone intervention or home visit on follow-up at the 3-, 6-, 9-, and 12-month intervals.

Prevention of Rape: Education and Community Coordination

A word needs to be said about the prevention of sexual assault. Families are concerned about this problem and very often will ask: How can we teach our children about sexual assault before it happens? Two suggestions can be made. First, parents and schools can help, and second, interagency program planning is important. The need for everyone to work together on this issue of prevention is essential. We emphasize that we do not have good data on how people successfully avoid sexual assault.[7] But we realize we must raise issues regarding prevention and thus offer the following issues for discussion.

Parents and Schools

Parents often ask: what can I tell my child about rape? How can it be prevented? If it happens, what should we do? In answer to these questions, we suggest some ideas that have been tried with children, offering them for discussion.

Before It Happens

1. Parents should be encouraged to talk with their children before anything happens. In these talks:
    a. Assess how much the child already knows about the subject. Some junior high and high schools are beginning to implement rape education programs in their curricula.
    b. Talk about encountering dangerous situations in general. What do children identify as dangerous; what dangerous situations have they already encountered, and how have they handled them?
    c. Role play some dangerous scenes with the children. Ask children what they would do if a stranger approached them to get in his car or if a man told them he would give them money if they did something for him. Also ask the children what they would do if confronted with a gun or knife, or if they were grabbed and pushed into a car. Talking it over and suggesting tactics they might think of provides an opportunity for parents to assess their child's reaction and point out alternatives in their thinking.
2. Parents can discuss with their children issues concerned with sexual assault. Parents can also reinforce previously taught general safety rules.
    a. Protection in the home. Rules such as reporting all strange telephone calls to parents; not to let any strangers in the house; telephoning the police if they suspect any emergency and a parent is not available.
    b. Protection of the self. Always travel with a friend or adult; avoid dark, deserted areas when outdoors; ask for directions only from authorized persons, such as a police officer.
    c. Psychological self. Keep your mind alert and watch where you are going; rehearse in your mind what you would say if a stranger asked you a question or stopped you.
    d. High risk areas. Talk with school officials and police officers about dangerous areas known in the community; be knowledgeable regarding teenagers who hurt or pick on children.
3. Parents can discuss with their children what to do if they are threatened or actually assaulted.
    a. If threatened, keep calm and try to talk your way out of the situation. Try to get out of the situation in as safe a way as possible.
    b. If attacked, try to keep a clear head. Observe the perpetrator for any identifying features. Focus your mind on survival and remember everything you can that will enable you to identify the person afterwards. Memorize the make of the car or license number, what he says to you, and any scars or distinguishing marks.
    c. After the attack, escape safely and report to parents, police, or the hospital. Many agencies have victim services that can help the child

and the family. Be sure to get follow-up care to decrease any chance of long-term symptoms.

4. The schools have a part to play in educating children to the laws of the society. History or social studies classes are excellent for having children study state laws that are designed to protect them. Such study would help children to know the legal terminology as well as the reporting laws. Schools can teach the legal definitions of rape, incest, and more general child abuse so that children have the knowledge to know when someone is breaking the law.

   a. If schools do teach the laws in class and children are aware that they can self-report, school nurses and police officers need to be prepared to work with children when they do report. Also, services, both immediate and follow-up, should be available.

Interagency Cooperation and Program Planning

The public health concepts of primary, secondary, and tertiary intervention are key to any program planning on a community basis. This book primarily addresses secondary prevention in sexual assault, that is, what to do immediately after the child has been assaulted, and tertiary intervention, that is, dealing with the unresolved aftereffects of sexual trauma and the rehabilitative aspect.

Primary intervention involves education and strategies to prevent the sexual assault of children. We rely heavily on Rape Crisis Centers for providing community education on the subject and for bringing the entire issue to the attention of the public. With the sexual assault of children being reported more, there is a stronger mandate for community education to continue.

At a statewide conference in New Mexico, sponsored by the Bernalillo County Mental Health/Mental Retardation Center of the University of New Mexico and the New Mexico Mental Health Association, panelists on Interagency Cooperation stated that interagency coordination is the key to rape crisis center development. The panelists emphasized that the eventual success of a newly formed Rape Crisis Center depends largely on its ability to form and maintain working relationships with existing community agencies.[8]

According to the panel, cooperative relations between agencies and organizations serving rape victims is essential for a variety of reasons. Comprehensive services are expensive, and usually cannot be provided through a single agency. Duplication of needed services is wasteful. Within each community, a wide range of services exist that can be beneficial to victims if they can be mobilized. A single agency or program is powerless to influence legislation or political groups; but combined, a number of agencies can work to bring about far-reaching changes. A lack of cooperation, or outright antagonism, between agencies can do much to further injure the victim of a sex crime.

Panelists offered the following suggestions for developing crisis centers, to assist in promoting interagency cooperation.

1. Locate sensitive people in the community who care about victims and are interested in the problem. Where possible, develop friendships in offices providing important services or support. Make personal and repeated contacts with agency personnel, and keep them informed of your progress. Frequently reinvite them to participate in your planning.

2. Identify agencies providing services, and work to develop a relationship with them. Recognize that many agencies and organizations need to be educated to the problem of sexual abuse, and provide opportunities for them to learn. In addition, identify the special concerns or needs that are barriers to agency participation, and develop strategies to overcome those barriers. Personal or political concerns frequently impact on professionals or agencies, making it necessary to approach community groups and representatives with caution and sensitivity.

3. Develop a public demand for the service. The fact that a rape program does not exist in your community is an indication that the community is not fully aware of sexual abuse as a social problem. The general public, as well as professionals, need to be educated and informed.

4. Develop and maintain concrete, workable agreements between agencies, and utilize services representing the widest possible base of funding sources. This can help provide for a secure future. Where possible, identify ways in which your program can be of help to existing agencies. Develop "trade-offs", things you can give up in exchange for things you need. Formulate contracts for the exchange of services, and establish referral procedures to smooth out transitions between your program and other agencies.

5. The primary mission of a rape crisis center is to provide timely, effective, and relevant services to victims of sexual abuse. The medical, psychological, and physical needs of clients should shape the development and operation of the programs.

The evolution of cooperative, community relations is a slow, and often tedious, process. Changes in personnel, political climate, and funding make the maintenance of these relationships an ongoing, continuous process. Above all, panel members stressed patience and persistence as the key variables in successfully developing workable, interagency agreements.

References

1. James E. Simmons, *Psychiatric Examination of Children,* 2nd ed. (Phila: Lea and Febiger, 1974), p. 17.

2. Erik Erikson, "The Initial Situation and Its Alternatives," in *Child Psychotherapy Practice and Theory.* Ed. Mary R. Haworth, (New York: Basic Books Inc., 1964), pp. 107–08.

3. Please note that although the common-law husband was not the biological father of Nancy, he was called "Daddy" by all the children.

4. A complete discussion of these four conceptual models of victim care may be found in Ann Wolbert Burgess and Lynda Lytle Holmstrom. *Rape: Victims of Crisis.* (Bowie, Md.: Robert J. Brady Co., 1974.)

5. Lynda Lytle Holmstrom and Ann Wolbert Burgess, *The Victim of Rape: Institutional Reactions* (New York: Wiley-Interscience, in press).

6. Ann Wolbert Burgess and Lynda Lytle Holmstrom, "Rape: It's Effect on Task Performance at Varying Stages in the Life Cycle" in *Sexual Assault: The Victim and the Rapist,* ed. Marcia J. Walker and Stanley L. Brodsky (Lexington, Mass.: Lexington Books, D.C. Heath and Co., 1976), pp. 23–34.

7. A Nicholas Groth and Murray Cohen, "Aggressive Sexual Offenders: Diagnosis and Treatment." In *Community Mental Health: Target Populations,* Ann Wolbert Burgess and Aaron Lazare (Englewood Cliffs, N.J.: Prentice-Hall, Inc. 1976) p. 222.

8. Reprinted with permission from *Noticias De Mujeres,* vol. 2, no. 2, June 1977, ed. Robert Knox.

13 The Child and Family During the Court Process
Ann Wolbert Burgess and Lynda Lytle Holmstrom

The availability of a person to assist the victim and family through the court process has been recognized as an important service need. Victim-witness advocate programs have been initiated, often from the district attorney's office, as one tactic to aid young witnesses. One Sexual Assault Center—based at Harborview Medical Center in Seattle, Washington—believes that criminal justice staff must adopt special techniques to encourage the cooperation of child witnesses and to acknowledge the inherent limitations on a child's performance. The Center staff state there are two negative effects that can result if a criminal justice system fails to do so: (1) further traumatization of the child by investigation and court procedures can occur, and (2) unsuccessful prosecutions result because the child witness is unable to convey the information necessary to corroborate the charge in court.[1]

The court process, for the child and the family, can be as much of a crisis as the actual sexual assault.[2] Victims and their families develop a multitude of intense reactions in going through the court process. Several general psychological responses are magnified.

First, time becomes suspended. The energies needed to continually go to court, to endure the court delays that interrupt schooling and family life are upsetting to the child. Victim and family become preoccupied by court and have difficulty going about their normal activities.

Second, the rape or assault is relived. The court process recapitulates in a psychological manner, the original assault situation. The child must relive the assault mentally and verbally in a public setting at least three times: at the hearing for probable cause, before the grand jury, and at superior court level. Court is a very formal protocol that is new and unfamiliar. The child does not know how the court system works and has to rely on preparation by the district attorney who often may not have the time to explain or prepare the child. In cross-examination, the defense counsel may try to discredit the child's story by implying that the child made up the story.[3]

Third, victims become aware that people are skeptical about their story, and a feeling of silent suspicion is felt. Few people, except in the courtroom, may be so blatant as to tell the child they do not believe her, but this suspicion is communicated in subtle ways. And fourth, the child and family may feel betrayed by people previously considered supportive.[4]

This chapter will focus on the preparation of a case by the district attorney (DA), what happens in the courtroom, and counseling techniques to help reduce stress for the child and family as they go through the court process.

205

Preparing the Case

To prepare and try a rape case, the DA needs evidence and witnesses. Likewise, the major witness in a rape case—the victim—has needs and requests to make of the DA. From the victim's point of view, two requests are important: (1) that the DA have some concern and understanding of the victim as a person and the rape as an upsetting experience, and (2) that the DA is professionally competent in trying the case. The first is a question of style, the second of technical expertise. The former is our main concern here.

Professional Style of the District Attorney

Professionals, as part of their training, develop a certain style or manner in which they present themselves to the client. In turn, clients react to this professional style from their own perspective, based on their past experiences. Professional style is related to the amount of human regard and respect one attaches to the client.

The importance to clients of these two components—professional competence and human understanding—varies. Lazare et al., for example, in studying the client requests of people seeking psychiatric services, state that, in mental health work, both qualities are essential in building and establishing a relationship. In certain other medical situations, however, the client puts less priority on the professional style. For example, a patient may settle for the "best surgeon in town" and forego the need to be understood and respected.[5]

It became clear in observing professionals react to and treat sexual assault victims that the issue of human regard for the client was important to the young person and the family. In analyzing the professional style used by the district attorneys toward the child and family in preparing the case, three types were noted: the indifferent, the task-oriented, and the humanistic.[6]

Indifferent Style. In the indifferent style, the DA provides little or no instructions to the witness, uses none of the usual social pleasantries, has minimal discussion with the witness, and, in general, displays little human regard for the witness. They generally lecture the witness, talk at the person rather than listening to the person, and interject their own opinions and biases. For example, one DA never said hello or goodbye to the victim or her family. In court, he would walk ahead of the family instead of with them. He ignored the group, even as he walked to the courtroom for the trial. Assigned to one case involving a 14-year-old girl, he prepared it standing by the elevator in the main corridor of the courthouse. He made judgmental comments, saying it was her fault to be out alone walking.[7]

This style is upsetting and confusing to victims. They are not sure if this is the DA's usual style or if he is acting negatively toward them on purpose. The victim counselor or advocate has to work hard to help neutralize the psychological insult caused by this style. If the counselor knows which DA has been assigned and knows that this is his or her typical style, some anticipatory work may be done with the young person and family to prepare them for its impact or work may be done to get a different DA assigned. If the DA uses this style with anyone, he needs to know that such a style is upsetting to people. If informal discussions fail to correct the situation, consideration might be given to having advocate groups put pressure on the system to consider the impact of this style on witnesses.

Task-Oriented Style. In the task-oriented style, the DA uses an authoritative, matter-of-fact manner. They are polite, use social pleasantries, acknowledge the victim and family, and give technical instructions for behavior in the courtroom. In one case of a 15-year-old girl whose parents pressed charges of statutory rape against a 23-year-old defendant, a DA prepared the case as follows:

The DA asked the girl what happened, and she was reluctant to say. The DA then said, "Not about the intercourse—we all know how that happens—but when, where you were before, and things like that." The girl was not able to volunteer the information, which prompted the DA to ask some of the following questions: what is your age, did you know the man, how long have you known him, what did he ask you to do, or where did you go, did you have intercourse, how many times, did he penetrate, did he climax, did you spend the night there? At the end of this dialogue, the DA then said, "Now you must tell the judge all this." The girl, with tears beginning to flow down her cheeks, said, "I have to tell all that happened?"

The DA replied:

"I'm not telling you that to make it hard, but so you'll know. We have to prove intercourse occurred—that penetration occurred. You have to tell the judge—but not the details—everyone here is old enough to know what it means and doesn't want to hear the sordid details. It's embarrassing, though it shouldn't be. We all know what it means. Tears speak well for your character. If you came in here and were not upset, we'd wonder."

The police sergeant added in an authoritative tone:

"You don't need to tell the details. Just say we went to bed together. And the DA will protect you from embarrassing questions. The defense will try, but he'll protect you. And above all, don't make up an answer. Say 'I don't know.' Or 'I don't remember.' Otherwise they'll catch you. For example, if they ask

you what kind of bed it was, and you don't remember, and you say it was a wooden bed, and then maybe later it turns out it wasn't really a wooden bed."

The DA added:

And don't answer in anger. You don't look like the type who would, but some witnesses do. And defense lawyers like that. They know they've gotten to you. And remember that the judge hears this stuff everyday. It's not new to him.

Then the DA continued his preparation of the case, saying:

"Now when you're on the stand, I'll ask your age. And you'll say '15.' And I'll ask you how long you knew him as an acquaintance. And you'll say '2 months.'"

The DA went over the list of questions and answers that he had on his legal pad and completed his preparation of the witness for testifying.

This style may be perceived as tolerable by the young person. Or the child may find the authoritative aspect scary. This style is often expected by adults who are used to dealing with bureaucracies and tolerated if instructions are given and are useful. But children have less experience in dealing with officials and professionals. In this style, the DA focuses on the task at hand, but fails to take into account the emotional impact this experience is having on the child and the fact that the rape has been a frightening experience. The victim counselor can help to soften the impact of this style after the case preparation is complete by engaging the young person in a nonstressful activity, such as the use of age-related toys or suggesting a diversional walk outside the courthouse.

Humanistic Style. In this style, the DA focuses on the task, but in addition, is sensitive to the socioemotional aspect of the interaction. The DA acknowledges the stress nature of the court process, tempers instructions with examples, adapts his or her approach to the level of understanding of the child, and is sensitive to the needs and feelings of the child. The following case illustrates such sensitivity. The DA obtained a relatively nonthreatening setting to interview the child and mother, provided practical points for the mother, and gave advice with his reasons. The DA called the victim counselor prior to talking with the family and requested her assistance. He said he would write to the family, requesting that they call him to arrange a time to get together to go over the story. The DA said he did not think the courthouse was a good place ("It is like a zoo here and would upset her. I could come to your office or go to her home"). The final arrangements were that the DA would drive to the victim's home and pick up the victim and her mother and then drive to the counselor's office at a University building. The following account illustrates the two hours preparation of the case. The DA used his observations of the child to judge her ability to testify, and decided he would not have her testify.

The child, Martha, cried as she walked down the hallway of the University building with her mother. She would not talk with the counselor and just buried her head in her mother's coat and continued crying. She did not respond to any of the counselor's questions. She refused to take off her coat and climbed onto her mother's lap once inside of the room. She stayed there for the first 45 minutes of the interview. Her only response for the first hour was at one point to utter a loud wailing sound as the DA asked the mother questions about the defendant. After an hour, the girl became bored and started playing with the swivel chair that was left for her. Then she agreed to go for a drink of water and a tour of the building with the counselor. She wrote her name on a blackboard in chalk, asked if the school had any toys. She did say "hello" to two people who passed, whom the counselor knew. When back in the room where the mother and DA were still talking, she started playing with various objects. She finally became so restless that the DA realized it was time to terminate the interview and said he would get her an ice cream on the way home as he had promised.

The DA went into extreme detail to describe to the mother what would happen in court and also carefully went over her story. He also made the following points, while talking to her:

1. "I want to make sure of everything."

2. "The defense lawyer will cross examine. That is his right and it may seem hard at times, but that is what he must do. He has to protect the defendant's civil rights."

3. "The mental status of the defendant might be an issue. He probably will have a sanity hearing, and he might plead guilty. I have entered a package [for a plea], but it is long and detailed and I do not think the defendant will go for it; i.e. he will go for trial and/or insanity."

4. "I want to put Martha on as an exhibit—that is, you would walk Martha up and down in front of the jury so they could see her, but she will not have to testify."

5. "It is important how witnesses look in court. I want the women to wear dresses and Martha to be dressed as cute as she can be. I will not have any male witnesses if they do not wear a uniform or a shirt and tie. I do not have witnesses who do not look proper. They hurt the case if they do not look good."

6. "The notes from the district court hearing say that you were a good witness and that the case is strong. Do you have any additional information that I should know?"

7. *"Will Martha's father be present, and is he in favor of the case going to court?"* (The mother said he was in the military, but he was home right now because one of their daughters was missing. It turned out that the girl was at a friend's but the father had been called home. The DA did not like that information at all and said for the mother not to tell anyone about that. That would hurt the case.) *"I do not want people thinking you do not watch the children— I know how easy it is for kids to be elsewhere. I am from a family of nine—but I do not want you talking about it to anyone."*

8. *"Be prepared for a long wait. The case could be delayed many times. The defendant has had a psychiatric examination and no evidence of psychosis was found."*

The DA told the mother that she should call him if she had any questions. He said it was his job to prosecute cases. He did not get any more money if he won or lost the case, but he always did his best. The defense lawyer was a public defender, and he would be trying to win the case. The DA wanted to be sure she had all her questions answered. He said he was hard to reach and that people were always looking for him, but to leave a message and he always picked up his messages at the end of the day. The DA asked the mother how her daughter was psychologically. The mother said she was doing OK—that they never talked about it except when she went to court. The rest of the interview was spent in going over in minute detail the case: the location of the incident, how the mother had dressed her daughter that day, if she noted any bruises that day, where the man lived, when she notified the police, how she heard about her daughter, how she got to the hospital, who she talked to, and where she went.

This humanistic style produced the most favorable response by young victims and their families. The people involved felt they were respected and cared about in a human way. The DA was thorough in preparation and instructions to the family. The family felt they could ask questions or call the prosecutor's office and their call would be returned.

DA's Requests of the Counselor

The DA may find the victim counselor a useful person with whom to talk. Counselors often have seen the child from the time of disclosure of the incident and thus have valuable observations regarding facts of the case, as well as the child's emotional status. DAs may have questions, look to the counselor for opinions, or wish to sort out their impressions of the child and seek verification from the counselor.

Questions and Opinions. In one situation, the DA specifically sought out the counselor and explained his concern as follows: "I am preparing this case and

I have two questions: Is she competent to testify, and what has been her psychological reaction to the incident?" Discussion focused on the information the DA had and the counselor's assessment of the psychological condition of the child. For example, the DA was concerned about whether he had evidence to prove penetration. The police could testify that they came in on the child, but it was dark and it was hard to see if the defendant was sexually penetrating her. He asked if the child could describe the sexual part. The counselor said the child was not able to talk at the hospital because she was in too much pain, too upset, and too tired. Also, the child had not been able to talk of that aspect of the rape since disclosure of the situation. The DA was concerned about how the child would react to seeing the defendant again. He decided not to have the child testify after learning the child still became upset when hearing the man's name.

In one case, the DA favored probation rather than prison. During a court recess, the DA asked the counselor, "Do you think the boy should be sent to prison?" Evidence and arguments in the courtroom had revealed many factors favorable to the defendant: his lack of record, his stable school history. Both his mother and father came to court and indicated their concern and active involvement with their children. The counselor felt pressured by the DA. She replied merely that one would have to take such factors into consideration. The ethical dilemma was how to answer without revealing any of the confidences entrusted to her by the victim. Thus she based her reply on the information available to all those in the courtroom and avoided saying anything based on information provided in confidence by the victim.

Sorting Out Impressions. The DA may react to information gained while preparing or trying the case. In most situations, the DA merely talks about his concerns in an attempt to sort out feelings and thoughts. In one case, the DA sorted out his feelings regarding the very small age difference between the adolescent victim and defendant, the nonvirgin status of the victim, and the fact the victim had lied to him. The last point was the most upsetting ("She said she hadn't planned on going there . . . and later admitted she had"). The DA expressed his opinion of the situation to the counselor. He felt it was a case of fornication rather than rape.

In another case, the DA sought out the counselor after a talk with the 12-year-old victim. The purpose was twofold: to sort out his impressions as well as to verify that his interpretation of the child's confusion was valid.

I was so confused talking to her. I would ask her a question and she would talk about Santa Claus almost. I just felt she was making up some answers to the questions I asked. I don't know what to do about this. I talked with the officer who saw her, and he said he thought she was in such shock that she reacted that way. He said he believed her. . . . I think I will just have to give a brief capsule of what happened to the jury and let her tell her story.

I tried to go over the notes from probable cause hearing but she just got too confused.

Defense Counsel's Requests

There are additional people in the court process that the victim and family are likely to encounter. Not only is the prosecutor working on the case, but the defense counsel is preparing the other side. The defense counsel may well use a variety of tactics (1) to gain information and (2) to add stress to the DA's witnesses.

Gaining Information. The victim and family need to be aware that the defense lawyer may try to contact them before the court hearing or trial. The family should be informed that they do not have to talk with the defense, and, if they do, the information may be used against them in court. In the following situation, the 16-year-old victim handled the defense lawyer quite effectively.

The defense lawyer introduced himself to the victim and her mother. Then he asked what the victim and counselor were doing (they were obviously studying a history book in anticipation of an exam the victim was scheduled to take for class). Wanting to make conversation, the defense lawyer asked the victim two times if she would speak with him. The victim quietly told him that she would prefer not to talk with him about the case. The defense lawyer told the victim she could ask the DA, but the DA could not prevent her from talking with him. The victim said she realized that but that she would prefer not to talk with him. The counselor, in an attempt to reduce tension, began talking with the lawyer about a current publicized issue in the newspaper, and suggested that the girl continue her studying.

In another case, one defense lawyer came over to talk with one of the counselors and privately conversed with her, ignoring the victim and her mother who were also sitting with the counselor.

Defense: *"Are you from the university involved with a rape project?"*

Counselor: *"Yes"*

Defense: *"You must hate defense lawyers."*

Counselor: *"Well, each person has their own job to do."*

The mother of the victim looked displeased over this intrusion and later astutely said, "He's the kind of person who tries to get information out of you."

There are legal ways in which the defense counsel can obtain information from the counselor. In one case, a newly appointed public defender called the counselor at home to try to obtain additional information from the court hearing. The counselor had taken notes at the hearing and had given a copy to the DA. The lawyer tried to pressure her to send him a copy. The dialogue was as follows:

Defense: *"I'd like to talk with you about the notes you took. What is your schedule?"*

Counselor: *"You can get the information from the DA."*

Defense: *"This is an adversary system and, although the DA and I may be friends, he doesn't have to tell me anything."*

Counselor: *"So why should I then?"*

Defense: *"I can subpoena you if I have to. This is a serious charge. This man, if convicted, could get a life sentence."*

Counselor: *"I realize it is serious and that is the reason for the trial. We're all after the same thing, aren't we? The truth?"*

Defense: *"But if the child lied, she could send a guy to jail for life."*

Counselor: *"I have no reason to believe the child lied."*

Defense: *"I talked with the school counselor and she clammed up too. No one will talk to me. It makes me feel like a second-class citizen. My client must have every opportunity to disprove that this in fact did occur. I have to see to that. I'd like to speak to you—informally—just take 30 minutes to go over the copy of your notes."*

Counselor: *"I am surprised the defense attorney at the probable cause hearing did not have a recollection that all this happened and am surprised that he didn't have a better memory of this or take his own notes."*

Defense: *"I will have my secretary issue you a summons and the judge will instruct you to talk with me."*

The counselor was subpoenaed by the defense and her notes taken at the probable cause hearing were used to try to discredit the police officer's testimony regarding his memory of the arresting scene.

Adding Stress. There are several ways a defense lawyer can add stress to a victim. He may ask an upsetting question and leave, he may ask for a sequestering of witnesses, or he may ask to speak privately with the counselor. All these tactics influence and add tension to the victim and family.

The defense lawyer quickly identifies the "other side" and at strategic points during court recess or before or after court seeks them out. The brief contact may include a statement or an out-of-the-blue question. In one case, the defense lawyer came over to a 14-year-old girl and her mother, before court started, and said, "Your father isn't coming today?" All three—the victim, her mother, and the counselor—looked at each other as if to say why should he ask.

In this same case, at the end of the trial, the following dialogue occurred, involving the defense lawyer and a mysterious telephone call.

The victim counselor was explaining the judge's instructions to the victim and the defense lawyer walked by. The counselor stopped talking until he had gone. He came back and said to the victim, "Why did you telephone me last night?" The victim indicated she had not telephoned him. Then the defense lawyer asked, "Did your family telephone me?" Both the victim and her mother indicated no and seemed most surprised by the question. The counselor asked the defense lawyer, "What makes you think that you were telephoned?" He replied, walking away, "Paranoia."

There is another strategy that has been reported informally by counselors who are serving the dual role in court of (1) providing support for the victim during the testifying phase, and (2) testifying as to information heard at the time of disclosure, or, in the case of nurse-counselors, the emotional and physical state of the victim at the time of hospital examination. Many times, if the defense counsel knows that a counselor is going to be present at the court, he or she will send a subpoena to the counselor to testify and request a sequestering of witnesses. In that way, the counselor cannot be present with the victim for purposes of support. The solution to this tactic is to send two counselors to court so that the one not testifying can provide the emotional support for the victim.

The defense counsel may use tactics to cast suspicion of betrayal onto the counselor. In one case, a defense lawyer asked a counselor while standing with the young victim if the counselor had the psychiatric records of the victim. There were no such records, but the question was heard by the victim who, in turn, reported the information to her mother.

The defense may approach the counselor in the guise of asking an opinion. Consider the following case, which adds stress for the victim and family as well as casts suspicion.

Late in the afternoon, when the victim and her mother were in another waiting area of the courtroom, the defense lawyer briefly came over to the counselor and asked, "Would it be inappropriate if I asked you if you believed she was raped?" The counselor replied, "I think it is inappropriate for you to talk to me when the victim is not present." The defense lawyer said, "Do you want me to get her?" The counselor got up and walked out and told the victim what he had asked and what she had replied. The victim who was alert to court procedure said, "I thought it would come to that." A policeman overheard the conversation and said, "The defense lawyer came over to you . . . you don't have to have any conversation with him."

The counselor or advocate is viewed in a variety of ways by people in the court process. The constructive ways in which the DA sees the counselor are as an advocate for the victim, as a source of information for preparing the case, and sometimes as a witness. The defense counsel may see the counselor as someone who is influential with, and has access to, the victim. The victim and family usually see the counselor as "being on their side." Thus, with so many people having access to the counselor, it is not surprising that there may be cross-pressures on her or him.

Counselors need to be especially careful that the cross-pressures are not misinterpreted by the victim and family. For example, many hearings and trials involving young people are closed court sessions. Thus the counselor may be called by the judge to explain her or his interest in the case, and then the judge rules on whether the counselor may stay. However, the family, not able to hear this conversation, may wonder what has transpired. The counselor should report to the family what the judge asked and what the reply was. The important counseling principle of providing this feedback to the victim and the family conveys the attitude that you are loyal to the victim, you respect the victim and take seriously the idea that every transaction should include the victim. Such action reduces the victim's feelings of suspicion and betrayal.

The counselor's goal in the court process is to help maintain a tolerable stress level for the victim and family. Thus the counselor's tasks in being in court with the family and victim are (1) to provide psychological support, (2) to interpret the routine courtroom protocol, and (3) to neutralize the stressful feelings that may develop between the victim and people encountered in the court process.

In the Courtroom

Observing Victim and Family Behavior

A young person often expresses his or her feelings and reactions through behavior and actions. Adult victims may be able to verbalize their tension, embarrassment, or anger, whereas the younger person may show a response through body language. Thus, to provide comfort and support for the child, it is important to first assess the child in regard to the tension or stress level being felt. This observation, when compared to the child's usual behavior under stress, will provide information on whether or not to decide to intervene.

Court is an unsettling experience. Young people and family members will show their nervousness in a variety of ways: increased body movements; facial expression; and verbal expression, such as talking or crying. The following examples provide some types of reactions within a normal range.

Arm and Leg Movements

A 14-year-old girl looked very nervous before the trial began as she was sitting in the courtroom. She put her hand to her face; looked possibly as though she were sucking her right thumb. She put her left hand flat against her left temple. The gesture seemed one of being distraught.

A 14-year-old girl kept moving her right leg up and down and, when sitting, kept rocking her body forward and backward. Also during testifying she moved her legs in nervous ways.

The mother of a 16-year-old rape victim picked nervously at her nails and said, "I'm getting a million hangnails."

Clinging Behavior

A 5-year-old girl clung to her mother almost the whole time. The mother held her arms around her daughter and patted her in a comforting way. Later the girl sat on the bench beside her mother, leaned over and put her head on her mother's lap. After a while a court official asked the mother to come into one of the interviewing rooms. She was going without the daughter. As soon as the mother got up, the child got visibly upset and was on the verge of crying. But the father said, "Come here" and she went to him. He calmed her down and she stood clinging to him and later sat beside him, again very close to him.

Verbal Style, Controlled

Throughout the hearing, a 14-year-old girl was visibly trembling and trying to control the tears which were welling in her eyes. She only spoke to her boyfriend. When she was asked questions by the judge or DA, she answered only yes or no.

Prior to the hearing, the 6-year-old boy sat quietly on the bench outside the courtroom. He stared straight ahead. If anyone caught his gaze, his eyes would fill up with tears. His brothers and sister sat on the bench with him and looked as frightened and upset as the victim.

Verbal Style, Expressive

A 16-year-old rape victim was obviously nervous, swinging her foot, picking her fingernails, and talking excessively to a girl friend.

In the courthouse corridor, one 13-year-old victim jumped up and said to her father, "See, I told you he wasn't in jail." The father told her to sit down and be quiet. Later, after lighting his third or fourth cigarette of the morning, he said he had quit smoking but seeing the guy come in had gotten him all worked up.

The counselor should consider intervening if young persons lose control of their behavior, such as crying or moving around loudly, and are unable to limit their behavior despite a firm request by a parent. The counselor knows the courtroom is stressful and can work with the DA to have the child in court only while testifying and for short periods. The decision of whether the child and parent wish to stay for the entire court procedings is usually given to the family.

Counselors may find themselves in conflict over their strategy in calming a young victim down after an upsetting experience in the courtroom and what a family member or person in the victim's social network uses to set limits on the child's behavior. In the following example, the counselor used a strategy aimed at allowing the girl to express her distress and feelings; the social network person's approach was just the opposite, designed to have the girl not express any emotion.

During a court recess, the 13-year-old victim, crying, grabbed the counselor's hand, held it a long time. The counselor let her cry—thinking she had been through a stressful cross-examination and had cried while on the witness stand. Then the family lawyer came over and told her sternly to stop crying. She stopped at his command. He said to the counselor, "I thought I'd try a little of my psychology."

When counselors find themselves in conflict with the method of discipline being implemented by a social network person, it is important to observe the child's reaction and, at a later time, when alone with the child, ask how the child felt about the situation. If there are feelings the child wishes to express, you have provided the opportunity. Such a technique helps to relieve any conflict the child may have in the situation as well as to provide you with feedback regarding the child's interpretation.

Child's Questions Regarding Court

Going to court is usually a new experience for many of the people involved in a rape case. Even though the DA may prepare the case and try to provide important information, the child and family may still have misconceptions and questions about procedure. It is always a good rule to inquire of the child and family members what they *heard* the DA tell them and what questions they still have. The information provided by the DA may have been misperceived because of their own anxiety about being in court or too technical or detailed and thus not understandable. As one mother said, "She was never in a court room before. . . . she looked at the room and thought it was awful." Later the mother said, "She had a million questions. She wanted to know where she would have to stand. I showed her the witness stand and she asked if she had to walk all the way up there. She said she was not going to do that."

People need to be told that the court officers help to maintain order and that the officer will usually indicate—or with small children lead them by the hand to—where they are to stand or sit as a witness. In courtrooms in which there is a microphone, there may be some discussion over whether the child should hold the microphone—as an adult might—or whether a stand microphone would be most effective.

Victim's Behavior While Testifying

The cross-examination by defense places added stress on the young person. For example, in the following situation, the defense put pressures on the 12-year-old girl and confused her to the point that she was unable to answer him.

Defense: *"Didn't you tell your father he raped you?"*

Child: *"Yes."*

Defense: *"But he didn't rape you."*

Child: *"Yes he did."*

Defense: *"Do you know what rape means?"*

Child: *(No answer)*

Defense: *"Do you know what rape means, I repeat."*

Child: *(No answer)*

Defense: *"Tell me what it means or say I don't know."*

Child: *"I don't know."*

Young people who have not had any preparation on tactics that help decrease the stress of being on the witness stand may experience the same type of dilemma. Witnesses can be told to look to the DA or a familiar person in the courtroom for encouragement during long cross-examination. In one case, a 14-year old, during her testimony, did not look at anyone—she either looked down or out the window when not directly answering a question. In this situation, it would have been helpful for the girl to have been given instructions on where to look while waiting for the next question or what to do as she was thinking how to respond.

Some young people will be quite spirited while on the stand. One 16-year-old victim of a gang rape by four men showed quite a bit of spunk on the witness stand. She would add things for emphasis, such as how much she cried. And when the defense tried to emphasize her lack of certainty regarding which man was the third or fourth, she insisted on saying that despite that confusion there was no doubt that the defendant had forced sexual intercourse on her.

Delays in the court process are usually experienced negatively, but occasionally, the long delays between court hearings and trial may work to the advantage of the prosecution. The detective in one case reported the following.

The guy was convicted and sentenced for 7 to 12. . . . There was no physical evidence—no medical testimony, no hospital report. They got the conviction on the girl's testimony. She was a poor witness at lower court and grand jury. I had to get someone to help her in district court—she wouldn't say more than yes or no. But in court at trial she was much better. In a year's time she turned into a good witness.

Reactions to Court

There are additional ways the victim can be affected by the court process. First, the victim may be tested by people in the court system; and second, the victim has to listen to testimony about herself or himself.

Testing the Victim. The victim may be tested by people thought to be on her side. In one case, the victim reported that a detective said to her, "I hear you've been going to bed with all the defendant's friends—that you are part of the group that goes together and sleeps around." The victim asked where he got such a story, and the detective said they had picked up more of the defendant's friends on other charges. Later the detective told her he didn't mean to accuse her, but he asked questions so she would be aware that they might ask her in court. The counselor asked how she felt. The victim answered, "I think he was just testing my reaction."

Listening to Testimony About Oneself. Not only do parents have to listen to upsetting testimony about their child, but victims themselves may sit through upsetting testimony about themselves. In the following case, a 13-year-old girl listened to her foster mother and a social worker give testimony.

The foster mother testified first for the prosecution. She said that Gerry had a learning problem but that she had not caused them very much trouble, except that she sometimes became very upset and despondent and it was difficult to say why. She said on the day that Gerry disappeared, she had scolded Gerry for having some cigarettes in her purse. Gerry was very upset and left the house. During the course of the next few days they tried to find Gerry.

The social worker then testified that Gerry had a learning disability and a passive personality, meaning that she could be easily led. She said that Gerry had been diagnosed previously as retarded, but a couple of years ago had been re-diagnosed as dull-normal.

Gerry sat through the testimony and was very quiet. She kept her head down and looked embarrassed by it.

Parents and Social Network in the Courtroom

Generally, one or both parents will accompany their child to court when the child is called to testify. The parent may wish to be present during the entire court session or come only for the period in which the child testifies. Parents may feel it is their responsibility ("I have to come to court. I wouldn't be a good father if I didn't"); or one parent may substitute for both parents when one finds the experience too stressful ("I didn't want to go and listen. I was too upset when it happened. I just didn't want to go and listen to the details. Her father went").

There are several tasks for the parent who does accompany the child to court. The parent may (1) neutralize other family member reactions; (2) provide support for their child; (3) testify as a witness; and (4) be asked an opinion.

Tasks in Court

Neutralizing Family Member Reactions. Family members—especially males—can be quite expressive of their negative feelings toward the defendant(s). This behavior is most visible immediately after the assault, when family members talk—and sometimes act—about "getting the guy." This reaction later surfaces during the court process. The negative reaction is intensified when the defendant is actually seen—as in the courtroom. If the strong reaction triggers the family member to act, another family member may have to provide the external control to stop the action.

In one case, the mother of a 14-year-old victim was sitting next to the counselor on the bench of the waiting area of the district court. Suddenly the mother jumped up, ran down the hall, even leaving her purse and belongings on the bench. The counselor did not see what had prompted her sudden concern, but when she came back she said that the brother was upset and that she had seen him go toward the defendants when they came in. She was worried that he might try to do something to them, and she didn't want any such thing to happen.

Supporting the Child. The physical presence of a parent is usually a supportive technique for the child who is going to testify as the principal witness for the state. Children can be observed clinging to their parents, whispering to them, as well as seeking comfort supplies of gum, candy, and tissues. In one case, a 12-year-old girl, after testifying, ran off the witness stand over to the long table where the DA, counselor, and father were sitting. Her face was flushed. She climbed into her father's lap and cried softly.

Testifying as a Witness. There are various reasons why a parent might be called upon by a DA as a witness: (1) to describe receiving the initial complaint from the child, (2) to report general observations of the child's overall behavior, and (3) to give an opinion. Parents may be asked to relate what the child said upon entering the home following the assault. They may find it difficult to answer.

"They asked the same questions as before. I got choked up and started to cry. I wasn't too much help. They asked me what my daughter said when she walked in the door. That upset me. I started thinking of that night all over again. I got so mad and I put it all into one word: rape. I think they wanted me to give some details, and I just couldn't."

The mother later said that she had to come home after the hearing and had to lie down because she was so upset over the experience.

In another case, the mother was asked to describe her daughter's reaction to the assault.

"They asked me my daughter's reaction when she came home; whether she was at the party, what time she came home, and what time the police were called. It made me quite nervous not to be prepared any better than that."

This mother was upset over the delay between the time of the rape and the trial and her being required to remember specific details during the 13-month interval.

Sometimes, on cross-examination, the defense may wish to try to establish that the child behaved in a certain way because of the rules in their house. In one case, the father was asked about the discipline in the home and if his daughter had ever broken the rules. The defense also wanted to know if the father has ever threatened to physically punish his daughter—trying to establish that this had been so and that his daughter was afraid of her father.

A parent may be asked for an opinion on various aspects of the case. In one situation, the judge asked the mother of the girl and the father of the boy for their opinion. The mother, after court, reported the following.

"The judge asked me how I felt about my daughter . . . did I believe her. The judge wanted to know did I want the boys to go to jail. I got upset and said I believed my daughter and, if the boys did it, and they confessed that night, then they should be punished. I don't think I should be the judge and say whether or not they should go to jail or for how long. The judge then asked the father of the boys if he believed his sons. The father said he did. His boys said my daughter did it willingly and on her own."

Listening in Court

The parents have to listen—if they stay for the entire hearing or trial—to other testimony. Thus the parent has to deal with his or her own feelings about being in court. Parents can react strongly to listening to the testimony of others. Sometimes they are upset over hearing testimony conflicting with that of their child, and other times they hear other people in authority make statements about their child; sometimes new information is revealed.

Contradictory Information. One mother complained, "There were some other boys there was witnesses, and they all told different stories that made me angry. . . . They contradicted each other."

Testimony to Discredit the Child. One father was upset with school officials that released school records and said, "the defense wanted to know how slow a child she was and what problems she had learning. It was irrelevant to the case such as her school record and her behavior at home and with other children." He later ventilated his feelings to the counselor:

"It was none of their business what my son was doing at home and why he wasn't in school and where my other son was. And what family doesn't have problems with their child. They talked like she was a behavior problem. She isn't. Just normal things she does, but it sounds like she was a big problem."

New Information. Sometimes information comes out in court that is a big surprise to everyone. Such a revelation may be upsetting to the parent. In one case, a witness for the prosecution revealed that the girls had planned to visit the boys. The mother of the girl looked upset and asked her daughter during court, if this was true. The mother later said to the counselor:

"I got really upset. Lisa changed her story and made my daughter sound bad. . . . Everyone knew I was upset. I was talking real loud, and I was really

furious. I said that no matter how it turns out, I wanted to know the truth. I just wanted to be sure everyone was telling the truth and not just changing stories."

Dealing with Feelings

One advantage to having a counselor present during the court process is the access to the parent after court. This intervention helps the parent in two ways. First, parents can ventilate their own concerns—as separate from their concern over their child's welfare—and decrease the intensity of feelings evoked. Second, it diminishes the chance of the parent expressing an immediate reaction to their child's behavior that could increase the child's stress level. For example, one mother, when asked what was most upsetting about the hearing said, "I just don't understand how she could have been so trusting."

A situation in which the mother's behavior could place a demand on the child and where the counselor intervened follows.

Mother: *"This has been a horrible experience for me. When you told me how long it would take and that it would get worse, I never dreamed it would be like this . . . you know, I have another daughter, but she never gets into situations like this."*

Counselor: *"What do you mean by 'situations like this?' "*

Mother: *"Situations where the girls are looking for it."*

Counselor: *"That is a popular way of looking at the problem—criticizing or blaming the lifestyle of a person."*

Mother: *"I suppose you are right. . . . I guess I do do that to her."*

Feelings Evoked. The feelings evoked through the court process are often quite strong. As one mother said, "I couldn't even talk with anyone. I was so scared, so shaky. I couldn't even drive home."

Identification with Victim. Sometimes the parent becomes as involved, or more involved, than the victim:

Attorney: *"You have to remember, this didn't happen to you. It happened to your daughter."*

Mother: *"If it happened to my daughter, then it happened to me. What happens to your daughter happens to you."*

Anger at the Defendant. Strong negative feelings may be evoked. For example, "When I looked at him, if I could have killed him with my eyes, he'd be dead."

Symptoms. "I have a headache for two days worrying about this. Am I glad I took the whole day off to go to the hearing." One mother waiting to testify said, "I'm glad to see what court is like before I testify. . . . I know he is going to tear me apart. I don't mind being a witness, but it is the terminal waiting that is awful."

What To Tell People

Family members—as does the rape victim—face the decision of (1) whether or not to tell other people about the rape and (2) whether to include any details of the rape. Time spent at court has to be accounted for to other people. Family and members of the social network talk about this dilemma as follows.

"I traded a day off work with someone . . . but I had to tell people at work why. . . . I told them my daughter was assaulted and it's going to court, but did not give any details."

A neighbor woman accompanying the mother of a 5-year-old rape victim asked how to handle all the neighborhood kids talking about the rape. The counselor suggested someone gather the kids together to talk about it in a group regarding (1) their feelings and what they saw, heard, and think; (2) how they intend to treat the victim when they see her again; (3) what they intend to tell others about the rape. The important point is (1) to get the children to ventilate their feelings and reactions and (2) to teach the children how to be supportive to someone who has been hurt.

One mother and daughter worried what to tell the younger children in the family as they asked why the sister was not in school. They decided to tell them she doesn't have to go to school again until it is exam time.

Sometimes the explanation that is given by a parent is upsetting to the child and requires the counselor to help neutralize the impact. In one situation, a father, explaining about his absence from work to be in court, said in a loud voice, "This is the little girl I was telling you about—and all the hanky panky."

Social Network Involvement

The court process pressures people in the victim's social network to assist in providing testimony. However, social network people—as do family members—have fears and feelings about "getting involved." Not only may they get involved, but they may be subject to the same treatment by court officials as are family members and the victim. For example, one neighbor woman expressed concern over one of the defense witnesses coming to her home the evening of the first trial day. She, suspicious over how he obtained her name and address, wondered if he gained that information during her testimony. She said, "I had nothing to do with this. Things are getting so stirred up. I don't want any trouble from all this." The following day at court she tried to be excused after her testimony, which coincided with the recess for lunch. The DA told her she should stay, and lectured her as follows:

"That's the price you pay. You leave now and it all goes down the drain. That's just the way it goes around here. If you want anything done about this, then you had better stay."

This encounter added to the stress and conflict the woman felt over being in court. It required input from the counselor and the victim's father to help neutralize some of these feelings and to provide a stronger reason for her staying.

Neighbor: *"I have things to do. Why do they need me? Why all the questions?"*

Counselor: *"The defense is trying to get the case off on technicalities and he is carefully checking each one's testimony for consistency and hoping to find a discrepancy."*

Neighbor: *"They are spending so much time on the outside of the building and what went on there. He had to have her in there. We all knew it."*

Counselor: *"The defense just wants to win his case. He doesn't necessarily care what went on. It is his job to get the guy off."*

Neighbor: *"I can't remember all those details. It happened so long ago. I could remember then. I get confused up there on the stand."*

Father: *"All that helps his case. He is trying to delay again. I can see that."*

Neighbor: *"We just wanted something done about the child."*

Father: *"But the police have to have a reason for breaking in without a search warrant."*

Neighbor: *"Everyone was so upset at that time. So much confusion. I don't remember who said what."*

Counselor: *"Just take your time and try to keep the story consistent, and if you don't remember, just say so. Don't say something you don't remember."*

Neighbor: *"Boy, you sure learn after going through this."*

Counselor: *"This experience might come in handy sometime."*

Neighbor: *"I sure hope there is no next time, but I know what you mean."*

Counseling Techniques

The following general techniques are suggested for use with the child or adolescent and family members during the court process. The techniques are aimed at decreasing the stress normally generated by having to go to court, as well as the stress from having to talk about the sexual assault.

Preparing the Child for the Court Process

The main point of preparing the child for court is to be sure the child and family members have some idea of what to expect and what their role will be. The counselor can help to reduce stress by going over the questions the DA may ask. A typical set of questions that have been observed in court include some of the following:

Do you know right from wrong?

Do you know about lying?

Do you know the words *intercourse, rape, penetration?*

Who took your clothes off; what happened to your clothes?

Did you call out for help; did you protest?

How did you get away?

Did you tell someone?

How do you know it was this man?

The questions may be posed in a role-play situation in which the counselor asks the questions and child responds. This type of anticipatory guidance helps to decrease stress over an unexpected situation.

Focusing

This technique is used to decrease environmental stimuli and to assist the person in concentrating on just one thing or person. One counselor helped a 16-year-old victim as follows:

Victim: *"I'm nervous. I don't know what's going to happen in there. . . . It happened two years ago. I won't be able to remember all the details."*

Counselor: *"The DA will get the facts by asking questions, starting with your name."*

Victim: *"What about all those people watching?"*

Counselor: *"Just talk to the DA and pretend he is the only one in the room."*

Encouraging Expression of Feelings

After testifying begins, the counselor can assume there will be considerable feeling evoked regarding the defense lawyer. During recess or lunch breaks, family and victim should have an opportunity to ventilate, as in the following case.

At lunch the three of us obsessed about the defense lawyer. He and his female coworker also came to the cafeteria for lunch. And per usual, he stared at us. Both mother and daughter wish they could tell him off but realize that they do not dare do so.

Telephone Contact

Use of the telephone as a counseling technique has been described in Chapter 12. The use of a telephone changes during the court process. Instead of meeting a therapeutic goal, in terms of eliciting feelings and working through painful issues, the telephone now is used to touch base with the victim and to keep the victim psychologically strong for the experience of testifying.

It is important that the child feel psychologically strong and prepared to testify. The telephone is often helpful to the parents in allowing them to express their feelings and reactions to the court process. In one case, the mother was asked about her neighborhood ("The neighborhood—it's not as nice as it used to be"); her education ("How far have you gone in school?"); playmates of her children ("Does your daughter play with black children?"). At one point, while testifying, the mother countered with, "This is new to me. I'm not familiar with court procedures." This mother utilized telephone follow-up to ventilate her anxiety over the stressful questions asked her by the defense lawyer.

Feelings about Court

Victims have a wide range of feelings about being in court, the preparations of the court, the people they see in court, as well as their experience in testifying. All these areas are important for the counselor to inquire into in follow-up counseling sessions.

Testifying

Although victims may be warned by the DA not to get a "bad attitude" while testifying, this reaction may indeed occur. If so, it is very important that the young person be able to describe the defensive reaction.

"The cross-examination was pretty rough. I got carried away. He was so caught up on the specific time and he was trying to wear me down. It was a pile of shit, and I was so bored with all those questions. I stopped listening, and they had to keep repeating the questions."

Dealing with Additional Crises

There often is a long time delay between the assault and the various steps of the court process. Additional family crises may occur that complicate the situation. The counselor needs to be aware of such events and to provide support at the time, as well as to acknowledge the crisis when there is another court appearance. Such information should also be available to the DA preparing the case.

In one situation, the father, who was influential in helping his daughter identify the two young men, and in locating them for the police, died unexpectedly of a heart attack about six months after the rape. His death had a major impact on his family. The young girl's comment to the counselor, when the date for a court trial was set, "I don't want to go to court. I forgot about it since my Dad died. I've been too sad."

The counselor had a dual task in helping the grieving family continue in the court process. Under certain conditions, as in this case, the counselor departs from the single issue-oriented approach used in counseling and includes a second issue for counseling. The conditions for such a departure include issues that directly relate to some aspect of the sexual assault or a crisis of greater or equal impact occurring since the rape. In this case, the death of the father represented a more tragic event to the family unit than the rape, and removed the strongest motivating factor for the daughter in pressing charges. The counselor helped the daughter and the mother with their grief and supported them through the court process.

Guidelines for Preparing the Child or Adolescent for Court

Table 13-1 is a list of guidelines that identify factors decreasing or increasing stress for the young witness. It has been prepared to serve as a checklist for counselors.

Table 13-1

Guidelines for Preparing the Child or Adolescent for Court

Factors Decreasing Stress	Factors Increasing Stress[a]
Talking about the court process: who does what in court.	Public setting of the courtroom
Visiting and walking around an empty court room.	Being unfamiliar with a court room and court personnel
Using a private, quiet room for interviewing about the assault	Speaking into a court microphone
Availability of crayons and paper and age-related toys for young witnesses during interview	Being sequestered and no familiar faces in court
Presence of a parent or familiar person in court	Different DAs at district court and superior court
Explanation of purpose of interview and testimony	Legal and/or technical jargon
Use of clear, simple language, as well as carefully chosen questions	Seeing the defendant
Practicing the style of the DA and/or defense counselor through role-play of testifying	Linguistic strategies of the defense
Flexibility of the interviewer	Rigid, indifferent style of some DAs
Including the family and/or familiar persons in the preparation process	Judgmental attitude of the situation
Keep a written account of the testimony for victims to refresh their memory	Long delays and postponements
Instructions about where to go in the courthouse	Memory loss
Instructions on how to respond to the DA and on cross-examination	

[a]Many upsetting features of the courtroom are described in detail in Holmstrom and Burgess, *The Victim of Rape: Institutional Reactions* (New York: Wiley-Interscience, forthcoming).

In summary, this chapter has presented some of the important issues for counselors to be aware of in their work with child and adolescent victims and their families involved in the court process.

References

1. Lucy Berliner and Doris Stevens. "Harborview Social Workers Advocate Special Techniques for Child Witness," *Response* 1, no. 2 (December 1976), Washington, D.C.: Center for Women Policy Studies, p. 1.

2. Lynda Lytle Holmstrom and Ann Wolbert Burgess, "Rape: The Victim and the Criminal Justice System" (Paper presented at the First International Symposium on Victimology, Jerusalem, September 1973, and published in *International Journal of Criminology and Penology* 3 (1975):101-110.

3. Ann Wolbert Burgess, Lynda Lytle Holmstrom, and Maureen P. Mc-Causland, "Counseling the Child Rape Victim," *Issues in Comprehensive Pediatric Nursing* 1, no. 4, (November–December 1976):46–47.

4. *Ibid.*

5. Aaron Lazare, Sherman Eisenthal, and Arlene Frank, "The Interview as a Clinical Negotiation," in *Diagnosis and Treatment in Outpatient Psychiatry,* ed. Aaron Lazare (Baltimore: Williams and Wilkens, forthcoming).

6. The district attorney's interaction with victims is discussed from another perspective—the role of the DA—in L. L. Holmstrom and A. W. Burgess, *The Victim of Rape: Institutional Reactions* (New York: Wiley-Interscience, forthcoming).

7. The preparation of this case is described in detail in Lynda Lytle Holmstrom and Ann Wolbert Burgess, *The Victim of Rape: Institutional Reactions* (New York: Wiley-Interscience, forthcoming).

14

Coordinated Community Treatment of Incest
Henry Giarretto,
Anna Giarretto,
and *Suzanne M. Sgroi*

We seek the French connection when we can't make a human connection.
Henry Giarretto

In the treatment of incestuous families, the capacity of the criminal justice system to intervene positively must be encouraged. Even though, at first blush, criminal justice system involvement appears to be a handicap, there are definite advantages if this involvement is incorporated into the treatment process. First, advantage can be taken of the expiatory factor: people who have committed incest feel that they have sinned and that expiation for their actions is appropriate. Second, criminal justice system involvement provides a powerful authoritative incentive for changing intrafamily behavior and stopping the sexual abuse. Lastly, it is advantageous for therapists to work cooperatively with the criminal justice system simply because it is *there* and frequently already involved or about to become involved with families whose incestuous behavior has proved so disruptive that the problem has somehow come to public attention.

Sexual abuse of children, especially if incestuous in nature, is, of course, a crime. Penalties for child sexual abuse vary widely across the country. However, direct punishment meted out to offenders in the form of incarceration has been conspicuously unsuccessful in the past in bringing about reformed behavior, despite its high cost to the community. Indirect punishment for child sexual abuse that is "found out" impacts not only on the perpetrator but also on the victim and other family members. Its effects can be devastating. Indirect punishment may take the form of widespread adverse publicity, loss of job for the perpetrator, and loss of social status and community respect for the whole family, coupled with a pervasive social stigma that may persist for all involved. The latter is deeply rooted in a horror of incest that is ubiquitous in our society. Criminal justice personnel and members of the helping professions are far from immune to feelings of hatred and fear regarding incest and frequently participate in the punishment process.

When there is little understanding, especially in civil servants, of what makes a human being behave the way he does (whether an offender, victim, policeman, social worker, judge, legislator, or oneself), the result is a contentious, destructive environment rather than one that is cooperative and regenerative. Someone

This chapter is adapted from a workshop sponsored by the Connecticut State Department of Children and Youth Services through the Connecticut Child Abuse and Neglect Demonstration Center (OCD Grant No. 90-C-399) on June 21, 1977.

231

has to take the responsibility of turning this situation around. The success of the Child Sexual Abuse Treatment Program (CSATP) in Santa Clara County (as opposed to other programs) is largely dependent on utilizing basic principles of humanistic psychology in working with victims, offenders, families, members of the criminal justice system, *and* coworkers. CSATP staff have learned that it is more effective to avoid scapegoating or indulging in righteous indignation with any of the preceding groups. Criminal justice system personnel will continue to use traditional methods until they are shown better ones. If the CSATP, or any other group, claims a better way of treating clients, it must be proven to the satisfaction of others. By internalizing the humanistic creed, the CSATP is developing a coordinated effort for creative management of cases involving child sexual abuse that is backed up by the authority of the criminal justice system but enables intervention in a nonpunitive fashion.

How does the CSATP work with the criminal justice system in dealing with sexual abuse so that the overall effect is regenerative rather than punitive? The program utilizes two basic principles of humanistic psychology. The first premise seems almost inane in its simplicity. Man's predominant drive is to feel good, and the maintenance of this state depends on how well his needs are met. When he feels good, he values himself and others and can develop nurturing relationships. The opposite polar state results when his needs are not met. He then feels bad and develops a self-hatred that he can discharge only by acts of abuse toward himself and others.

The self-hate/destructive-energy syndrome in an individual starts early in life. As a child, the individual is raised by parents who themselves feel deprived. When the child acts with hostility, he or she is punished by the parents out of their own distress. As the punitive measures become increasingly harsh (the worst being desertion), there is a corresponding increase in the level of self-hatred and in the severity of the abusive behavior. Families composed of parents and children with unmet needs constitute the so-called dysfunctional or troubled families. Child neglect, sexual abuse, and battering are some of the many symptoms.

Maslow has identified a number of needs ranging from the individual's fundamental needs for food, shelter, and security upward to the needs for self-respect, social recognition, and actualizing one's latent abilities. To these must be added the needs for self-caring, to be cared for by others, and to care for others. Caring is a practical and biologically determined human need. If mankind did not care for its children, the human species would die. Any society that does not provide for the needs of all its people must be classified as dysfunctional and will be eventually overwhelmed by its casualties.

It is at the point when symptoms in dysfunctional families or individuals result in behavior that is criminal that criminal justice system intervention can either accelerate the self-destructive cycle or have a creative effect. If civil servants, because of their own low self-worth, react impersonally and punitively (as the individual's parents did initially), the old cycle is perpetuated. But if the offender is started on a path of self-reeducation in which he or she learns how to meet unmet needs, including the higher needs that foster social responsibility, creative intervention by the criminal justice system will have taken place.

How does the CSATP help to accomplish this in Santa Clara County? This involves utilization of the second premise, also deceptively simple. Humanism operates on the realistic assumption that people are what they are. At any moment, they act as they know how to act. If they knew how to meet their needs more effectively, they would do so. No one "holds out" on himself. The same evolutionary rule holds true for societies. They, too, add up to what they are. Denigration, angry diatribes, hindsightful contempt, and punishment do not improve past conduct. Instead, they produce a defensive backlash that, for the moment at least, deters progress. Society has such high expectations that the sum total of an individual at any given time can always be characterized as "not good enough." When incestuous behavior is occurring within a family, each family member is very apt to feel burdened by a "not good enough" label. To intervene creatively in this situation, it is necessary to forget about labels and, instead, meet the person nonjudgmentally as an evolving human being. The only significant place to confront any person is the "place where he is" at that time.

Operation of the Child Sexual Abuse Treatment Program

The experience with more than 600 families since 1971 who have been involved with the Child Sexual Abuse Treatment Program of the Juvenile Probation Department in California's Santa Clara County has been that no profile of a typical incestuous family exists when a large sample is examined. The program has for the most part worked with white middle-class families whose average length of involvement has been six months. The average age of target children has been 10 to 11 years. Father-daughter incest has occurred in 75 percent of the cases serviced thus far. Fewer than 1 percent of the cases have been shown upon investigation to be based upon lies or false allegations of sexual abuse or incest by the child. Although it is difficult to quantitate the long-term success of the CSATP since it has been in operation for only six years, the following results indicate that the approach is effective.

1. No recidivism has been reported in the more than 600 families who have been treated and formally terminated.
2. Compared to the situation prior to the CSATP, children have been returned to families sooner, 90 percent within the first month.
3. Early treatment for offenders has been provided instead of deferring treatment until after the father was released from jail.

4. Reestablishment of a normal father-daughter relationship has been achieved in most families (versus just living together and tolerating each other).
5. A much higher level of coordination and cooperation between previously competitive and fragmented services has been realized.
6. CSATP and Parents United have received a high degree of visibility, with many requests for consultation and assistance from troubled families and professionals from across the program.
7. A training program in the CSATP methodology has been funded by the State of California with the aim of beginning similiar effective programs in other counties.

A primary emphasis on maintaining family integrity has been the keystone of the CSATP. Its goals are to teach people to assume personal responsibility for their actions, to reunite families whenever possible, and, of course, to eliminate all incestuous relationships among family members. There is close interaction between the CSATP and the police, probation officers, district attorneys, and judges. In the early stages, a great deal of effort was expended to enlist the cooperation of a few judges and prosecutors to permit fathers who had been convicted or were being prosecuted for incest to participate in the program. Now that a successful track record has been established, more people within the criminal justice system in Santa Clara County are willing to refer cases to CSATP.

The authority of the criminal justice system has proved to be absolutely essential in treating incest. Most of the small number of "drop-outs" from the CSATP have been families who were not involved with the police. On the other hand, incestuous families must be offered something positive if they are to become engaged in any treatment program. In addition to the authoritative incentive afforded by involvement with the criminal justice system, family members have to perceive that the treatment program is designed to help them. In most cases, intervention that "feels like help" will consist of satisfying significant unmet psychological needs of the individuals involved via a course of treatment aimed at reuniting the family.

Although approaches may vary depending on the situation, the CSATP usually combines initial individual therapy with subsequent group therapy. Self-help groups guided by a therapist comprise an important ongoing treatment entity. Every therapist or counselor needs to confront and deal with his or her own feelings of inadequacy and hostility brought forth by the incest situation. Such reactions are universal and should be anticipated at the outset. Self-knowledge is very important for "helping professionals." Whenever a therapist perceives his or her own anger and frustration being directed at a client, these feelings should be carefully examined and dealt with. Positive intervention cannot occur in an atmosphere of tension and distrust generated by the therapist's unresolved judgmental feelings toward clients. The CSATP staff meets weekly to help each other ventilate and resolve negative feelings.

The first tendency is for therapists to want to protect the victim—usually by removing the target child or children from the parents. Accompanying the tendency to be protective of the child is much anger directed against the father and the mother for allowing the father-child incest behavior to be perpetrated. However, the therapist soon discovers that the child is frequently unhappy in an outside placement. It is not unusual for the child to feel isolated and victimized by separation from the rest of the family and to want to return home. So the second tendency is for the therapist to reconsider his or her feelings toward the mother and be willing to reunite and work with mother and daughter but to continue to exclude the father. At this point, the mother, whose initial reaction in most cases is to opt for divorce or permanent separation from her husband, will now have reassessed *her* situation and may well begin to want to maintain her marriage. Under these circumstances, family members may be expected to react with fear and denial when the therapist projects enmity. If the long-term intervention plan is to separate rather than reunite the family, clients will be quick to perceive that the therapist is a danger to them. Family members who want to be reunited will be unlikely to cooperate if they fear that information and confidences will be used to dismember their family.

In the CSATP, if the family has requested help, the target child (usually a daughter) is frequently permitted to decide for herself if she wishes to remain at home or be separated from her family. If the daughter wants to leave home, the staff respects her decision and arranges a temporary placement for her, pending the outcome of the treatment efforts and the disposition of the case within the criminal justice system. If the daughter prefers to stay at home, the treatment staff usually will support her in this decision, especially if the mother appears to be able to function as an ally of the child. Some exceptions are made, however, especially if any of the following conditions are present: (1) the mother does not want the child to remain in the home, (2) the mother appears to be dangerously abusive, (3) the daughter is so beaten down and passive that she really cannot make this decision for herself, and (4) the father's level of impulse control is extremely low and he will have access to the family. Under the foregoing circumstances, the CSATP staff may well advise that the daughter not be permitted to stay in the home.

The therapeutic approach employed by the CSATP with families in which father-daughter incest has occurred usually begins with individual counseling of the daughter. The next step is individual counseling of the mother. The following step, joint counseling of mother and daughter, constitutes the core around which the family is rebuilt. After that, all the children in the family join with the mother in counseling sessions. Meanwhile, the father is being given individual therapy. Marriage counseling begins when both partners are ready. Eventually, the father is included in therapy sessions with the entire family.

Although the remedial approach to each family incest situation must be individualized for that particular family, the CSATP has developed a number of techniques that have been successfully applied in many cases.

Working with Child Victims

The child victim needs to be convinced that he or she is not to blame for the incestuous behavior or for the family disruption that ensued when the incest secret was disclosed. Regardless of how seductive or provocative the child's behavior, all family members must acknowledge that the total responsibility for incest rests with the adults involved. The child victim must hear from the mother, "You are not to blame. Daddy and I did not have a good marriage. That is why Daddy turned to you." Likewise, the child victim must receive an acknowledgement of complete responsibility for the incest behavior from the father and an apology from the father.

A girl who has been a victim of incest needs to receive the message that sexual feelings are good and normal, despite the guilt and confusion attending the sexual relationship with her father. Great care must be taken to prevent girls from coping with the enormity of what has happened to them by "turning off" sexually. Contrary to popular opinion, most victims do not enjoy the incest relationship, especially on a long-term basis. It is an oppressive relationship for the child victim and an exploitation of parental authority. Daughters often describe a feeling of "a heavy weight pressing on me." This feeling is lessened and frequently will disappear after counseling, if the daughter has been successfully relieved of her guilt and helped to become comfortable with her sexual feelings. The individual and mother-daughter counseling is supplemented by participation in self-help Daughters United Groups, sponsored by the CSATP.

Working with Mothers

In absolving the child victim of blame, the mother no longer views the child victim as her rival but as an innocent bystander in a dysfunctional marriage. The mother's first reaction in most cases after acknowledging the father-daughter incest situation is to want to divorce her husband. But soon after, she starts to take inventory of the good and bad aspects of her marriage and to wonder if it is salvageable. Parents United helps the mother a great deal in making this decision. She sees that the majority of couples have decided to remain together. This gives sanction to her own inclination to try to reunite the family. The thrust of Parents United is not just to salvage the marriage, but to improve it through special couples groups that work toward enhancing marital relationships.

Working with Fathers

The father must be given hope that the family will be helped and worked with, not destroyed. The key to treatment of fathers who are perpetrators of incest is to be able to hold out the hope that they will be able to maintain a relationship with their loved ones and, ideally, rejoin a strengthened and regenerated family circle. At the same time, the incestuous relationship is never condoned. In addition to accepting full responsibility for his sexual behavior toward his child, the father must admit and believe that the behavior was wrong and cannot be repeated. The father (along with the rest of society, which has ambivalent feelings, at best) must acknowledge that incest is extremely destructive for the entire family. The myth that incestuous relationships are benign or less destructive for the child victim than a sexual assault by an outside perpetrator must be repudiated entirely.

In working with fathers, its is crucial to establish human contact and to try to reach the lonely and isolated part of this human being. Again, projection of judgmental feelings by the therapist will sabotage the treatment process. Another goal is to work on developing the father's capacity for gentleness and tenderness and to try to help him channel these feelings toward his wife, as well as to integrate these qualities into his adult life and behavior. Many men in our society do not know how to receive gentleness or tenderness, much less how to express these feelings toward others. It is well to avoid blaming the husband and wife for the quality of their emotional and sexual relationship. Instead, the approach should start with the strengths that are present and encourage them to learn the skills that enhance marital relationships.

Working with Families

Parents are introduced and integrated as quickly as possible into Parents United. These self-help groups of parents are led by male and female cotherapists, one a professional and the other a Parents United member who has been trained in group leadership. The father's and mother's reaction to attending their first Parents United meeting has been most frequently characterized by a sense of relief and a feeling that, after all, they are not alone, that this group will not reject and ostracize them because of the incestuous behavior. New members also quickly sense an ongoing process of help and growth generated by the group, as well as a sense of unity and togetherness. Parents United fills an important therapeutic need for its individual members. It functions as a body of people who provide good parenting and guidance for the incestuous family. The group process helps to convey by example to its members that a good parent is neither permissive or tyrannical. The body of people that constitute a successful Parents United group has to be so strong that evasive maneuvers by individuals do not succeed. In addition to conveying firmness and an insistence that they conform to a nonincestuous mode of family interaction, the group must also offer enough support and nourishment to individual members to keep them involved.

In addition, Parents United has a significant function as a political entity that speaks out on behalf of better services and more humane treatment for families in which child sexual abuse has occurred. It is hard to overstate the positive impact that can be made on legislators, administrators, and even the general public by a committed and articulate group of people who have "been there" and are responsibly trying to help themselves to overcome the stigma and despair of incest and regenerate their lives.

Parents United also enables the treatment unit to handle a larger caseload than would otherwise be possible. All parents meet weekly for the first eight weeks in an orientation group. They then are transferred to another group. These currently include two intensive couples groups (limited to six couples each), an open group comprised of men and women who are not currently living with a sexual partner, a men's group, and a mothers and daughters group. There are several Daughters United groups comprised of girls 14 to 18 years old. There is an adolescent group of boys that includes victims, young offenders, and boys who are siblings of victims. Recently the program has added a play therapy group for children 5 to 10 years of age and a group for preadolescent girls. A separate group of adult women who were themselves sexually abused in childhood serves as an excellent resource of volunteers to assist in the family treatment program. The CSATP staff continue to believe that their now burgeoning caseload still represents only a fraction of the actual incidence of child sexual abuse in Santa Clara County.

How To Start a Child Sexual Abuse Treatment Program

The key components of the Santa Clara County Program are potentially available in most communities across the United States. The most essential exportable ingredients are the will to begin and a "can do" attitude to put against the inevitable obstacles. A core team could consist of a child protective services worker (or Juvenile Probation Officer), a police officer, and a mental health professional. This core team must immediately begin to develop a focused effort in treating child sexual abuse cases while building a body of expertise within the program. All team members must be prepared to deal with their own anger toward the parents in the families who are served without projecting hostility toward their clients. The first two families served will constitute core Parents United and Daughters United groups. As the caseload increases, additional part-time staff can often be recruited from faculty and students from nearby colleges with programs in psychology, social work, and counseling.

The successful development of a child sexual abuse treatment program within a community will depend heavily on enlisting the cooperation of local police, probation officers, child protective services, prosecutors, and judges. All these professionals need to become convinced of the program's credibility. Enlisting their cooperation will often require an individual person-to-person approach. Societal attitudes toward incest are, in general, so punitive that a treatment program must be characterized by an approach that combines hard-nosed practicality with compassion. A heavy emphasis on helping clients to assume personal responsiblity for behavior that is wrong and to regenerate family members so that there is no repetition of incest will win far more allies from the criminal justice system than a hearts-and-flowers approach. Everyone involved in the sexual abuse treatment program must understand that it exists to provide a humane alternative to family dismemberment and incarceration, *not* to assist offenders to evade punishment and responsibility for their actions.

The CSATP of Santa Clara County has developed a number of exercises and techniques to assist counselors and clients to facilitate a "human connection." Those aimed at counselors are designed to assist them in dealing with their own hostility toward their clients. These include having paired counselors alternate playing the roles of counselor and perpetrator. They are encouraged to exaggerate the judgmental phase against the perpetrator and to express all their hatred and revulsion of the incestuous behavior toward their partners. Then the two exchange roles, and the partner proceeds to express *his* self-righteous anger toward the perpetrator. In similar fashion, the counselors alternate playing counselor and mother and thus can discharge their anger against the mother for failing the child. The use of off-hand humor is also helpful. The obvious purpose of these exercises is to assist those who would function as therapists and counselors to resolve their negative feelings toward parents so that they can begin to perceive their clients as troubled human beings in need of help.

Exercises for Parents United groups are more likely to be aimed at assisting clients to move beyond their own feelings of loneliness and isolation and to be able to enjoy positive interaction with others. Every Parents United group meeting in the Santa Clara County Program begins with a light meditative exercise (e.g., sitting with eyes closed and silently observing their breathing), which is designed to assist individuals in becoming inwardly calm and "in the mood" for the group experience. Introductory exercises for new groups usually involve pairing individuals who do not know each other. One exercise involves having each individual make a list of all the important events in his or her life and then relate them to a partner. This is a timed exercise; after an interval, the partners reverse roles of autobiographer and listener. A similar exercise entails having each individual write a motion picture script of his "life story" and then "act out" the story with others. Still another exercise requires the individual to recall and then relate all the sexual experiences of his or her life. This is usually done personally and related to a small group. The object of all these exercises is, again, to enable individuals who have multiple reasons to feel lonely and alienated to establish connections with a group of accepting, supportive, and nurturant people who will assist them to reunite and regenerate their families.

240

Replication

An outreach teaching component has now been built into the CSATP of Santa Clara County, with the goal of training individuals who will then set up treatment units within other counties in California. Judging from experiences to date, a staff of three people plus volunteers with creative use of local resources should be able to manage the child sexual abuse cases from a population of one million people. Since the staff will probably be made up of present employees in agencies already responsible for dealing with sexual abuse, the start-up cost to a typical community should be minimal. As the public learns of this new resource, an increased referral rate and a need for additional hours of caseworker services can be anticipated. This cost will eventually be paid by the taxpayer. However, the savings realized through decreased use of other county and state services (e.g., welfare, law enforcement, prisons, medical and mental health services) should offset the cost. There is no hard dollar figure for estimating what a treatment program will cost or save a community. The validity in core democratic values of the CSATP method of enabling the criminal justice system to react creatively in child sexual abuse cases is obvious; i.e., families are reconstituted rather than fragmented; child victims are more likely to become productive adults; and offenders are returned to society as responsible citizens rather than banished to the outlaw subculture.

As a long-term goal, there may well be justification to establishing a national network of Family Resource Centers. These would be official arms of the criminal justice system (a name more suggestive of social justice would be better) and would be used for the prevention and early treatment of child sexual abuse and other problems manifested by troubled families. Each center would have to be strongly rooted in the community. The Family Resource Centers' operation would be based on humanistic principles translated into a self-help format of interpersonal enhancement for not only the clients but the volunteers and professionals as well.

Index

Abraham, Karl, 96
Accessory-to-sex syndrome, 60, 85–98; disclosure of activity, 90; dominant-subordinate role, 89; signs and symptoms, 91; type of activity, 89; victims' reaction, 87–88
Adolescent adjustment reaction, 57
Adolescent sexual offenses, 57
Aggression, 13, 15, 16, 28, 29, 52, 53, 92, 131
Alcoholics Anonymous, 41
Alcoholism, 5, 134
American Academy of Pediatrics, 145
American Humane Association Study, 162
Anxiety, 100
Assault, 174; assessing impact, 179–180
Associations, 103–106
Austen, Jane, 138

Battered child syndrome, 138, 232
Battered child workup, 150
Behavioral model, 193, 196–197, 200
Bender, Lauretta, 96
Bernalillo County Mental Health/Retardation Center, 202
Blaming the victim, 135, 136
Blau, Abram, 96
Blitz attack, 61
Branch, Geraldine, 146

Child abuse, 21, 130, 150, 154
Child neglect, 130, 150, 154, 232
Child protective services, 155
Child Sexual Abuse Treatment Program (CSATP), 140, 232–236, 238–240; operation of, 233–236; starting a program, 238–240
Child sexual assault, 11, 23, 127, 143–158, 238; access to victim, 149–150; comprehensive examination, 143–158; dynamics, 131, 141; frequency, 129–130; guide-lines for intervention and assessment, 129–141; impact of, 183; incidence statistics, 159; mechanics, 130–131, 141, 146; parents' ability to deal with, 195–196; police investigation, 159–170; primary prevention of, 181; spectrum, 130
Coconspiracy dyad, 94–95
Communication barrier, 89
Comprehensive examination, 143–158; collection of evidence, 144; entry into system, 143–144
Confidence attack, 61
Connecticut Public Health Code, 149
Counseling: Child Sexual Abuse Treatment Program, 234–240; crisis, 72, 117, 118, 120, 126, 171; families, 181–204; gang rape victims, 61–66; handicapped victims, 68–75; multiple victims, 69; techniques during court process, 226–229; victim of multiple assailants, 66–68; young victims, 181–204
Counselor: in court, 208, 215–225; and defense lawyer, 212–215; and district attorney, 210–211; goal in court process, 215
Counselor's role, 77, 78, 79, 82, 83
Court, 78, 137, 145, 168, 181; appearances, 47; recapitulation of crisis, 199; victim and family reaction, 48
Court process: child during, 205–230; in the courtroom, 215–225; family during, 205–230; preparing the case, 206–215; protocol, 205
Crisis counseling, 117, 118, 120, 126, 171

Dangerousness, issue of, 28–32
Data, types of, 33
Daughter's United, 236, 238

241

About the Contributors

Mary L. Keefe, M.C.J., is retired from the New York City Police Department, where for the last three years she was commanding officer of the Sex Crimes Analysis Unit. As a lieutenant in charge, she was responsible for implementing the Rape Report Line, Forced Choice Form (for the collection of information), and an Information Van. She served on the Mayor's Task Force on Rape, which was instrumental in changing many of the laws relating to rape in New York City. The cases cited in her chapter are from her work with child and adolescent victims.

Henry Giarretto, M.A., and **Anna Giarretto**, M.A. founded and expanded the first Child Sexual Abuse Treatment Program in San Jose, California. As part of this program they designed a state-wide demonstration and training program for professionals dealing with incest problems. Their client population currently averages six hundred referrals a year. This program, established through the Juvenile Probation Department, is fully discussed in this volume.

Maureen P. McCausland, R.N., M.S., is assistant director of nursing, Department of Health and Hospitals, City of Boston. Prior to this Ms. McCausland was coordinator of victim services at Boston City Hospital. The cases cited in her work represent children and adolescents seen at the Pediatric Walk-In Clinic at Boston City Hospital.

About the Authors

Ann Wolbert Burgess, R.N., D.N.Sc., F.A.A.N., is professor of nursing at Boston College. She studied at Boston University and the University of Maryland, and received the Doctor of Nursing Science degree in psychiatric-mental-health nursing at Boston University. In addition to her teaching, writing, and clinical practice, she serves as chairperson of the Rape Prevention and Control Advisory Committee of the U.S. Department of Health, Education, and Welfare.

A. Nicholas Groth, Ph.D., is the director of the Sex Offender Program for the Connecticut Department of Correction at Somers State Prison and is co-director of the St. Joseph College Institute for the Treatment and Control of Child Sexual Abuse in West Hartford. He is a member of the advisory board to the National Center for the Prevention and Control of Rape (NIMH) in Washington, D.C., and a training instructor for the Massachusetts Criminal Justice Training Council. A clinical psychologist, Dr. Groth received the doctorate from Boston University and has specialized in the area of sexual assault working with both victims and offenders in institutional and community-based settings. He is the author of *Men Who Rape: The Psychology Of The Offender* as well as numerous professional papers on rape and child molestation.

Lynda Lytle Holmstrom, Ph.D., is chairperson and associate professor, Department of Sociology, Boston College. She received the B.A. from Stanford, the M.A. from Boston University, and the Ph.D. from Brandeis University. She and Dr. Burgess cofounded the Victim Counseling Program at Boston City Hospital, which serves as the research base for their writings on sexual assault. Drs. Holmstrom and Burgess also have written *The Victim of Rape: Institutional Reactions* and *Rape: Victims of Crisis*.

Suzanne M. Sgroi, M.D., received the A.B. from Syracuse University and the M.D. from the State University of New York at Buffalo. Dr. Sgroi is attending physician in the Department of Ambulatory and Community Medicine, Mount Sinai Hospital, Hartford, Connecticut, and medical director for the venereal-disease clinic jointly run by the hospital and the Hartford Health Department. Dr. Sgroi serves as Project Internist and Chairperson of the Sexual Trauma Treatment Pilot Program for the Connecticut Child Abuse and Neglect Demonstration Center, a demonstration grant funded by the National Center for Child Abuse and Neglect, Department of Health, Education and Welfare. Her publications include *VD: A Doctor's Answers* (Harcourt Brace Jovanovich) and several articles on sexual child assault.